HEROIC FLIGHTS

HEROIC
FLIGHTS

by

John Frayn Turner

LEO COOPER

First published in Great Britain in 2003 by
LEO COOPER
an imprint of Pen & Sword Books,
47 Church Street,
Barnsley
South Yorkshire,
S70 2AS

Copyright © John Frayn Turner 2003

ISBN 0 85052 970 0

A CIP catalogue record for this book is
available from the British Library.

Typeset in 11/13pt Sabon by
Phoenix Typesetting, Burley-in-Wharfedale, West Yorkshire.

Printed in England by
CPI UK

CONTENTS

AUTHOR'S NOTE

This book recalls some of the human highlights in a century of flight. It is more concerned with the fliers than the machines they flew. I have been associated with the air for fifty years – and I even watched the Schneider Trophy races long before the war.

As a number of my books have had aeronautical themes, it is inevitable that in this present one I have quoted from several previous titles. Most prominent among them is *Famous Flights* (Arthur Barker). I have also drawn on material from *Famous Air Battles* (Arthur Barker), *VCs of the Air* (Airlife Publishing), *Fight for the Air* (Airlife Publishing), *The Yanks Are Coming* (Midas in Britain, Hippocrene in USA) and *Fight for the Sky* (Sidgwick and Jackson) on which I collaborated with Douglas Bader. Chapters 36 and 37 are adapted from features I wrote originally for *Officer* magazine, published by the Ministry of Defence.

Finally, I remain grateful to authors and publishers who originally granted me permission to use brief extracts from any of the above titles.

1

THE WRIGHT BROTHERS
The Birth of Powered Flight

The seventeenth of December 1903 was the day that man first flew an aeroplane – when the Wright brothers made the very earliest sustained, controlled flights in a powered plane at Kitty Hawk, North Carolina, USA.

This brief but historic event, a week before Christmas, was the culmination of years of thought and effort not only by the Wrights but by other aeronautical pioneers.

Wilbur and Orville Wright of Dayton, Ohio, began to take a passionate interest in the problems and possibilities of flight from the time of the death of the great German gliding pioneer Lilienthal in 1896.

Starting from the findings of Lilienthal they determined to develop further the art of gliding and eventually to provide power to drive and control flight and make it more or less independent of the elements. But before they could consider powered flight, they had to get as much practical knowledge as possible of the behaviour of gliders.

They kept their bicycle business going, but spent every spare second building a glider. They found the perfect place to test it at Kitty Hawk, North Carolina, which gave them the climatic conditions they sought: a steady prevailing wind blowing at around twenty miles an hour. This small settlement stood on a long bleak sandbar that bridged the waters of Albemarle Sound and the Atlantic Ocean.

It was there in September and October 1900 that the Wrights started the series of trials which would have their climax three years later. The trio of sandhills they chose for the work were about thirty, eighty and one hundred feet high. That first glider was a biplane

1

with an area of 165 square feet, and an eighteen-feet wingspan designed and built from the findings of Lilienthal and others, and intended to fly with a man in a wind of anything over twenty miles an hour.

The Wrights tried it out first as a kind of man-carrying kite-cum-glider. Either Wilbur or Orville would lie flat on the middle of the lower wing to minimize head resistance, and then try to fly from one of the sandhills selected. But although the wind blew at twenty-five – thirty miles an hour they found that no matter how they tried, they could not get the upward thrust anticipated, and that the pilot could not control the glider properly.

So they started to modify their ideas, substituting weights for the pilot and flying the glider as a kite. This enabled them to measure the forces operating on the glider in various conditions. They were eventually compelled to the conclusion that this design would never soar but only glide short distances downhill. When they did resume gliding tests again, they took every precaution possible against accidents, although both they and the glider did have one or two close calls in their free glides a couple of yards off the sand.

But by the last week of October 1900, they realized that they had learned all they could from glider number one. Anyway they were getting a little worried about the business, and the weather showed signs of deterioration.

Throughout that winter at Dayton, they busily built glider number two, which was bigger than its predecessor. They increased the wingspan to twenty-two feet; the weight was nearly double, at just under 100 pounds; and it had an overall area of 308 square feet. This glider had the distinction of being the biggest ever made to date. Among other changes, the Wrights decided to try a greater curvature of the wings.

In late July 1901, they carted the new version to Kitty Hawk on what was the equivalent of their summer holidays. The initial test results disappointed them, for it seemed that they had curved the wings too much and produced a loss of control. Each successive test was followed by trial and error modification, but gradually they were coming to understand the concept of control by balancing planes and rudders.

Their glides in August did in fact gradually grow longer in distance and time, but they still felt dissatisfied and made the long trek home to Dayton pretty depressed.

They next turned their attention to the most vital question of all – wing design. They started to devise and carry out small-scale tests with model wings in a wind tunnel they rigged up at home. The tunnel measured about five feet long and sixteen inches square, and by injecting a flow of air from a fan they could observe the reactions of it on miniature metal wings which they developed literally daily.

In this tiny tunnel they could simulate wind speeds of twenty-five – thirty miles an hour and see precisely what effect these produced on as many as two hundred different designs they tried. For hour after hour that winter the Wrights made notes and readings about the various shapes of model wings. And from all the thousands of notes emerged the design of glider number three.

An impartial observer would have been able to detect signs of real advance, but the two brothers were too close to it all and too involved to be able to see it in proper perspective. They only knew they had to fly – somehow.

The wingspan went up from twenty-two feet to thirty-two. This extra width helped to give it greater hoisting power. Other innovations included a double fixed vertical tail and a front elevator. The area of the new glider was about the same as the previous one, at 305 square feet, and it weighed some 116 pounds.

The Wright brothers felt more optimistic this summer and first tried out the glider at Kitty Hawk in September 1902. Kitty Hawk had become their summer residence, but the weeks they spent there were far from a holiday. From dawn to sunset they slogged away, flying the glider again and again.

A few days after their arrival Orville Wright was the pilot during one glide when the right wing started to rise. Trying to control it, however, he made it worse and the wing went on rising, throwing the glider more and more out of balance. The whole glider was now tilted up at a nasty angle.

While Orville grappled with the controls, his brother and a few onlookers below suddenly saw the glider stall and then float backwards and downwards. This was the sort of situation the brothers had struggled to avoid, yet here it was, and those on the ground could only call out vainly. Orville and the glider hit the ground in a spray of sand. The others ran to the wreckage, but luckily Orville was not hurt.

By the following week they had repaired the glider, or rather reassembled it, and at the same time they set about remedying what had gone wrong by changing the double tail into one movable fin.

They now reckoned that they could control the glider reasonably in three dimensions – and proceeded to prove it.

Wilbur Wright said:

We made nearly 700 glides in the two or three weeks following. When properly applied, the means of control proved to possess a mastery over the forces tending to disturb the equilibrium. We flew it in calms and we flew it in winds as high as 35 miles an hour. We steered it to right and to left, and performed all the evolutions necessary for flight. The machine seems to have reached a higher state of development than the operators; as yet we consider ourselves little more than novices in its management.

Before they left Kitty Hawk that autumn, the brothers had made no fewer than a thousand actual glides averaging about fifteen seconds each. In one hectic week they clocked up over 375 individual glides, one exceeding 600 feet and lasting nearly half a minute. For those days, that represented an eternity. Most important of all, however, they could now control their flights.

Their next planned step was to add an engine to produce a powered plane – and make the first powered flight of all time. At once a fresh set of difficulties appeared, for as the brothers said subsequently:

What at first seemed a simple problem became more and more complex the more we studied it. With the machine moving forward, the air flying backward, the propellers turning sideways, and nothing standing still, it seemed impossible to find a starting point from which to trace the various simultaneous reactions.

Contemplation of it was confusing. After long arguments we often found ourselves in the ludicrous position of each having been converted to the other's side, with no more agreement than when the discussion began.

The brothers had not only to design and build an aeroplane, but the engine as well, for when they looked around for a suitable petrol engine on the market, none existed. And at the same time they had to experiment with propellers, for next to nothing was known about the precise behaviour of these strange new devices.

First they designed the aeroplane. They based their design on the third version of the glider, extending its linen-covered wing area still

4

further to 510 square feet. It was a wooden frame biplane spanning just over forty feet and measuring twenty-one feet long, with a twin elevator in front and a twin rudder at the rear.

The Wrights then set about making the components that would produce powered flight – the engine and propellers. They built a four-cylinder engine developing some twelve horsepower at 1,200 revolutions a minute which they mounted on its side on the lower wing in a position calculated to counteract the pilot's weight.

They christened the aeroplane the *Flyer* and took it to Kitty Hawk well crated towards the end of September 1903, together with glider number three. They were full of excitement at the prospects ahead of them, but they had to be superhumanly patient. Stormy weather all through that autumn made it out of the question to test the *Flyer*, but they went on with their glider, getting in all the practice they could before the first attempt to fly a powered aircraft – and sustain and control it.

The wild weather abated at last, and the Wrights made ready on 14 December to test the *Flyer*. The two undercarriage skids of the machine were placed on a trolley, which in turn ran on a monorail. A wire would hold back the *Flyer* while the engine revved up; the wire would be slipped; the *Flyer* would thrust forward and, with any luck, be airborne. That was the theory.

Wilbur and Orville tossed up to see who should have that first flight. Wilbur called correctly, but was less lucky with the actual attempt. The *Flyer* shuddered down the rail all right, but went up in the air too steeply, stalled, and then crashed. The repairs took a couple of days.

Despite this further setback the Wrights remained so completely confident they were about to make history that they invited the few locals of Kitty Hawk to come and witness the event. Five turned up; three men from the local life-saving station a mile or so away, a lumber buyer and a sixteen-year-old boy. This was the scene on those desolate dunes, as described by Orville Wright:

During the night of December 16, 1903, a strong, cold wind blew from the north. When we arose on the morning of the 17th, the puddles of water, which had been standing about camp since the recent rains, were covered with ice. The wind had a velocity of 22 to 27 miles an hour. We thought it would die down before long,

5

but when ten o'clock arrived and the wind was as brisk as ever, we decided to get the machine out.

Wilbur ran at the side, holding the wing to balance it on the track. The machine, facing a 27-mile wind, started very slowly. The course of the flight up and down was exceedingly erratic, partly due to the irregularity of the air and partly to lack of experience in handling this machine.

The control of the elevator was difficult on account of its being balanced too near the centre. This gave it a tendency to turn itself when started, so that it turned too far on one side and then too far on the other. As a result the machine would rise suddenly to about 10 feet, and then as suddenly dart for the ground. A sudden dart when a little over 100 feet from the end of the track or a little over 120 feet from the point at which it rose into the air, ended the flight.

This flight lasted only 12 seconds, but it was nevertheless the first in the history of the world in which a machine carrying a man had raised itself by its own power into the air in full flight, had sailed forward without reduction of speed, and had finally landed at a point as high as that from which it had started.

One of the men, John T. Daniels, had clicked a camera aimed at the end of the monorail runway and recorded for all time the *Flyer* in flight, with Orville Wright lying prone on the lower wing. In the photograph, beside the starboard wing, trots Wilbur Wright in a peak-cap, just having let go of the wing and now surely willing the *Flyer* forward with all his soul. And there too is the *Flyer* itself, a maze of struts and wires and wings, with no wheels, its skids some three feet off the ground. And it is flying.

It was just after 10.30 a.m. on that memorable morning. Then Wilbur took over the controls, while Orville watched and guided. Again the *Flyer* sailed forward at some thirty miles an hour for eleven seconds. Orville did a third trip for fifteen seconds, and then came the fourth and longest flight of the day.

The time was noon. Wilbur shot forward and upwards. The *Flyer* steadied and flew on at a good thirty miles an hour, forcing itself forward in the icy Atlantic wind.

A quarter of a minute passed, then half a minute, three-quarters. then Wilbur made rather too sharp an adjustment after negotiating a slight sand hillock. The *Flyer* dipped, dived, and struck the sand. But by then it had travelled 852 feet from its starting place and remained airborne for fifty-nine seconds.

A few minutes later, a gust of wind caught the *Flyer*, overturned it, and did damage to various vital parts of it. But although the machine never flew again, the air age had arrived.

The fantastic fact, though, was that none of the press were there to see it – and no one really took much notice of it at the time.

It was not really until five years later in France that the world realized the significance of the Wrights' achievements, when throughout that year, Wilbur Wright astounded Europe by a succession of sensational flights, culminating in his record at Le Mans on 31 December 1908, of 2 hours 20 minutes 23.2 seconds in the air. It was no accident then that the next famous flight, in the following year, was by a Frenchman, Monsieur Blériot.

2

BLÉRIOT

First to fly the English Channel

A thousand pounds to the first person to fly the English Channel. That was the offer Lord Northcliffe made in the *Daily Mail* on 5 October 1908. Despite the achievements of the Wright brothers, only a handful of people really recognized the potential of the aeroplane – either for peace or war. Northcliffe was one of these.

This offer of a prize for the Channel flight fired the imagination of the public as well as that of the select band of pioneer aviators in Europe at the time. None of these pioneers wasted any time in trying to win the award – and the prestige deriving from the first successful flight over such a famous stretch of water as the English Channel.

Blériot, who had already covered considerable distances in his No. XI machine, was determined to win this honour for France. But two more airmen appeared on the scene and Blériot realized he would have to hurry if he were to be the victor.

The odds were against him from the outset, for he had suffered quite a bad crash only a matter of days before he finally attempted the Channel project. Blériot's usual method of extricating himself from fatal or serious injuries was to clamber out on to one of the wings just before crashing, but he had not managed to make his customary exit from his seat on this occasion. One of the inevitable faults had occurred when he was in the air: the fuel pipe snapped and the resulting flow of petrol had flared up frighteningly, forcing him to stay in his seat and bring the plane down as best he could. The blazing fuel ignited the flimsy fuselage and the aeroplane hit the ground in a shambles of smoke and fire. The heat had burned one of his feet badly, but he managed to pitch out of the plane as his helpers hurried up to it.

At the time of the Channel flight he still had the foot bandaged and walked with a limp. Nevertheless he protested he would be all right to fly.

Meanwhile one of his rivals beat him to the first shot at the goal on 19 July. Since the Channel separates England from France, it seemed appropriate that the man making the opening move in the exciting experiment was half English and half French.

His name was Hubert Latham, and he had an English father and a French mother. Latham had the use of an elegant Antoinette IV monoplane, distinguished by its slender lines. For those early times, the plane was unusually graceful, as its name might suggest.

Latham got his crated monoplane to a place called Sangatte, not far from Calais. He assembled it in one of the small group of sheds originally constructed in connection with the scheme for building a Channel Tunnel. Yes, they were talking about it as long ago as that and even earlier! But now the idea had been temporarily shelved and the sheds stood neglected. It was significant, therefore, that he should have chosen a shed associated with this submarine means of bridging the Channel when he was about to try and demonstrate a more effective and expeditious way – above the water.

Latham knew he had to make his effort promptly to stand a chance of winning. So soon after daybreak on 19 July 1909, he helped to get the Antoinette out of the shed and in a matter of minutes he was ready for the flight. He carried a camera to record any details he could of the flight, and he glanced out over the cliffs to see the French destroyer which was standing by some way out in case of accidents. And with these primitive aeroplanes, there usually were.

Latham rose up over Sangatte, circled, and headed out to the calm sea. He set his compass in the direction of Dover and sat back and hoped for the best. The hard work had gone on before, while the aeroplane was being assembled and tested. He had flown it only a day or so previously and it had seemed to be working well.

But before seven o'clock that morning, when Latham had only flown a very few miles, he began to have sparking plug trouble. The engine started spluttering ominously, missing, and eventually failed completely. As the propeller slowly stopped turning, Latham realized with a jolt that he had to set the machine down somehow on the water.

He glided gently down over the smooth surface at an angle as small as he could possible manage. Fortunately he was a skilled pilot; the sea scarcely rippled; a French destroyer was steaming towards the area, churning up the sea in its haste.

So six miles out from the Calais coastline, Hubert Latham juggled with his controls to keep the plane as level as possible – and came down to water-level. It would have been a marvellous landing if the ground had not been liquid. At first, the sleek Antoinette fuselage floated on the surface and the wings hardly got wet, but soon the aeroplane did start to submerge slowly, so Latham calmly climbed out on to a wing, where he waited for rescue, which soon came. So expertly had Latham set the plane down on the sea that he remained completely dry the whole time, but the aeroplane was virtually a write-off.

Latham sent an urgent message to Paris for a replacement and was glad to see one arrive at Sangatte only three days after his abortive attempt. It was now 22 July and the race was really on. Latham and his team started to assemble and test the second model at a frantic pace, for he knew that Blériot had by then appeared and that his rival would be likely to prove highly dangerous to his hopes.

The second of Blériot's rivals was some miles off at Wissant, near Boulogne. He bore the imposing title of Comte de Lambert, but despite this and a Wright biplane, the other two did not really see him as a serious contender.

Blériot had heard, of course, of Latham's fall into the water, but this did not deter him at all. He had had far worse spills himself. And hadn't he actually flown his No. XI machine at a distance equal to the Channel crossing quite recently? The Blériot No. XI was a monoplane, like Latham's, and powered by a 25-horsepower Anzani engine. Now it had been uncrated, assembled, and awaited its moment amid the tufty sand-dune coastline at Baraques, just outside Calais.

After Blériot's wife had bade him farewell, she was taken aboard the French destroyer on rescue duty. There would be no problem in recovering an airman up to about ten miles from the French coast, but if an aeroplane should come down after flying about halfway across the Channel, the destroyer would have been outpaced. Blériot reckoned to fly at a speed around fifty miles an hour, far faster than any ship could manage at that time. So there were very real hazards in this venture. Twenty-odd miles of sea can seem an ocean to a pilot in trouble.

The two chief opponents had been right about the Comte. He was not yet ready to try his luck.

By Saturday, 24 July, both Latham and Blériot were ready for the flight. Then the weather intervened quite dramatically. All day the wind whined up the Channel from the south-west, so that neither of them could possibly hope to succeed in their little light aeroplanes. The weather did not look likely to change much as dusk fell, but Blériot felt that the prospects could improve during the night, so he made arrangements to rise well before dawn and travel by motor car the short way to Baraques to be ready in case any attempt were possible on Sunday, 25 July.

As the night died, so did the wind.

The rival machines were housed only a mile or so from each other, and the first that the Latham team knew of any activity by Blériot was when Latham's friends actually glimpsed No. XI being wheeled out on the sand flats below the cliffs. Through the dawn haze, they saw four men steadily pushing the little monoplane along on its spoked wheels. The curved propeller quivered in the faint breeze. And the pilot himself stood in the cockpit, his helmet flap dangling under his chin, superintending the movement of the machine towards its starting point. Then he sat down between and behind the two broad wings, and made last-minute checks to his controls, clearly anxious to be up and away.

Before the final formalities, Blériot turned to one of his friends and asked in his usual ultra-casual way: 'Incidentally, where *is* Dover?'

'Over there,' came the response, with an equally casual wave in the general direction of the English coast. Blériot did not carry a compass. It was all a bit haphazard! With that Blériot was ready to take off.

They swung the large propeller manually and the motor started. An engine of the kind in this aeroplane ran without becoming badly hot in the realms of twenty minutes. But Blériot would need twice that time to cross the Channel. That was a measure of the risk involved, though there were others as well.

The official take-off time read, 4.41 a.m., 25 July 1909. Most of Europe was still fast asleep, unaware that history was about to be made.

Before the Antoinette's team could even call Latham to his machine, and still scarcely believing that Blériot was attempting anything more than a trial, they saw their rival's aeroplane signalled

11

away, ascend over the sands, and set its nose out to sea on the course so casually indicated.

'He's heading for Dover,' one of them cried out in panic. But by then they knew it was already too late to do anything, so they merely watched mesmerized as the Blériot XI veered round and vanished into the morning mist over the Channel.

The grey light showed through the open framework of the fuselage, which ended in the upturned tail at the rear. And the same light pierced the three landing wheels which had stopped spinning by now and would not be able to turn again till they made contact with the ground of another country – England.

Blériot vaguely made out the smoke of the destroyer *Escopette* ahead and below, but then the little monoplane sailed steadily up to, and past, the warship. For a moment or two, Blériot continued to turn round to see if she were still visible, but after ten minutes' flying he realized she could help him no more: he was on his own. From now on if the aeroplane failed and fell he would probably drown.

By this time, the French coast had also faded far behind him and he could not see anything ahead of him. At this low altitude visibility was limited to a few miles anyway. So there he was, surrounded by morning mist; below him, the sea; and somewhere ahead, England – he hoped.

He did not feel too happy knowing he was the first man to be suspended in space in this unhealthy position miles out to sea. With each passing moment, the destroyer fell further astern.

'I was amazed,' he said. 'I could see nothing at all. For ten minutes I was lost. It was a strange position to be alone, unguided, in the air over the middle of the Channel.'

In fact he flew the aeroplane along the approximate line indicated to him at the start by the destroyer. Not exactly advanced navigation but at least an improvement on the original briefing!

Twenty minutes had passed and he was barely half way across. That was the average time the engine was expected to run without showing signs of overheating. Could it hold out?

Then the engine began bumping. He sucked in his breath through his great moustache. He knew the signs. The scorching engine; the audible reaction; the effect on the aeroplane's performance. But luckily he ran right into some gentle drizzle which cooled the small engine sufficiently for it to go on chugging and churning away.

Blériot flew on.

Thirty minutes gone.

Suddenly he saw the rippling silhouette of the clifftops of Dover rising into shape several miles ahead of him. England! He was within sight of success. No one had ever been more delighted to glimpse those famous cliffs. Surely he couldn't fail now? That half-hour had seemed endless – but the final ten minutes were worse.

As he approached the coast he realized that he had been blown east by the breeze and was heading straight for St Margaret's Bay. He swung the aeroplane round to the south-west towards Dover, where he had arranged for a landing-place to be marked for him by a French journalist. The method of identification was for a French tricolour to be exposed flat on the ground, clearly visible from the air.

But the wind was fiercer now, and in this area where it blew off the sea and over the cliffs, it created currents that made the little aeroplane increasingly awkward to handle. Blériot zoomed up over the actual clifftop, not missing it by much. He could not really control the aeroplane properly, so decided to come down quickly in the first possible place. His leather-helmeted head peered out over the side of the aeroplane and he settled for a stretch of green grass not far from the cliffs where Dover Castle stood proud.

The aeroplane had done its duty well, and Blériot brought it down thankfully. The landing-strip turned out to be a steep slope just across a meadow from the castle, and the machine came down with a considerable crack. The front wheels spreadeagled and smashed, and with them went the propeller. The heavy landing gave Blériot a sharp shock and hurt him a little, but not enough to stop him vaulting out of the damaged machine and taking stock.

No one was in sight!

Several minutes later a policeman came up breathlessly, followed by the French journalist, till gradually a knot of onlookers had arrived to see this strange French flier on English soil. Where did he come from? There was a sailor, a straw-hatted man, several cloth-capped workers, and as it was England – a customs officer! And in the midst of them stood the triumphant, boyish Blériot. He'd done it. Thirty-one miles in forty minutes.

Lord Northcliffe, in a moment of vision, said at once, 'Britain is no longer an island.' How right he was.

And if men could cross the English Channel by air, why not the Atlantic Ocean? Ten years later they did.

3

WARNEFORD
Destroying the First Zeppelin

The first man to destroy a German Zeppelin, and one of the first famous flyers of the First World War, was Flight Sub Lieutenant Reginald Alexander John Warneford of the Royal Naval Flying Corps.

The enemy made their earliest Zeppelin raid on England on 19 January, 1915. Two airships reached the East Coast, dropped bombs on Great Yarmouth and King's Lynn, and killed four people. This was a fresh peril for the people of Britain, especially as more raids followed on places as far north as the Tyne.

The spring of 1915 was a worrying time altogether for Britain. The submarine war was under way with a vengeance, and then came news of the alarming headway being made in building bases in Belgium for housing the military raiding Zeppelins – German gasbags as they were called.

Towards the end of April, it was known that the first of the new military Zeppelins, L.Z. 37, had arrived there. The sister ships L.Z. 38 and L.Z. 39 soon followed in huge sheds of their own, and they lost no time in carrying the air war to London. The enemy High Command was confident in its campaign to reduce the British people to panic by airship attack. After a few skirmishing raids on various English towns, L.Z. 38 got through to drop the first bombs to fall on the capital, on 31 May, 1915.

Even before this, though, the British naval air unit based at Dunkirk had got in their initial blow at the Zeppelins. At 3.15 a.m. on 17 May, the L.Z. 39 was seen off Dunkirk nosing slowly east-wards. She had set out with her two sister ships for a raid along the Channel on both French and English towns. The warning that the airships were out had been received from England some time before, and two of the Dunkirk aircraft were already patrolling the area. Seven others took off as soon as the Zeppelin was sighted, and three pilots quickly closed with the enormous enemy.

Squadron Commander Spenser, D.A. Grey and Flight Sub Lieutenant Warneford attacked first, with machine-gun and rifle fire from below the L.Z. 39. But the Zeppelin put up her nose in disdain and proceeded to outclimb them. Their fire fell away harmlessly in an arc short of the great gasbag. The Zeppelin commander achieved this increase in altitude, of course, by dropping a load of ballast which at once caused the airship to spurt up hundreds of feet.

Piloting an Avro, however, Flight Commander A.W. Bigsworth kept on climbing after the ship as she veered off in the general direction of Ostend. At 10,000 feet over the town, he was actually a couple of hundred feet above her. This was high flying for those early days, yet Bigsworth flew right along the line of her back – and dropped his little load of four 20lb bombs. Smoke was sweeping from the tail of the airship as he turned back, but she still flew on, apparently little the worse, towards her shed at Evère, the Belgian base. It was learned later that the ship made a rough but safe landing. The bombs had caused the death of an enemy officer and injuries to several men in one of the gondolas. Five of the individual gasbags sustained damage and the airship lost her starboard after-propeller. Her two sister ships got back to base unscratched but their respite was to be brief.

From the beginning of 1915, if not before, British airmen had been awaiting a chance to challenge the Zeppelins. These huge airships never indulged in legal warfare as it was understood at that time. Instead they were clearly intended to terrify by gliding ghostlike at night over undefended towns and dropping their bombs. When these raids really got going, they aroused the immediate indignation of the whole civilized world, and as they began to be aimed at London itself, the only answer seemed to be to try and attack the Zeppelins at their bases. A conference of officers at Dunkirk, where the British naval air unit already in action was based, decided to attack from the air the Zeppelin sheds at Evère and Berchem Ste Agathe.

Just after midnight on 7 June, exactly a week after the first raid on London, four pilots stood by on their aerodrome at Dunkirk, ready to set out to bomb the airship sheds. The ground crews stowed the bombs in their racks and checked the machine guns. Then mechanics warmed up the engines of the first pair of planes. Flight Lieutenant

15

J.P. Wilson and Flight Sub Lieutenant J.S. Mills were piloting these two Henri Farman biplanes for the raid on Evère. After taxiing down the runway and taking off at 12.40 a.m., they at once ran into heavy summer mist over the Belgian coast, so that they had to fly blind on a compass course towards Evere.

Unknown to the British pilots, this mist was also vitally affecting an enemy operation, for by coincidence there was German activity at the same time around these bases.

The enemy High Command had ordered a raid on England that night by naval Zeppelins from North German sheds and also by the three military airships from Belgium, L.Z. 37, 38 and 39. The plan was to rendezvous and sail on a strafing raid of the English Home Counties. But they reckoned without the mist. All three duly got off the ground with their load of bombs, but L.Z. 38 had some trouble in the air, landed again, and was returned to her shed at Evère. The other two ran into the thick mist over the North Sea, lost their way completely, cruised around anxious and bewildered for some time, and then began to nose their way homeward again. They did not drop any bombs on England at all. The four British pilots knew none of this at the time, of course, and as they flew from Dunkirk across Belgium to the attack, the L.Z. 38 was shut up again in her shed at Evère, and the other two ships were groping their way home from a fruitless flight.

Meanwhile, Wilson reached Evère at 2.05 a.m. As he started to circle, peering out to try to penetrate the gloom, a searchlight stabbed on, signalling a series of long flashes in the air. Wilson thought quickly, and promptly replied with short flashes on his pocket lamp, which seemed to satisfy the searchlight party near the airship base. At any rate, he was free from anti-aircraft fire for the further fifteen minutes he spent circling over his target, waiting hopefully for the first faint tinges of dawn to outline the airship shed. At 2.20 a.m. he could just see the shed slightly. He pushed his joystick forward till he had dived to 2,000 feet and then he released his three 65lb bombs. One of them hit the centre of the shed and sent up black billows of smoke – but no flames. Wilson did not wait to watch longer than that, as anti-aircraft guns were already spraying the sky.

Ten minutes later, at 2.30 a.m., Flight Sub Lieutenant Mills arrived overhead to the accompaniment of such shatteringly accurate fire that he had to swerve clear of his target as he was actually diving down to the shed. He swung wide, circling to gain precious height, and returned at a reasonable 5,000 feet to drop his four 20lb bombs. There was still only smoky light as the bombs fell towards the buildings, grouped in vague shadows below.

Then the whole Belgian countryside became brilliantly lit up as the bombs hit home and L.Z. 38, the first of the London raiders, frizzled in fierce flames.

A great glow followed Mills as he turned back towards his base, but soon he flew into thick white mist. For two hours until 4.30 a.m. he steered solely by compass. When he judged he must be near home, he dived low in search of somewhere to land – and nearly struck the sea. He hauled on his joystick and managed to avoid crashing into the water by literally a few feet. Then he straightened up and turned south. At exactly 4.45 a.m. he landed on the beach between Calais and Dunkirk. Wilson also had trouble with the mist, not managing to land until half an hour later, in a field near Montreuil.

So to Flight Sub Lieutenant Warneford's own action. At the time when the attack on Evere was in full swing, he was having a lone duel with one of the two returning airships, L.Z. 37, at close quarters. Warneford and the fourth pilot had set out to bomb Berchem Ste Agathe a few minutes after the others had taken off. But before he got near his objective, Warneford suddenly distinguished, against the milky night horizon, the faint pencil-slim shape of an airship far off towards Ostend. She was flying fast at about 6,000 feet. The time was 1 a.m. and he gave chase at once. His companion, meanwhile, was out of luck. The lights over his instruments failed as he got lost in the dark, and he had to land in a field near Cassel, where his plane turned turtle. The pilot suffered no injuries, however.

The L.Z. 37 was 521 feet long, with a capacity of 953,000 cubic feet. Its useful load was eight tons. Eighteen gasbags held it aloft, and it was powered by four 210hp engines, which could thrust it at a top speed of some fifty miles an hour. It could carry a ton and a quarter of bombs and its armament comprised four machine guns. In short, it was quite an opponent for one pilot.

Warneford was flying a Morane single-seater monoplane. At 1.50 a.m., having tailed the airship for forty-five minutes, he caught up with her a few miles past Bruges. He had no doubt that they had seen him, since the airship opened up with heavy Maxim fire from the gondolas. He realized that the airship was no sitting target, tremendous as she might be. He realized also that he must force his bomb-laden plane still higher – but he could not climb at that range and under fire. So he turned and retreated to gain height. With supreme – and excessive – confidence the Zeppelin commander swung the ship round after the impudent little monoplane, and continued to keep it under fire for some time. But Warneford had speed and manoeuvrability on his side, and he cleverly outclimbed the giant he had challenged to such strange combat.

By 2.15 a.m. the firing seemed to have stopped, and so the pilot considered it comparatively safe to approach from behind, but well above, the airship. His altitude had then reached 11,000 feet.

Over two miles high, in the middle of the night, piloting a primitive aircraft, Warneford turned back on the Zeppelin, switched off his engine and dived to descend on top of her. The little Morane monoplane glided silently down to 7,000 feet and went into the run from one end of the airship to the other, at about 150 feet above the envelope. No sound emerged from his engines. The Zeppelin crew were completely unaware how near he had flown to them. This is how Warneford described what happened next:

> When I was almost over the monster, I descended about fifteen yards and flung six bombs. The sixth struck the envelope of the ship fair and square in the middle. There was instantly a terrible explosion. The displacement of the air round about me was so great that a tornado seemed to have been produced. My machine was tossed upwards, and then flung absolutely upside down. I was forced to loop the loop in spite of myself.

Warneford had been trained to keep his head at all times – even the wrong way up, above a disintegrated Zeppelin. As the great airship plummeted, leaving a trail of smoke and flames, the Morane got into a nose dive. Yet Warneford somehow clung to the joystick as if it were his link with life. Precious seconds passed as the little plane plunged and lunged all around the sky, losing even more precious altitude. Then Warneford managed to jerk the joystick and regain some slight control.

He brought up the nose from the dreaded dive, and once more saw the scene the right way round. Scanning the sky for the enemy, he saw nothing, so he leaned over his cockpit and spotted the Zeppelin already on the ground in a ragged heap of flames – and there were pieces of something still burning in the air all the way down. All

18

Zeppelin L.Z. 37 being attacked and destroyed by Reginald Warneford flying a Morane single-seater monoplane

except one of the Zeppelin's crew of twenty-eight perished. The flaming wreckage of the airship fell on the Convent of St Elizabeth, in a superb of Ghent, killing two nuns. The sole survivor actually leaped out of the doomed 'dirigible' when still 200 feet in the air. He crashed through the roof of the convent, where a bed broke his fall. He suffered slight injuries and in fact flew again for the enemy.

Warneford's amazing adventure was far from finished, however, when he found himself in control of the aircraft again. He heard a spluttering sound from the engine of the Morane and discovered that the whirlwind violence of the explosion had broken the joint on his petrol pipe and pump from the back tank. He had to land at once. Choosing a field faintly visible at the back of a forest, he brought the battered plane safely to earth close to a farmhouse. Continuous changes of course, coupled with the persistent mist, made it impossible for him to guess where he was. In fact he must have been some thirty miles behind the enemy lines at 2.40 a.m. Acting in accordance with orders on what to do when forced to land in enemy-held territory, he prepared to destroy the plane to avoid it falling into German hands. When he had everything ready for firing the petrol – and so burning the plane – he suddenly had an idea. Perhaps he could still escape back to British lines.

Listening acutely, he could hear nothing to suggest that he had been seen or heard, so he started to work furiously repairing the broken joint. Half an hour passed with sickening slowness. At last the joint was made and Warneford could try to restart his engine. Shot after shot failed and he felt that soon someone was bound to hear him. When he had almost despaired it suddenly shook into life, and he scrambled into the cockpit as the Morane actually seemed to be jogging over the grass in eagerness to be airborne.

Still he was not safe. He had survived a sojourn of thirty-five minutes inside enemy lines, but he found himself flying in fog, groping south-west, ignorant of his position, and in a patched-up plane. Several times Warneford descended through the clouds to try and spot a landmark amid the mist, but he could not. He flew on by compass direction alone, however, and eventually came clear of the fog. He landed to learn that he was safe and sound behind British lines again.

'Where am I?' Warneford asked the first person he could find.

'Why, Cap Gris Nez.'

He took in some petrol and waited for the weather to clear, before taking off for the second time on the adventurous sortie. He flew through clear sky back to his base at Dunkirk, arriving in time for a late breakfast at 10.30 a.m. – and to break the news of destroying the dirigible.

Tragically, Warneford was killed only ten days after this exploit. He was piloting a Henri Farman plane near Paris when it broke up in the air at 700 feet, indicating how fallible were those early designs even for simple flying, let alone for combat. But Warneford's deeds did not die. He and his two fellow-pilots routed the three Belgium-based Zeppelins. The sole survivor, L.Z. 39, was moved to the eastern front of Europe where she was destroyed by fire later the same year. As a result of the Dunkirk pilots' two brilliant successes, the Germans completely abandoned the Belgian bases except for emergency landings. This was the first victory against the Zeppelins. The decisive one followed in 1916.

4

ALBERT BALL
The Earliest Air Ace

In the early days of the First World War, fighting in the air was unknown. For all practical purposes, the use of aircraft was limited to reconnaissance over the enemy's lines. Then came young men like Captain Albert Ball, who flew 'crazy crates' and became air aces in a matter of months.

Ball first flew across the Channel on 15 February, 1916, to join 13 Squadron of the Royal Flying Corps in the battle line in France. At that particular period, things were not going well with the Allies in the air. Their planes were still inferior to those of the enemy, who could choose their own time and place for combat. It was hardly an auspicious moment for the nineteen-year-old Ball to arrive. He was soon sitting in the cockpit of a B.E.2C ready to fight the better equipped Fokkers. By May he had been transferred to 11 Squadron, then using the Nieuport Scout – considered to be the best single-seater aircraft in France.

Ball was not brilliant from the beginning. He was not even an exceptionally good pilot, but one who was becoming better all the time by practising. One of his brother-officers said that he was never for a moment what pilots called a star performer. He never swanked in the air – or on the ground. He was not a fancy pilot, but he was a great man.

After a long air duel with a German airman in those early days of 1916, neither Ball nor the enemy pilot could outwit the other, and their ammunition was all gone. Suddenly there was nothing either of them could do, high in the air over the battlefields of France. So they both burst out laughing; they could not help it, the situation seemed so ridiculous. They flew side by side, laughing at each other for a few seconds, and then they waved adieu from their respective cockpits and flew off for their own bases. 'He was a real sport, was that Hun,' Ball said later.

During the early battles of the Somme, Ball would be aloft from 2.30 a.m. till 9.30 p.m. From the front, he wrote home for some seeds for a garden he had out there. 'You will think this idea strange but, you see, it will be a good thing to take my mind off my work; also I shall like it.' Clearly Ball was no typical pilot.

On 25 June, 1916, Second Lieutenant Ball – as he was at that date – scored a success which proved to be the first of many. He brought down an enemy kite-balloon used for observation. He did not feel it to be much of a triumph, but the manner in which he accomplished it was a sign of his thoroughness.

Ball banked steeply to get into a position to bomb the balloon for the first time, and then released his load. It missed. Ball maintained the traditions of the Nottinghamshire and Derbyshire Regiment and the Royal Flying Corps by returning to his base for a fresh supply of bombs. He took off again and returned to the spot where the long balloon still hovered in the sky with its observer dangling from a little gondola. Despite the pounding he had received from enemy ground guns the first time, Ball made no mistake on this return trip. The balloon caught fire and fell to earth, enabling the Allies to continue operations without the hindrance of an enemy air observation on fire and movements.

Just a week after this, Ball shot down his first plane. Patrolling over the Mercatel–Arras road, he spotted six enemy fighters setting on a group of British F.E.s. He did not hesitate, but flew straight towards the fray, peeled off a German and sent him spinning out of control. Another time, Ball took on six fighters single-handed with methodical calm, although several miles behind enemy lines. He tore into the attack, got first one in his sights, then another, and brought both of them down, despite the presence of the remaining four, whom he drove off one by one. Already he was being heralded as the most brilliant air fighter of the war, a claim he would never have accepted, of course.

'Pluck, not luck,' was the phrase used to describe Ball's deeds. Thought, insight, experiment, and perpetual practice – these things were his aids. Within a short time, he had become an ace of the air. His knowledge of how to use sun, wind and clouds, coupled with an instinct for the blind side of any enemy machine he had in view, made him a master in the art of approaching unobserved. And once at close quarters, he usually took up his favourite position under the German's tail before opening fire. His experience taught him to anticipate any move an unprepared enemy might make, and his quick wits how to take advantage of it.

About this time, his commanding officer wrote the following brief report of Ball's service since joining 11 Squadron:

Lieutenant Ball has had more than twenty-five combats since May 16 in a single-seater contest. Of these, thirteen have been against more than one hostile machine.

In particular, on August 22, he attacked in succession formations of seven and five machines in the same flight; on August 28, four and ten in succession; and on August 31, twelve.

He has forced twenty German machines to land, of which eight have been destroyed vertically with flames coming out of the fuselage, and seven seen to be wrecked on the ground. During this period he has forced two hostile balloons down and destroyed one.

These are the bare facts. This is what happened on those occasions when he attacked groups of enemy planes. On 22 August, 1916, Ball saw seven of the enemy flying in formation. He immediately attacked one of them, and shot it down at a mere fifteen yards' range. The remainder retired at full throttle. Only a few minutes afterwards, Ball saw five more hostile planes and did the same again. This time, though, he shot one down when it was precisely ten yards from his own cockpit. Flames trailed out of the fuselage as it gradually got more and more out of control. Ball did not stop at this. He swung his aircraft around at another of the enemy which had been firing at him while he had been previously engaged. A burst of machine-gun fire holed it in a dozen places, and the plane fell into a village nestling below, landing on top of a house.

But by now, Ball's own plane bore signs of the scrap, being badly shot about in various places. Yet although he had run out of ammunition, he did not want to break off the battle. So he hurried down to the nearest Allied aerodrome for fresh supplies and returned to take up where he had left them. Three more machines met him this time. He flew in cleverly among them to attack – and caused all three to dive and go out of control. Only when he had nearly run out of petrol did he reluctantly swing his stick back to base again. When he had landed safely, he saw the fuselage riddled from the fire he had intercepted.

By August 1916, Ball was at his best, joining 60 Squadron in that month. Over the Somme during August and September, he had become the first flyer to make what could be called a business of killing Huns. He allowed nothing to interfere with his duty, although he did not enjoy the actual execution of it. This is a story of air aces and air battles, but one should always remember the men behind the names who achieved such amazing feats. This letter from Ball to his mother reveals more about him than almost anything else. It was written after his refusing a job as an air instructor back in Britain.

I have offered, dear, to go out again and have another smack. I don't offer because I want to go, but because every boy who has loving people and a good home should go out and stand up for it. You think I have done enough, but oh, no, there is not, or at least should not be, such a thought in such a war as this . . . It is an honour to be able to fight and do one's best for such a country as this and for such dear people. I shall fight for you and come home for you, and God always looks after me and makes me strong; may He look after you also.

I only scrap because it is my duty, and I do not think anything bad about the Hun. He is just a good chap with very little guts, trying to do his best. Nothing makes me feel more rotten than to see them go down; but, you see, it is either them or me, so I must do my best to make it a case of *them*.

I am, indeed, looked after by God; but oh, I do get tired of always living to kill. I am beginning to feel like a murderer. I shall be pleased when I have finished.

Oh, won't it be nice when all this beastly killing is over, and we can just enjoy ourselves and not hurt anyone. I hate this game, but it is the only thing one must do just now.

So it went on. One day Ball went on escort duty in a bombing raid. Suddenly seeing four enemy machines in tight formation, he dived on them, shattered their neat grouping, and shot down the one nearest to him. The enemy fell on its nose, and Ball flew down to about 500 feet to make certain it was wrecked. Enemy gunfire made it unhealthy to remain low for long.

Soon after this, he encountered three times as many enemy. A formation of a dozen flew in typical Teutonic style, oblivious of his presence above them. He dived down at top speed and fired a complete drum into the nearest plane, which went down. Ball's strategy and aim were both unerring by then. Several more hostile planes pitched into him, so he let off three more drums at them, driving down another one. Then he called it a day and returned, crossing the front line at a very low level with his machine in a drastically damaged state.

It began to be almost a matter of mere numbers, as if nothing, no one, could stop his stream of successes. Attacking three of the Huns, he shot down one. Then within a very short space of time, he accounted for eight enemy and forced many others to land.

On his twentieth birthday, he had been presented with the honorary freedom of his native Nottingham. It was while home at this ceremony that he told how he had added four more victims in a single flight on the very night he was to come home on leave.

I had done three and used my last drum of ammunition when another arrived on the scene. I thought it was all up. He had his gun trained on me, and ought to have smothered me with bullets. Then I saw him shaky and seized my chance. I had only my revolver, and I emptied it into his face. He went on a little way, turned over – and fell.

So from the Battle of the Somme in 1916 to the Battle of Arras in 1917. The air offensive of the Battle of Arras opened along the whole British front on 4 April, 1917, five days before the infantry action began. The object of this offensive was to force the enemy airmen away from the immediate battle area so as to allow maximum measure of freedom for corps planes.

As had happened often before, this offensive opened in conditions of low clouds and rain, yet the fighting was intense and the losses severe. On the five days from 4–8 April, the British lost seventy-five planes in action, with the loss of 105 men. In addition there were an abnormal number of flying accidents. In those same five days no less than fifty-six aircraft were wrecked and struck off the strength.

Meanwhile, back over Arras, in contrast to the mass fighting, Captain Albert Ball, now of 56 Squadron, flew alone on roving commissions in a series of successful encounters with the enemy. He had perfected his combat technique. When he attacked a two-seater enemy plane with the observer sitting behind, his tactics were to dive from the half-rear until the observer had got his gun in that position. Then Ball would swerve suddenly, pass to the opposite side, and fire from below at close range before the observer had time to swing his gun round.

Flying one of his beloved Nieuport fighters on the morning of 23 April, Ball launched into two German two-seaters and peppered one so precisely that it crashed to the ground upside down. Later that same morning, in an S.E.5 this time, he was over Cambrai at 13,000 feet when he saw a formation of five Albatros fighters. He gave chase, came up with them over Selvigny, dived at the nearest and dispatched it in flames. The other four all put batches of bullets into Ball's S.E.5, but he made good his escape, having chalked up just one more victory. For good measure on his homeward run, he attacked another stray two-seater, forcing it to land.

From the start of May, the casualties to British planes dropped drastically and the air fighting was pushed away from the front lines towards the German back areas. This had been the aim of the offensive from the outset.

Ball was still thoroughly in the thick of it all, and did not confine himself to lone sorties and single combat. On the evening of 2 May came a clash of air arms east of Arras involving forty fighting planes – quite a crowd for those days. Luckily, twenty-five of these were British, and these planes gradually drove the enemy pilots east to Donai, but most of the individual combats ended in stalemate. Ball added one more to his list. The British did not lose a single person or plane.

Following this action, a major British infantry attack opened before dawn next day, supported by bombing from the air. The German pilots came back into the battle on 4 May, and on the next day the British pilots were given a rest from bombing, reconnaissance and offensive patrols. This did not apply to Ball, however, and that evening he took off in an S.E.5 and sighted a couple of enemy single-seaters coming from Cambrai.

Adapting his tactics to the current conditions, Ball allowed them to approach his tail before doing a rapid turn and attacking one from underneath. As it fell, he was already manoeuvring for a perfect position to get at the second. In fact, he found his plane and the enemy approaching head-on – a position which would frighten most people but one he welcomed, having often exploited it successfully.

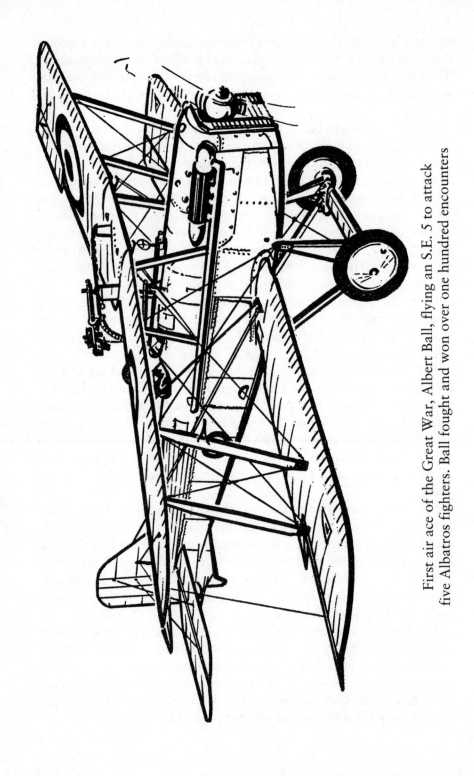

First air ace of the Great War, Albert Ball, flying an S.E. 5 to attack five Albatros fighters. Ball fought and won over one hundred encounters

Ball had found from experience that if he held his course firmly the enemy pilot always swerved away at the last moment to avoid a collision. This split-second, when the German lost the cover given by his engine, was usually enough for Ball to finish the fight. If not, he was ready for a rapid climbing turn and dive, which would put his enemy at a disadvantage.

In this case, the two planes came towards each other at speed, almost to the point of junction, when the German began to fall out of control. Presumably Ball had hit him or his engine. The engine of the S.E.5 had been hit, too, and oil spurted out into the cockpit, covering Ball. But he went down low to look at his victory before returning in the sunset to base. The two German planes lay on the ground within a few hundred yards of one another, totally wrecked.

By 7 May, 1917, Ball had fought and won 100 encounters. During this century of success, he had six machines so badly damaged that he was forced to make temporary landings for repairs. Yet he escaped without serious personal injury – until 7 May.

To try and catch the Germans while they had the most possible planes in the air around their aerodrome at Donai, patrols were ordered by eighteen fighters of the British North Wing. One of these patrols encountered severe fighting in the evening. The planes chiefly involved were ten S.E.5s all of 56 Squadron. Out of six Spads patrolling with the S.E.5s, only one joined in the fighting, which was confused by rain and poor visibility and took place through rolling layers of clouds. The other five Spad pilots lost touch with each other and saw nothing at all of the combats.

It was in this fighting that Captain Albert Ball was killed.

Flying in three layers, the ten S.E.5s met a group of red Albatros fighters near Cambrai, in similar layers. Amid the befogging cloud and blurring rain, a dramatic dogfight developed. Two of the enemy went spinning fatally through the clouds. After a while, the S.E.5 pilots lost touch in the atrocious weather, and one of them, Captain H. Meintjes, flew off alone in the direction of Lens, where he unexpectedly came across a single red Albatros. The two planes exchanged bullets, which not only pitted the fuselage of the British fighter, but hit Meintjes in the wrist. Losing blood badly, he had to dive steeply to escape from a worse fate.

Another detached group of four S.E.5s, headed by Captain C.M. Crowe, made for Vitry and shot down an enemy fighter apparently all on its own. Almost at once, however, a horde of other enemy aircraft swooped on them from above, scarred and then shattered one of the S.E.5s, wounded the pilot in another, who managed to land providentially near a Canadian hospital, and damaged a third S.E.5 so seriously that the pilot had great difficulty in getting back to base.

Crowe then flew back to the prearranged point above Arras and rejoined Ball and the remaining three pilots. The five closed formation and resumed their patrol towards Vitry and Lens. Then they got involved with four red single-seaters. The rain was streaming steadily now, and they were still hampered by the clouds and general foul visibility. The five planes became split up soon after the fight started. Three of them returned home safely.

Ball and Crowe, however, continued to patrol independently, although out of touch with one another. At about 8 p.m., they met over Fresnoy and flew together. The next thing that happened was when Ball fired two Very lights into the fading evening sky, indicating that he was about to dive on a single red fighter he had spotted through the gloom. Crowe reacted instinctively and also dived, while a stray Spad joined in as well.

All three British pilots attacked the enemy in turn, and then Ball and the German disappeared into the gloom-grey of a cloudbank – still scrapping. Crowe followed them, but when he emerged from the clouds he could see nothing of either plane, so he had to return to base.

The body of Captain Albert Ball was recovered by French civilians from the wreckage of his biplane, and he was buried by the enemy at Annoeullin. The Germans later stated that he fell in a fight with Richthofen's younger brother, Lothar, who was himself forced to land with his petrol tanks torn by bullets.

Ball was officially credited with forty-three planes destroyed, but he had in fact scored many more than this. And he went down as one of the three or four leading air aces of the war.

By June the Battle of Arras was over, and interest moved to the Flanders front for the next stage in the bloody battles that added up to the First World War.

5

LEEFE ROBINSON
Defeat of the Zeppelins

Despite the defeat of the three Zeppelins based in Belgium, many more continued to cross the North Sea and English Channel during the following months. Bombs burst on London and the Midlands, as well as other far scattered points. From January 1915 to January 1916, in a total of twenty-one raids, some 1,900 bombs killed 277 people and injured 645. The attack on the Midlands on 31 January, 1916, ended the worst period as far as frequency, damage and casualties were concerned. But the threat remained and at regular intervals Zeppelins loomed out of the gloom to release their loads on some unsuspecting town, Canterbury or Preston, perhaps.

London received renewed attacks in August 1916, Zeppelins reaching the capital with comparative ease on the night of 24–25 August. This may have been the reason for the enemy's most dramatic demonstration against London on the night of 2–3 September.

In the afternoon of 2 September, sixteen airships – twelve naval and four military – set out for a combined raid with the City of London as their only objective. The Admiralty heard of their departure by 5 p.m. and the usual warning went out to the East Coast, where Zeppelins had the habit of crossing.

Out of the great load of bombs carried by this armada of airships, 261 high explosives and 202 incendiaries were destined to fall on English soil, but not one of them on London itself. The casualties from this load of some sixteen tons were four killed and twelve injured, but damage to buildings was only slight.

The failure of the raid was due partly to bad weather but mainly to the moral effect produced by the first night-flying victory for the defence planes, achieved against the only one of the four military airships definitely identified. This success came just in time, too, for the public was starting to doubt the much-praised anti-aircraft defences which had so far failed to shoot down a single Zeppelin.

Then came the Schutte-Lanz S.L. 11. The airship arrived unheralded at Foulness Point – the extreme tip of that part of Essex – at about 10.40 p.m. and proceeded to make a wide sweep over Essex and Hertford to approach London from the north-west. All the defence posts could do was to keep an accurate check on her movements. They reported her over St Albans at 1.10 a.m. and ten minutes later she dropped her first bombs, on London Colney. They did no damage. Other bombs followed, falling on North Mimms, Littleheath, Northaw, Gordon Hill, Clayhill, Cockfosters and Hadley Wood. From here the airship passed to Southgate and on to London itself, over the northern district of Wood Green. At this stage, she was picked up by the questing searchlights in Finsbury Park and Victoria Park.

From then on, the searchlights really kept her lit up, enabling the anti-aircraft guns to open fire. The shells split the air uncomfortably close to the S.L. 11, turning her off rapidly towards Edmonton, where she dropped six bombs – two falling fairly harmlessly in Eley's Explosive Works! The trail of bombs traced the course of the airship, as two on Ponders End were followed by more along Enfield highway and the last on Forty Hill and Turkey Street. Not one of the sixty bombs brought over by the S.L. 11 caused casualties, and the only damage was to houses and water-mains. Right out to Turkey Street, the guns fired at the Zeppelin continuously. Several shells burst close to her but none actually hit. It was left to a lone flyer to account for the S.L. 11.

On the first warning of the approach of the raider, planes had taken off in the dark from the three detached flights of 39 Home Defence Squadron at Hainault Farm, Suttons Farm and North Weald Bassett. Each flight sent up single planes at two-hourly intervals, the first pilots leaving their fields about 11 p.m.

Lieutenant William Leefe Robinson (of the Worcestershire Regiment and Royal Flying Corps), based at Suttons Farm, was to patrol the line from there to Joyce Green; Second Lieutenant C.S. Ross, from North Weald Bassett, had the line from there to Hainault; and Second Lieutenant A. de B. Brandon the line from Hainault to Suttons Farm. The second set of patrols was slightly different. Second Lieutenant F. Sowrey and B.H. Hunt had the line Joyce Green to

Farningham and Second Lieutenant J.I. Mackay the line North Weald to Joyce Green. The pilots ascended for these second patrols at about 1 a.m., when Leefe Robinson had already been in the air for nearly two hours.

Three of these officers, Leefe Robinson, Mackay and Hunt, all sighted and pursued the S.L. 11 and it is difficult to see how the airship could have escaped. Leefe Robinson came up with her first, when she was between Enfield highway and Turkey Street. Shells were rending the air around her – but he went straight into the attack. So he was liable to be hit by his own ground defences as well as by the substantial armament of the airship.

This is his account of his adventures, which included an earlier attempt to engage an unidentified military airship that made an abortive attack near Gravesend:

I have the honour to make the following report on night patrol made by me on the night of the 2nd/3rd instant.

I went up at about 11.8 p.m. on the night of the 2nd with instructions to patrol between Suttons Farm and Joyce Green. I climbed to 10,000 feet in fifty-three minutes. I counted what I thought were ten sets of flares. There were a few clouds below me, but on the whole it was a beautifully clear night.

I saw nothing until 1.10 a.m. when two searchlights picked up a Zeppelin SE. of Woolwich. The clouds had collected in this quarter, and the searchlights had some difficulty in keeping on the aircraft. By this time I had managed to climb to 12,900 feet, and I made in the direction of the Zeppelin, which was being fired on by a few anti-aircraft guns – hoping to cut it off on its way eastward.

I very slowly gained on it for about ten minutes. I judged it to be about 800 feet below me, and I sacrificed my speed in order to keep the height. It went behind some clouds, avoided the searchlights, and I lost sight of it. After fifteen minutes' fruitless search I returned to my patrol. I managed to pick up and distinguish my flares again.

At about 1.50 a.m. I noticed a red glow in NE. London. Taking it to be an outbreak of fire I went in that direction. At 2.5 a.m. a Zeppelin was picked up by the searchlights over NNE. London, as far as I could judge. Remembering my last failure, I sacrificed height (I was still 12,900 feet) for speed and made nose down in the direction of the Zeppelin. I saw shells bursting and night tracer shells flying around it.

When I drew closer I noticed that the anti-aircraft aim was too high or too low and in some cases falling 800 feet behind. A few tracers went right over. I could hear the bursts when about 3,000 feet from the Zeppelin.

I flew about 800 feet below it from bow to stern and distributed one drum along it – alternate New Brock and Pomeroy. It seemed to have no effect. I therefore moved to one side and gave it another drum distributed along its side – without apparent effect.

I then got behind it. By this time I was very close – 500 feet or less, below. I concentrated one drum on one part, the underneath rear. I was then at a height of 11,500 feet when attacking the Zeppelin.

I had hardly finished the drum before I saw the part fired at glow. In a few seconds the whole rear part was blazing. When the third drum was fired, there were no searchlights on the Zeppelin and no anti-aircraft gun was firing. I quickly got out of the way of the falling, blazing Zeppelin, and being very excited fired off a few red Very lights and dropped a parachute flare. Having very little oil and petrol left, I returned to Suttons Farm, landing at 2.45 a.m. On landing I found I had shot away the machine-gun wire guard, the rear part of the centre section, and had pierced the rear main spar several times.

That is Leefe Robinson's modest version of his victory.

At first the S.L. 11 glowed like a great incandescent gas-mantle. Then the fire from the pilot's bullets spread and tremendous tongues of flame tore jagged patterns in the night sky as she fell. Her huge wooden frame collapsed in a blaze of heat at Cuffley, a village some fifteen miles north of London, and the airship continued to burn for nearly two hours before she and her occupants were all gone. The instantaneous effect of this success was for the other Zeppelins to take fright at the fate of S.L. 11 and head for home as fast as their great forms could float in the air.

Captain W. Leefe Robinson led a formation of six Bristols on an offensive patrol. They ran into the German air ace Richthofen with catastrophic results. Two of the Bristols fell to the guns of the remarkable Richthofen and two more to junior officers of his squadron. The other two Bristols got back but much shot about in the process.

During the action, Robinson became a casualty. The enemy shot his engine out of action, forcing him to bring the Bristol down in hostile territory. The British hero was made a prisoner of war, suffering from shortage of food in the remaining eighteen months of the war. When he finally returned home to England in December 1918, he contracted the influenza, then rampant, and died.

With the collapse of the S.L. 11 there also collapsed any attempt to launch mass dirigible raids on London. The S.L. 11 had tested the defences, and the crews of many of the other enemy airships had actually witnessed her fate. From that moment, bombs were dropped not on targets but at random to try to lighten their loads as quickly as they could.

This first airship brought down on British soil naturally had the opposite effect on the public here. Even after the cheering of that night had died down, they were never as afraid of Zeppelins as before. Leefe Robinson in a B.E.2C could beat one single-handed – and with bullets, not shells or bombs. They could not be so serious after all – that was the general conclusion.

But in fact this merely marked the beginning of the end of Zeppelin raids. The Germans were not going to give up lightly, certainly not after the loss of only one airship. They did operate much more cautiously, however, and for the next attack three weeks later only their three super-Zeppelins, L. 31, L. 32 and L. 33 risked raiding the London area. The result of the raid did not exactly encourage the enemy to consider Leefe Robinson's action as a fluke.

The L. 33 came in over the Crouch Estuary and after dropping a few stray bombs en route, appeared above the outskirts of London about midnight. By way of Wanstead and West Ham, the L. 33, on her maiden flight, actually had the nerve to drop bombs on Bromley-by-Bow and Bow itself, her sleek shape moving amid a mass of shells and tracer.

'She's hit,' one of the gunners called, after a shell seemed to explode almost inside her. But the L. 33 showed no sign of damage and dropped twenty-seven bombs before nosing round for the Essex coast and home. She left a trail of eleven people killed and twenty-six injured.

But the gunner had been right. One shell passed through her flimsy fuselage, another damaged her propeller, and shell splinters punctured some of her gasbags. Losing gas steadily, she started the long stretch for the Continent. Near Chelmsford, Second Lieutenant A.

de B. Brandon was waiting for her. For twenty minutes he kept up a running attack on the airship, firing from every possible point, but although he saw his shots streaming into her, she failed to catch fire.

Eventually the Zeppelin crossed the coast at West Mersea, but by then the commander realized he had no hope of navigating her home, so he turned the great dirigible around again and calmly landed in a field. Only when she was on the ground did flames finally emerge from the airship, but she had lost so much gas that the fire burnt itself out without much damage to her structure as a whole. So this was the first and last voyage of the L. 33 – and the latest type of Zeppelin thus fell into our hands.

That left two of the super-Zeppelins to be accounted for on the night of 23–24 September. Second Lieutenant Sowrey was patrolling in roughly the same area as Leefe Robinson had been, when the L. 32 caught his eye in a trellis of searchlights at about 12.45 a.m. At once he manoeuvred his machine into an attacking position underneath the airship. He was flying a B.E.2C. Although the searchlights were on the 500-foot monster and moved a degree at a time to follow her, Sowrey could not see a sign of gunfire.

So close did he get that he could distinctly see the propellers revolving. The Zeppelin was moving as urgently as she could to avoid the searchlight beams, but her length made manoeuvring a slow process. Sowrey saw his chance. He fired at her.

The first two drums of ammunition did nothing, but then he loosed the third. They were all loaded with a mixture of Brock, Pomeroy and tracer ammunition. Suddenly he saw the envelope catch alight along several strips of it length. He went on with his traversing fire until he had nothing left.

Sowrey watched while the scorching airship struck the ground, then he headed back to Suttons Farm, after an exciting patrol. The L. 32 fell on a farm south of Billericay, where her wreckage burnt for three-quarters of an hour, many of the crew being charred beyond recognition. The descent of her flaming form was even seen from a British submarine, surfaced out in the Straits of Dover.

The L. 31 was the only one of the three super-Zeppelins to escape on that night. This airship was commanded by the German ace Heinrich Mathy, who managed to cross London swiftly and at a safe height. Leaving a trail of blasting bombs across south London, the Zeppelin killed twenty-two people and injured seventy-four. Three of the H.E.s weighed 300kgs, or 660lb, each. Mathy took advantage of a mist which completely shrouded the ship across the northern defences of London. The L. 31 hurried out to sea south of Yarmouth under heavy fire from shore and ships. But unknown to Mathy then, he and his crew had only a week left to live.

After another raid two nights later, the next came from a clear sky on 1–2 October. Eleven started but only seven crossed the coast. And L. 31 never re-crossed it. Coming in over Lowestoft, she set straight for the capital, but was soon spotted by searchlights.

The first of four pilots in the air to come up to her was Second Lieutenant W.J. Tempest, who had already been patrolling for an hour and three-quarters when he found himself over south-west London at a remarkable altitude of 14,500 feet. Apart from a heavy ground fog and biting autumn cold at this height, the night could be called beautiful and starlit.

As Tempest gazed over towards north-east London, where the fog was lighter, he noticed all the searchlights in that particular part concentrated in an enormous pyramid. Following them up to the apex, he saw a small cigar-shaped object, which he recognized as a Zeppelin. She looked so small, since at that stage she was some fifteen miles away and heading straight for London.

In the past, Tempest had chased many imaginary Zeppelins, only to find on closer acquaintance that they were clouds! He began to approach the airship at speed, as they both were on opposite sides of the city and heading for the centre. Throughout these minutes, Tempest also had a very nasty time from the ground guns, passing right through a succession of shells.

All at once it seemed to Tempest that the Zeppelin must have sighted his tiny plane, for she suddenly dropped her entire bomb-load in a single volley – even the 660-pounders – and then swung round, tilting her nose, and proceeded to turn, racing away northwards and climbing as she went. Her height before she started to climb must have been about 11,500 feet. Tempest made maximum speed at 15,000 feet and gradually overhauled her. The gunfire from the ground grew really intense now and he had an even worse time as he tried to close the five-mile gap between himself and the ship.

At this precise point, his mechanical pressure-pump went wrong, and he had to use his hand-pump to keep up the pressure in his petrol tank. At such an extreme altitude, this proved terribly tiring, besides occupying one of his arms. He had only one hand left for firing when the time came.

As he drew up with the Zeppelin, he felt relieved to find himself free of the ack-ack, the nearest shells bursting three miles away. The Zeppelin was now nearly at 15,000 feet and still ascending. He decided to dive at her, for though he held a slight advantage in speed, she was climbing like a rocket and leaving his plane standing. So he gave a great pump at his petrol tank, dived straight at her, and loosed a stream of fire. He let her have a second burst as he passed right under the belly of the craft, before banking his machine over and sitting under her tail. For a few seconds Tempest flew along underneath her, pressing his trigger for all he was worth.

He could see tracer bullets flying from her in all directions, but he was actually too close beneath her to become a target. As he went on firing, he noticed the vault of the monster glow red inside, like an enormous Chinese lantern. Then a flame shot out of the front part of her, and he realized she was on fire. She rose up 200 feet, paused as some stricken giant, and came roaring down straight onto Tempest, before he had time to get out of the way.

He nose-dived for his very life, with the ship tearing after him – expecting every second to be engulfed in her flames. He put his machine in a spin and just managed to corkscrew out of the way as she shot past him, roaring like a furnace. Tempest righted his machine and watched the airship hit the ground with a shower of sparks.

That moment marked the end of Heinrich Mathy and the start of the defeat of the dirigibles.

6

AVERY BISHOP

Shot down Seventy-two Planes

The most successful and spectacular air ace of all was Captain William Avery Bishop. This Canadian officer shot down seventy-two enemy planes – and lived.

By the time Bishop crossed the Channel to France in March 1917, Albert Ball and his colleagues had already been at it for months. And months could seem – and often were – a lifetime in that hour-to-hour existence of the Royal Flying Corps. Bishop joined Ball's squadron at once, and a fresh, fantastic chapter opened in the story of air warfare.

On 25 March, Bishop's first flight nearly became his last. The enemy were making a strategic withdrawal to their Hindenburg Line, and British flyers were trying to impede this as much as possible from the air. Bishop was flying a Nieuport Scout on a defensive patrol, covering the work of bombers and observation planes. This was his baptism of fire and almost his funeral.

At 5 p.m. he was piloting his Nieuport at 9,000 feet between St Leger and Arras, when three Albatros scouts approached his group. One of the enemy separated from the rest, lost height, and tried to come up behind Bishop's second-to-rear machine. The Canadian dived, firing a dozen rounds. Tracers flew all around the German, who dived suddenly, steeply, for 600 feet and then flattened out.

Bishop followed him, opening fire from forty to fifty yards. Two score of rounds rasped out of his guns. A group of tracers tore the enemy's fuselage and centre section; one entered just behind the pilot's seat and another seemed to strike the man himself. The machine hurtled horribly out of control, spinning its way earthwards.

Bishop followed, diving and firing. When he reached under 2,000 feet, his engine had oiled up, but he managed to spot the scout going vertically down at only 500 feet. Sometimes pilots pretended to be out of control to try and escape; this was why Bishop took no chances.

As he peeled off, satisfied that the Hun would hit the ground, he had to think fast of his engine. He was at a mere 2,000 feet and falling each second his engine had died on him, and he was still over hostile ground. It was a question of how far he could glide before coming down, so he aimed the Nieuport for Allied lines and sat back and hoped for the best. He had not long to wait. The little plane left the chatter of machine guns behind it, and just wafted over the line to bring Bishop home safe and sound. For if he had not been killed, at the very least he would have become a prisoner of war.

Safe and sound was perhaps an exaggeration, for the plane actually landed barely beyond the front-line trenches. After jolting to a halt in this highly undesirable spot, he dived into a dugout occupied by gunners, who helped him to move his machine at regular intervals to prevent the enemy getting a line on it and shelling it. That night, Bishop borrowed a toothbrush from the gunner officer and used this to clean the sparking-plugs of his charmed aircraft. Eventually he flew it back to base, where he had already been reported missing. But it was going to take more than this little incident to stop Bishop.

He had joined the war at the vital Vimy Ridge phase. Here on 9 April, his compatriots would be flinging themselves at the enemy in an all-out ground attack. Bishop escorted reconnaissance and photographic planes over enemy lines daily and on 31 March he won his second success.

Flying a Nieuport with its open cockpit and one Lewis gun, Bishop was suddenly shocked to see another similar plane attacked by an Albatros. Recovering composure instantly, he jerked his joystick to close with the German. Only fifty yards separated the pair of planes – with the second Nieuport still under attack – when Bishop's tracers struck the centre section of the Albatros, which seemed to fall mortally. It never recovered, crashing ten miles north-east of Arras. This position far behind the German lines was typical of the territory over which the British pilots had to fight. The enemy were almost always within their own lines, the British beyond theirs.

Now it was two days to go before the Vimy Ridge onslaught. His orders for Saturday 7 April, were to destroy a balloon five miles behind the Boche lines. An enemy scout plane disturbed him on the job, but Bishop soon shot this down. Whereupon he returned to the balloon, only to find it taken down. This presented no problem to the resourceful flyer. He hounded it to earth, bursting its bag with tracer from his Lewis, and scattering the scared German crew in charge of it. The balloon caught fire and crumpled in shreds. But Bishop had another shock in store for him before he got home.

His engine coughed apologetically and died. No coaxing could revive it, as Bishop drifted down towards enemy-held ground. He practically shook it trying to bring it back to life again, and as if in response it answered with a welcome sound. Only a few feet from the ground, he gained height and then hedge-hopped the miles home.

Ironically, this was Easter weekend, and with the Vimy Ridge assault timed for Monday 9 April, Easter Sunday turned out to be a busy day for Bishop. Under the wing of his squadron leader, Major Scott, Bishop flew one of six Nieuports on offensive patrol that morning. The engines of the little group throbbed on for mile after mile towards the enemy. Then they met. They soon lost one pilot killed. Enemy anti-aircraft fire hit the plane of another officer, forcing him to land in hostile-held ground.

Bishop became separated from the others, but saw Scott diving on a two-seater, so went after him. There seemed to be enemy aircraft all around them. After opening fire on the two-seater, he engaged an Albatros single-seater, pummelling the enemy with forty rounds of tracer. The machine made maximum speed with gashes ripped in its fuselage and wing surfaces – like some injured animal seeking shelter.

Bishop's next target was a balloon. Diving from 3,000 feet, he drove it down to the ground, but was disappointed not to see it smoking. After that interlude, he set his nose up to 4,000 feet, came across an Albatros, fired the rest of his drum, dodged away to reload, and swept back again. After two brief bursts, this plane signified defeat by diving vertically and was still in a steep nose-dive at only 500 feet.

Bishop was really in his stride by then. A few minutes had to elapse before he could continue the fight. Painstakingly he climbed to 10,000 feet and intercepted a couple of single-seaters hopefully flying towards the British lines. Three more machines flew above and behind, none of them looking friendly.

Bishop used up the rest of his drum on the pair. The first turned abruptly and flew away with its nose down, and the other spun spirally downward, with tracers having hit the pilot's seat and probably its occupant. Bishop climbed as quickly as he could and contrived to get behind the other three in the vicinity of Vitry. One double-seater dived, but was still partly under control. There was no point in saving any ammunition, so Bishop pressed on until the rest of the third drum had gone towards the last pair of planes. During this fantastic three-quarters of an hour, it was later learnt, he had totally wiped out two of the enemy planes.

Easter Monday arrived and with it the awaited attack. The Canadian Corps succeeded in sweeping over the Ridge, with the aid of their airmen overhead. On that fateful day, Bishop's flight went out without its commander, and only one man returned. This meant that in the three days of Easter, ten out of eighteen pilots were lost . . .

From then on, 'Billy' Bishop, as he was known, flew and faced death every day – almost every hour. Fight after fight, always the same pattern yet always in a different form. The numbers and conditions varied. Only Bishop's skill remained constant. On 24 April he had a change from personal combat, attacking a balloon actually on the ground. He fired twenty rounds from an altitude of 800 feet but then his Lewis gun suddenly stopped. In a very vulnerable position he reacted at once – and flew away fast. No ground guns got a hit on him and he had a chance to clear the jammed Lewis. Pilots always needed more hands than they had. Here was a case in point: trying to fly a plane out of enemy range while remedying a fault in his gun. He managed it, though, and five minutes later was roaring back to the attack, from 800 to 300 feet. Firing the rest of the drum at the balloon, he saw some of the bullets hitting home, but no smoke or flame appeared. At any rate, it was a hit. This did not satisfy Billy Bishop, however, so on 27 April he again attacked this same Vitry balloon.

While proceeding towards the target, he lost his way in the clouds. Flying blind through clouds can be unnerving, but Bishop took it in his stride. Suddenly he made out the blurred shape of a balloon half a mile east, suspended 600 feet up. He made the necessary adjustment to the joystick and flew perilously close to it, firing some sixty rounds of Buckingham into it. Then he passed over it again, intending to finish the drum, but already smoke poured out of the balloon, merging with the clouds. So instead he used some of the ammunition by firing into the observation basket beneath it, as he had seen no one jump out. Then he went on to the Vitry balloon and finished his drum on that.

A certain inevitability seemed to surround everything Bishop did during the following weeks and months. Hardly a day passed in April or May without his destroying at least one Hun machine. Sometimes there were more.

Just a couple of days after the balloon attack, he was 17,000 feet above Epinoy at noon. Cruising along at this high altitude, he spotted a hostile plane 3,000 feet lower. Diving from the sun side, to approach unseen, he opened fire at 150 yards. Bishop used bursts of three and after a dozen shots the enemy spun away hit. The Canadian pressed home his attack and the machine flickered into flames. That was the end of just one more combat.

Climbing back to 15,000 feet he dived at another single-seater who had witnessed the fight and dived out of range. After loosing his Lewis at the retreating tail, Bishop then spotted another hostile plane on his own level. With quick wits, which meant the difference between life and death, he climbed, and dived out of the sun at the intruder. But even Bishop could not catch him, and the plane sped off.

If that was a quiet day, the next one went down as a record: he had nine flights in the space of two or three hours.

At 10 a.m. on 30 April, Billy Bishop was leading a patrol at 10,000 feet near Lens. He saw an enemy plane, dived, and fired at it, but it rolled rapidly away eastwards. This was just a warm-up. Ten minutes later he climbed up to an enemy two-seater over the Allied side of the front line. Launching the attack with his Lewis gun, he fired from underneath it – but after only fifteen rounds the gun jammed. The wire cocking device caught in the slide, and he could not free it while in combat. The danger of his position did not occur to him, but he was especially annoyed at having to break off the fight when he realized that these two enemy planes were great Gothas, which would become familiar in air raids over London.

In two minutes under an hour, he was once more over Lens. Not having found his patrol, he went solo at a couple of enemy doing observation for artillery. Bishop dived on the leader, who hared off for protection under five Halberstadt scouts. Bishop had only just become aware of this formation, but was not daunted by the ratio of seven to one. As he had 500 feet to spare, he attacked from above and then flew off as soon as this advantage of altitude vanished.

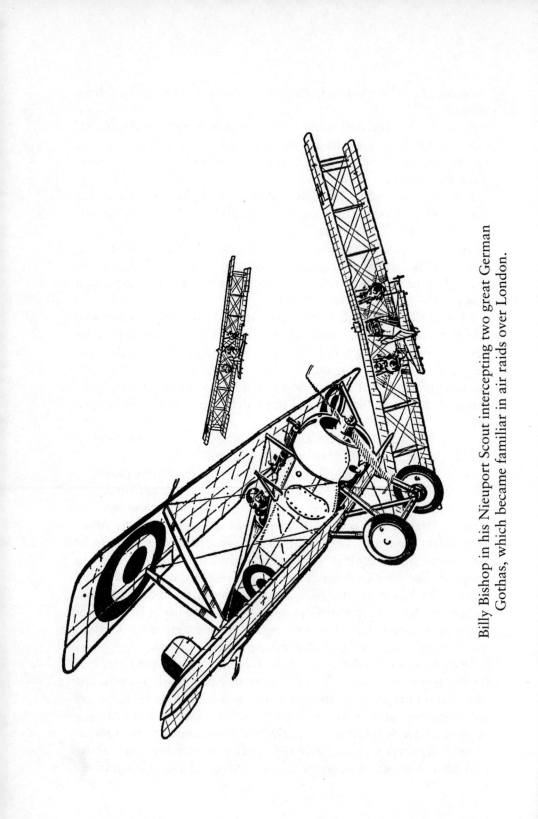

Billy Bishop in his Nieuport Scout intercepting two great German Gothas, which became familiar in air raids over London.

Bishop was bold but not foolhardy enough to risk five enemy dead level with him.

He had scarcely recovered from this little brush when at 11.15 a.m., just seven minutes later, the three hostile planes returned from observation duty. Twenty rounds sent the second spinning towards the mud-ridden no man's land far below them. As this one spun out of the fight, Bishop turned to the next, which dived desperately to try and avoid his attention. Bishop followed, firing steadily until he had emptied his drum. The second enemy went on his fatal fall, but this other one must have chosen to land rather than remain and risk fighting it out. Despite the fact that the three enemy planes carried six machine guns between them, Bishop had defied, dispersed and defeated them.

Yet this epic was still far from over. At 11.25 a.m. he made another amazing attack over Monchy at 6,000 feet. He spotted five scouts heading as if to take on some B.E.s, which were acting as observers for Allied artillery. As he zoomed down at them from a favourable angle, a shudder of fear must have rippled right through them all, for after another two such dives they all decided to quit, glad to get out of range of this petrifying pilot. The three dives and twenty rounds did the trick and they all turned tail and fled. The B.E.2Cs could continue their spotting service.

Five more minutes and Bishop flashed into two enemy aircraft at 5,000 feet. These also set their noses east in panic. Several times he narrowed the gap and fired at them, but they got away. The important thing, though, was that neither returned that day. As the faithful B.E.s – Blériot Experimentals – went on with their work, Bishop had one more brush, at 12.08 p.m., on this memorable morning. He had sixty rounds left, so, diving on an enemy south of Lens, he finished his last drum on it, to the last bullet. He did one of his vertical dives for this final attack, and the enemy must have been paralysed by the sight of the plane screeching straight down at him. Stunned, the German himself dived down with an open throttle and landed thankfully in a field just behind his own lines.

After a hurried lunch on landing at 12.15 p.m., Bishop and Scott were up together by 3 p.m., actually taking on four Albatros. Billy suddenly glimpsed four more machines preparing to swoop on him from above, so he turned the tables and zoomed up at speed. He discovered they were British naval triplanes. At that the enemy gave up and Bishop called it a day, too.

Bishop scarcely ever seemed to be on the ground at that time. When he did land, bumping slightly over the make-shift advance aerodromes quite near the front line, a big black dog would always be there, bounding over the grass to meet his master. This was Nigger, Bishop's beautiful pet and faithful mascot. It was as if the animal knew the risks the man took, and waited for him patiently every day. He would leap up at Bishop, who could just about carry him, holding his forepaws in his right arm and back paws in his left, with the dog's head pressed firmly over his shoulder. And by a strange coincidence, the dog had the same name as the pet of an equally immortal flyer in the Second World War, whose exploits will be described in due course: Guy Gibson.

But Bishop had little time to spare for Nigger on 2 May, 1917, over the Western Front. For this was the day he engaged altogether twenty-three enemy planes, destroyed two of them, fired seven drums of ammunition, and had as much if not more aimed at him. His official narrative records this dramatic day, when he made out three separate combat reports. This is how they read:

At 9.50 at 13,000 NE. of Monchy while returning from photographic escort, I attacked one single-seater H.A., and fired two bursts of five rounds each. I was unable to catch him and evidently did not hit him.

Later I saw five H.A. about 6,000, doing artillery observation. I manoeuvred to catch one party of three when just W. of the Queant-Drocourt line, as that was the nearest they were coming to our lines. I attacked the rear one and after one burst of fifteen rounds, he fell out of control and crashed near Vitry, just E. of Queant-Drocourt line. While watching him, another two-seater came up under me and opened fire. I attacked him firing about forty rounds. He fell out of control and I followed about 1,500 feet, finishing my drum. He was in a spinning nose-dive and my shots could be seen entering all around the pilot's and observer's seats. Three more H.A. being above me, I returned.

The second narrative reads:

At 12.15 E. of Lens 8,000 feet I attacked two H.A. doing artillery observation, firing twenty rounds into one. They then escaped.

Watching five minutes later, I saw only one H.A. there, the other evidently having been forced to land.

At 12.35 E. of Monchy at 6,000 feet, I attacked two H.A. doing artillery observation, but only succeeded in driving them away. At 12.40 over Monchy at 9,000 feet, I attacked from underneath a two-seater returning from our lines. I fired a whole drum into him but there was no apparent result. At 1.5 over Peloes at 6,000 feet, I attacked the same two H.A. as above and fired a drum from long range. No apparent result. I returned to aerodrome as I had no more ammunition.

The third narrative reads:

At 3.45 S. of Vitry at 11,000 feet. While leading the offensive patrol I attacked two H.S., firing into the rear one. He turned and I fired sixty rounds at him. He dived on me while I was correcting a stoppage. I then turned and finished my drum at him. I opened fire again from underneath, firing twenty rounds, but he flew away and I was unable to overtake him. At 4.30 Wancourt, I attacked one H.A. from above, firing seventy rounds at him. He turned on me while I was changing my drum and I fired a whole drum with the exception of about five to ten rounds at him. At 5 o'clock I fired the remainder from long range at six H.A. attacking one of our machines.

After more days of heavy aerial combat, Bishop shot down an Albatros on 7 May, the day that Ball died. Bishop went on leave soon afterwards, already having been credited with over a score of enemy aircraft destroyed in only six weeks' combat.

By the time he returned to France, he found fresh duties for the scouts. After the enemy had withdrawn to their massive Hindenburg Line, the artillery came into action on the ground more than ever, which meant more planes acting as observers. Scouts bent on catching these enemy observation planes had to be exposed to the unpleasant blend of bursting shells and machine-gun fire from the ground – as they had to fly extremely low to get to their destinations. Bishop did some of this scouting and attacked enemy observation machines, adding three more to his total. Then came June and a day that marked a climax, though not an end, to his courageous career.

A certain Corps complained of enemy machines flying low over its line, so Bishop received a free hand to deal with the problem as he thought best. The obvious answer, he decided, was to beard the Boche in his own den: in other words, to attack them on their own aerodromes. Bishop did not think there was anything unusual about this scheme of pitting himself against an enemy aerodrome.

In the pale, pellucid dawn of 2 June, Billy Bishop took off hopefully, heading straight for the particular aerodrome he had in mind. He had no fixed plan of attack, but waited to see what opposition he met. He crossed the front line slightly south of the main battle area, and aimed for the aerodrome. At that early hour of day, all was complete quiet for a while, so quiet in fact that when he finally saw it stretching below him, not a single sign of life could be detected. Bishop circled for a few moments wondering what to do, and then he decided to try and find another aerodrome farther south-east. It would have been a pity to have wasted the journey.

He was lucky. Just three miles to the south-east, and twelve miles behind the German lines, he stumbled across another one. He could hardly believe it. The place was near Cambrai, and there below him lay seven nice new Albatros machines all exposed on the field. Several actually had their engines running, either for test or before take-off. He had to hurry.

He was at only 300 feet at the start, but that would be too high. Bishop tipped the tail of the Nieuport up and the nose down as he dived for the 'drome. The ground crews stood stunned as they saw him swooping and screaming towards them: 300, 200, 100, 50 feet. He flattened out, firing spray after spray at the parked planes. One of the enemy mechanics fell hit, as the Nieuport nosed over the hangar and cheekily started to climb. Then Bishop got the chance he had wanted and waited for ever since the idea of the raid had been born: to attack an enemy in this unprepared state. The rules of war were not polite now. He had to win to stay alive – and he meant to do so. This is how it happened:

I heard the old familiar rattle of quick-firers at me. Then one machine began to taxi off down the aerodrome. It increased its speed quickly, and I immediately tore down after it, opened fire from dead behind it – just fifteen rounds – and it side-slipped to one side and crashed on to the aerodrome beneath.

Turning quickly, I saw another machine just off the ground. The

Hun saw I was catching him up and pushed his nose down, then, gazing over his shoulder at the moment I was firing at him, he crashed into some trees near the aerodrome . . . This time my heart sank, because two machines were taking off at the same time and in slightly different directions. I began to climb. One of the enemy machines luckily climbed away at some distance, while the other made straight after me. At 1,000 we made two circuits round each other, neither getting a very good shot, but in the end I managed to get in a short burst of fire, and this machine went crashing to the ground.

At 1,000 feet, every conceivable kind of gun had begun blasting at the little Nieuport. The fourth Hun had climbed to get an advantage, so Bishop followed suit. The two of them indulged in a chase for the next two or three minutes. Just as the Hun turned to give battle, the fifth Albatros got well under way and looked like sandwiching the single British plane. Bishop kept pegging away at the fourth, however, until the pilot became scared at his audacious counterstrokes and made off. The litter of other machines lay spread-eagled all around the aerodrome, and he had no wish to be added to the pile. So in that spell of chaos over the Cambrai airfield, Bishop had destroyed three or four machines and caused complete panic.

Low on petrol and ammunition, Bishop decided that the party was over. He waved the last Hun farewell with his empty drum and veered round to start the long haul for home.

All the way he was extremely exposed to anti-aircraft fire. Machine guns around the aerodrome had already carved great gashes in the furrowed fuselage of the plane, when more machine guns in the front-line trenches took up the attack on him. Bishop was almost unconscious now, as the whine and splatter and splutter echoed from dozens of guns along the way. He had only the faintest notion of where he was and how he could get home. Yet somehow through it all, he did direct the plane across the lines and actually chugged safely down again.

When he did touch down and stagger from the cockpit, tired and dazed, the ground crew stared astounded at the Nieuport. Its whole fuselage and other areas had been hit a hundred times, leaving only torn tatters fluttering on its airframe. Pocked and pitted, slashed and scarred, the plane had flown home. No one had ever seen such a mess.

That was merely one morning in many months' operational flying,

49

and Bishop went on to record seventy-two victories – as well as surviving many miraculous escapes. Once his machine caught fire and fell in flames for 4,000 feet before he managed to regain control and land. So Bishop lived to be acknowledged as the greatest Allied air ace of them all.

7

ALAN ARNETT McLEOD
Wing-Walking to Live

'M' seemed to be a magic letter among the many notable names in the First World War. At least five flyers with surnames starting with 'M' won undying fame, even though more than one of them died in the act. Their deeds ranged from wing-walking to save a plane, to bringing back an aircraft with the pilot actually on fire.

Sergeant Thomas Mottershead was the man who performed the latter miracle. It happened early in 1917 over the French trenches, while he was patrolling in an F.E.2D with his observer, Lieutenant W.E. Gower. Suddenly set on by a whole host of enemy scouts, they found themselves in drastic danger as Mottershead tried to manoeuvre the plane at 9,000 feet for Gower to open fire. The inevitable happened, however, and out of the hundreds of bullets focused on the British plane, an incendiary pierced the petrol tank with an ominous plop.

Fire broke out instantly in this vital and vulnerable spot. While Mottershead went on flying, the flames were fanned by the draught. Gower tried vainly to control them with his extinguisher, but only a minute or two after being hit, the plane had become a torrid trap. The flames engulfed Mottershead himself, and Gower turned his efforts from trying to save the plane to training his extinguisher on his pilot. In the heat of the holocaust, Mottershead continued at his controls. With Gower still spraying him as the plane lost height, he fought the torture of burns to try to bring the disintegrating aircraft back to British lines. They were still over enemy land.

Mottershead and the plane were both engulfed, yet he managed to manoeuvre it so that the fire did not reach his observer. They were over their own lines by now, and each moment the watchers below were dreading seeing the entire aircraft explode. It did not. Mottershead screwed up his eyes in search of a field for landing, his body on fire. He found one and sufficiently steadied the wrecked machine to urge it down.

They landed, but the instant the plane touched ground, it collapsed completely, flinging Gower clear of the furnace. The pilot was pinned in the wreckage as Gower struggled to subdue the fire. Rescuers got Mottershead out of it in a few minutes, but the shock had been too severe. Ravaged by burns, he died the following day, certainly having saved Gower's life by his self-sacrifice.

The feat of an Australian pilot, Lieutenant Frank Hubert McNamara, serves as a reminder that this war was fought not only on the Western Front, but in the Middle East, too; in Egypt, Darfur, Palestine and Turkey.

On 20 March, 1917, during an attack on the railway station near Tel el Hesi, between Gaza and Palestine, Captain Rutherford of 67 (Australian) Squadron was forced to land his B.E.2C with engine trouble behind enemy lines – right amid the Turks.

During this bombing raid on a hostile construction train, Lieutenant McNamara had already been badly wounded in the thigh, but despite this injury he decided to try and rescue his friend. McNamara took his Martinsyde scout down, descending through heavy enemy rifle fire. His thigh throbbed terribly, but he put the machine down safely as near to the stranded plane as possible.

In fact, he landed about 200 yards away from it, but his wound prevented him from getting out of his plane to go to the rescue. Instead, Rutherford ran across to ask his help in restarting the engine. But McNamara's wound put this out of the question, and in any case the approach of hostile cavalry confirmed the fact.

'There's nothing for it, we'll have to try and get off in this one,' McNamara shouted.

Rutherford nodded and climbed on the fuselage behind the pilot. But McNamara's leg was troubling him so much that he could not keep the machine straight on take-off – and it turned over. The two men extricated themselves somehow and set the plane on fire. The enemy cavalry were much nearer now, the horses disturbing the dust over the rough track. It was a tense moment.

Just in time, the pilots of two other planes had seen what had happened, and also spotted the cavalry. They dived down at full throttle and sent sweeping bursts of fire among the riders, holding them from the two Australians on the ground.

Rutherford then helped McNamara over to the B.E.2C and lifted him into the pilot's seat. Still under fire from the closing cavalry, Rutherford swung the propeller and by a miracle it started. Rushing back into the observer's seat, he signalled he was safely aboard, and McNamara managed to take off, though weak and dizzy from loss of blood. Somehow sticking it out, he piloted the plane back to their aerodrome, a distance of seventy miles, taking the best part of an hour.

Fifty-four enemy aircraft were shot down by Captain James Byford McCudden, and it would be easy to describe in detail how each one occurred – such as the two of a force of five scouts he tackled all alone. On that occasion, he broke off and returned only when he had driven the remainder far off, his Lewis gun ammunition was finished, and the belt of his Vickers gun had broken. In fact, he actually chased the other Huns with no guns at all, and nearly ran into the tail of one, at whose pilot he could have thrown a bad egg!

Instead of other incidents like this, though, here is his own account of how a colleague of his, Second Lieutenant A.P.F. Rhys-Davids, shot down the most famous German air ace after Richthofen. He was Werner Voss.

We were just on the point of engaging six Albatros scouts away to our right, when we saw ahead of us, just above Poelcappelle, an S.E. half spinning down closely pursued by a silvery blue German triplane at very close range. The S.E. certainly looked very unhappy, so we changed our minds about attacking the six V-strutters, and went to the rescue of the unfortunate S.E.

The Hun triplane was practically underneath our formation now, and so down we dived at a colossal speed. I went to the right, Rhys-Davids to the left, and we got behind the triplane together. The German pilot saw us and turned in a most disconcertingly quick manner, not a climbing nor Immelmann turn, but a sort of flat half spin. By now the German triplane was in the middle of our formation, and its handling was wonderful to behold. The pilot seemed to be firing at all of us simultaneously, and although I got behind him a second time, I could hardly stay there for a second. His movements were so quick and uncertain that none of us could hold him in sight at all for any decisive time.

I now got a good opportunity as he was coming towards me nose on, and slightly underneath, and had apparently not seen me. I dropped my nose, got him well in my sight, and pressed both triggers. As soon as I fired, up came his nose at me, and I heard clack-clack-clack-clack, as his bullets passed close to me and through my wings. I distinctly noticed the red-yellow flashes from his parallel Spandau guns. As he flashed by me I caught a glimpse of a black head in the triplane with no hat on at all.

By this time a red-nosed Albatros scout had arrived, and was apparently doing its best to guard the triplane's tail, and it was well handled too. The formation of six Albatros scouts which we were going to attack at first stayed above us, and were prevented from diving on us by the arrival of a formation of Spads, whose leader apparently appreciated our position, and kept the six Albatroses otherwise engaged.

The triplane was still circling round in the midst of six S.E.s, who were all firing at it as opportunity offered, and at one time I noted the triplane in the apex of a cone of tracer bullets from at least five machines simultaneously, and each machine had two guns.

By now the fighting was very low, and the red-nosed Albatros had gone down and out, but the triplane still remained. I had temporarily lost sight of the triplane whilst changing a drum of my Lewis gun, and when I next saw him he was very low, still being engaged by an S.E., the pilot being Rhys-Davids. I noticed that the triplane's movements were very erratic, and then I saw him go into a fairly steep dive and so I continued to watch, and then saw the triplane hit the ground and disappear into a thousand fragments, for it seemed to me that it literally went to powder.

Strange to say, I was the only pilot who witnessed the triplane crash, for even Rhys-Davids, who finally shot it down, did not see its end.

It was now quite late, so we flew home to the aerodrome, and as long as I live I shall never forget my admiration for that German pilot, who single-handed fought seven of us for ten minutes, and also put some bullets through all of our machines. His flying was wonderful, his courage magnificent, and in my opinion he is the bravest German airman whom it has been my privilege to see fight.

Next day he heard who the pilot was – Werner Voss, the famous ace. Both McCudden and Rhys-Davids wished they could have brought him down alive. It was in this generosity of mind that much of the air fighting was conducted.

So to the wing-walker Second Lieutenant Alan Arnett McLeod. Bombing became a more and more important part of flying operations as the war progressed, and when the enemy let loose a major offensive in March 1918, the Royal Flying Corps received orders to undertake long bombing raids. One of these was to be on Bray-sur-Somme, near Albert, where the Germans were gathering in masses for a fresh attack on an area already shaken by blows.

Despite appalling weather, McLeod and his observer, Lieutenant A.W. Hammond, took off in an Armstrong-Whitworth to try to attack the enemy infantry east of Albert. To tackle these, they had both bombs and machine guns, but it was obvious that they would have to face two foes: the enemy and the elements.

Taking off after an early lunch, they reached the target zone by flying below the base of the clouds. They were isolated well to the rear of the German lines, when they had no difficulty at all in spotting an enemy gun battery blazing away near Bray. Just as McLeod was angling to get in a bombing run, an enemy triplane suddenly assailed them from a range of only a couple of hundred yards and below them.

It was the latest fighter from the German factories: the fast Fokker. Cumbersome by contrast, the bomb-laden Armstrong-Whitworth looked to be in dire danger, the eternal inequality of fighter versus bomber. But McLeod actually attacked, thinking this to be the best means of defence, which it was, for triple bursts of fire from his guns sent the Fokker falling over on its back and straight into a spin. McLeod and Hammond hardly got over this easy if unexpected success when seven more Fokkers fell on them from every point of the compass. They were, in fact, from Richthofen's famous Flying Circus, and they fired their front guns at the lone Armstrong-Whitworth.

But by supremely skilful control, McLeod managed to swivel the sluggish bomber about, to enable his observer to fire at each machine in turn. He had to take care not to waste ammunition, as they had a lot to handle before they could hope to get away again. One point-blank burst from Hammond's gun struck with such ferocious force that the bullets bit into the triplane and snapped off its body at the pilot's seat. Flames did the rest.

That was two down, but they were still swarming all around. The gallant McLeod and Hammond made it three down before the eventual end. Five bullets lodged in McLeod. Another triplane came up from under the Armstrong-Whitworth, bullets raking and ripping it. Both McLeod and Hammond were hit now, and the petrol tank, too. The bomber caught fire, as they knew it would, and the flames were fanned nearer and nearer the bombs.

Still some 2,000 feet up, the pilot put the plane into a shallow dive to try and land safely. Neither of them could think very clearly. Hammond had as many bullet wounds as McLeod by this stage. Next the actual floor of the machine fell out, and with it the stool where Hammond normally sat, although he was then on the ledge around the top of his cockpit.

If either of them had paused to ponder the position, they must have given themselves little logical chance. But they did not. Instead, McLeod realized he had to try and keep the flames out of the way – and so climbed out on to the left lower wing, actually controlling the machine from the side of the fuselage. By side-slipping the plane steeply, he continued to keep the flames to one side, thus enabling Hammond to carry on firing as long as he could in defence. McLeod went on wing-walking all the way down, hanging on literally for life.

The enemy must have assumed they were powerless now, for one dived foolishly near, and Hammond, despite having one hand utterly useless, staggered to his gun again and shot the triplane down. He could hardly have missed, but the miracle was being able to fire at all. Their ordeal was only half over yet. Another Fokker followed them still lower, silencing the observer's gun at last, and peppering them all the way.

The steep side-slip continued, as the war-torn earth raced up at them. McLeod just managed to flatten out the Armstrong-Whitworth a matter of a few feet up, and Hammond was poised on an upper wing, clasping a strut, as the aircraft crashed into a shell hole.

One more miracle was recorded, as neither of them was killed. The next hazard loomed up in the shape of eight bombs still aboard, not to mention the rest of their machine-gun ammunition. Hammond lay helpless with his six wounds, but McLeod, though losing a lot of blood, somehow summoned up strength to drag him away from the immediate area. Already the burning wreckage had set off the machine-gun bullets, which zipped and zoomed all around them. Hammond's form felt like lead to McLeod but he did not pause till they were both far enough from the plane.

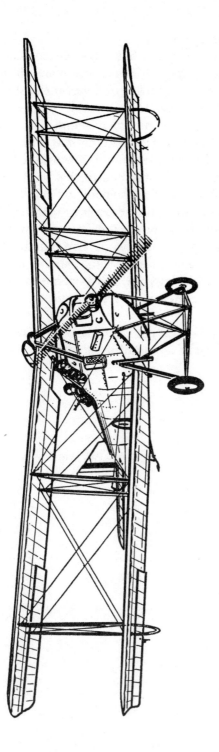

After this Armstrong-Whitworth was set on fire by Fokker triplanes,
Alan McLeod had to wing-walk to side-slip the plane and check the flames

Then the bombs began to burst.

Splinters flew fearfully near them, but still their luck held – if you could call it luck. The next danger dawned on them when McLeod stopped dragging Hammond any farther and they realized where they had landed. Between the two lines!

Two wounded men lying alone in no man's land. The spit of rifles and stutter of automatics reminded them of this real peril. So McLeod girded himself again and dragged Hammond towards the British lines – and was wounded again before the end of this epic. So with six wounds each, they both collapsed from exhaustion and loss of blood. By that time, McLeod had hauled his observer to within a short way of the Allied trenches, and it was not long before they were rescued.

Yet even then their ordeal was not over. Throughout the rest of that day they had to lie in a front-line trench, unable to be carried back before darkness. In appalling pain, they bore it bravely and were eventually borne back by stretcher for several miles, and thence to Amiens.

McLeod died from his wounds the week the war ended, although Hammond recovered after the amputation of a leg.

8

WILLIAM BARKER
Survived odds of 50 to 1

The final and most fantastic air ace was Major William George Barker, whose career culminated in the last weeks of the war, when he fought fifty enemy aircraft single-handed – and survived.

But the Barker epic goes back to 1915 when he transferred from the mud and monotony of the infantry to the Royal Flying Corps. He received his first flesh wound just before the Battle of the Somme started in 1916, when an enemy scout's bullet scorched through his skin in early combat.

One year and many missions later, Barker received another wound, again comparatively slight. During the Flanders offensive in the summer of 1917, he was spotting for a huge howitzer battery on an enemy emplacement, and just as he signalled the annihilation of this battery, anti-aircraft guns engulfed his biplane with a series of shells. Despite weaving and wheeling to try and dodge the enemy's aim, shrapnel hits holed his wings, and the plane see-sawed wildly from side to side. Not surprisingly, one of the flying splinters hit him. Luckily it bounced off his cheekbone and missed his eye. Barker got back to base, had the wound dressed, and was up in the air again next day.

At the climax of the famous Flanders offensive of autumn 1917, Barker had orders to take his flight of six Sopwith Camels and attack enemy relief forces on the Ypres–Menin road. After flying at tree-top height to carry out this attack successfully, diving down to the level of the tall poplars lining the road, Barker and the others suddenly ran into ten fast Albatros D.5s which tried to decimate the slower British machines. After a daring dogfight conducted at almost zero altitude, Barker eventually decided it was time to return, as he could not see any of his flight.

Climbing to a respectable height of 10,000 feet through low-lying cloud, he realized all at once from a glance at his control panel that the Camel had gone into a hopeless spin. Among the thick clouds, he had lost all idea of the horizontal. Barker cut off the engine and grappled with the controls as he stared appalled at the altimeter. Nine thousand, eight, seven, six, five, four, three, two, one thousand . . . Still the engine was not running, and he had fallen 9,000 feet in a few minutes. Clear of the clouds at last, he restarted the engine and straightened out of the spin at an altitude of only 500 feet.

Immediately after this escape, the Italian Army started to collapse against the Austrians, and Barker and his squadron were sent to support this front. During the next twelve months Barker's score of successes leapt from five to fifty.

Barker decided to celebrate Christmas 1917 with some spectacular flying. After accounting for an enemy balloon, he penetrated deeper behind the Austrian lines, leading two other young pilots. Below them, Barker noticed an Austrian aerodrome alive with men but peculiarly lacking in machines – which must have been safely stored away in their hangars. Safely, so the enemy thought. Barker had already realized that an attack on a hangar from directly overhead, or even at an angle, was less likely to succeed than one actually on a level with it. In other words, he wanted to try and fire *through* the hangars and not down on them. The incendiary bullets would have a better prospect of hitting home, and certainly a better one of setting the hangar alight. A condition for such an attack, of course, was that the airfield should be clear, like the one below him now.

Barker wheeled into a sharp dive just short of the aerodrome and came into the attack skimming the ground. If he were not careful, he would find himself inside a hangar! He roared over the amazed Austrians, pressed his triggers, and poured a drum of Buckingham bullets right into the entrance of the hangars. At the perimeter, Barker raised his nose into the wind, wheeled right round and gave the ground crews and hangars a second dose. Flying in at forty feet, the three planes let off six bursts of this treatment at the aerodrome, and the hangars were soon blazing brightly in the winter light.

Then Barker led the others over to a trench, where the Austrians were huddling for shelter, and sprayed a drum of devastating machine-gun fire on them. Despite the enemy retaliating with rifles and automatics, which ripped and rent part of their wings, the three planes got back to base feeling more like Christmas dinner than before they had started. From enemy pilots captured a couple of days later, it was learned that Barker and his colleagues had wiped out nearly an entire squadron in the attack on the hangars, as well as killing a dozen and wounding many more men.

Barker followed this up with another low-level attack that happened so swiftly and suddenly that he surprised the enemy completely. His target this time was the Austrian Army Headquarters at San Vito. To avoid detection by enemy scouts up above the Venetian Plain, Barker led the little band of bombing planes out to sea and flew parallel to the coastline until he was abreast of San Vito. Then they veered round in a right-angle and sped straight for the town, having achieved 100 per cent surprise at Austrian Army H.Q.

The building projected slightly above others adjacent to it, and so Barker was able to dive down to the level of the main windows. The first that the enemy knew was the sudden sound of six aircraft, quickly confirmed by the shattering of dozens of panes of glass as their bullets pierced the windows. After Barker had led the flight on several more machine-gun attacks at low level, they peeled off one by one and gained height to drop their loads of four bombs per plane.

The onslaught had happened so literally out of the blue that the Austrians barely got any opposition airborne before Barker and his men were away again. They did meet some on the way home, however, running into ravaging fire. But none was lost. The Austrians naturally felt far from comforted that such bold bombing could be directed against their actual headquarters.

Throughout the winter, Barker frequently flew high above the Alps of the Asiago area, where the mountains meant danger and usually death to any pilot unfortunate enough to experience engine failure. Once Barker did, in fact, have just such an experience, but miraculously managed to live through it.

Flying alone in his Sopwith Camel, with its twin guns pointing forward, he was hit by anti-aircraft fire from a gun sited up in the mountainous zone. Almost at once, the little biplane began to lose height, but fortunately Barker was over the edge of the Alps area proper. A few miles farther and he must have been killed on the spur of a snowcapped peak. As it was, he coaxed the stricken machine to glide gradually into the shallowest dive he had ever flown. Spluttering in protest, the engine died on him, only the whine of the wind through the frail-looking struts remaining as company. Lower and lower the Camel dived, until the dots of houses and patterns of upland fields took more definite form. He was away from the snows – that was something anyway.

Then he saw a group of large white buildings in front of tall trees typical of the region. All his experience went into the next minute or so, as the wings of the Camel fluttered up and down. A narrow strip of grass on a slope confronted him from below. Nearer he came to the foothills of the Alps. The plane suddenly struck the earth hard, bumped violently, and then turned turtle, completely upside down. Its tail traced out a semicircle in the air before coming to rest, and Barker banged his head. He surveyed the scene the wrong way up, looking beyond his guns, which were only a couple of feet from the ground. He was even closer.

Somehow he struggled out of the cockpit, quite calm and in one piece, to see one of his wheels wrenched off and lying forlornly near by. The propeller had snapped in half, and the plane had suffered other disastrous damage. But he was all right. And in no time at all, he was being photographed standing beside the wreck, wearing his full flying kit of boots, breeches, tunic, belt, helmet, goggles, and a pair of enormous fur-lined gloves. It was just one of several hundred days in Barker's brilliant flying life.

The next exploit in this remote region of the far north-east of Italy was for Barker to drop a spy behind the enemy lines to gather information for the Allies. And the method he would use to convey any news he might manage to find was, of course, carrier pigeon.

Barker and Captain Wedgwood-Benn took off with the spy on a bright but moonless night and headed for the agreed spot. It all went well, the man fell through a trap arrangement in the floor of the plane, and his parachute brought him slowly to earth near a particular farmhouse. Barker did not waste this journey, going on to bomb an enemy supply dump.

After what seemed ages of waiting, Barker and Wedgwood-Benn heard with excitement that the spy had found vital intelligence, which a faithful pigeon had borne back to their headquarters. So successful did the man become, in fact, that he ran out of pigeons quite soon and Barker and Wedgwood-Benn had to fly over with a fresh supply of birds in cages. The sight must have been unique: carrier pigeons being dropped in cages by parachute.

Barker's forced landing in the Alps foothills was far from his only narrow squeak. Already back in France, he had landed a plane with its nose dug deep in the ground and its tail dangling high above him.

He climbed out of that riddled aircraft, just as he survived the next shock.

After a prolonged encounter in the Benta Valley of Italy, the enemy had hit his machine in a number of places; not sufficiently serious to destroy it, yet bad enough for it not to be able to fly any farther. Barker looked down more in hope than expectation. He knew that nothing he could do would keep the Camel aloft much longer, so it was a case of finding any likely spot to try and land. But by mischance he was right over Lake Garda, with nothing but water within range. There was nothing for it but to bring the crippled Camel as gently as possible towards the water. Nearer it loomed, as he urged and egged it on to the side of the lake. He could see that he would not reach the beach, so he just got close to it and the plane suddenly splashed down to a wet 'landing'. Barker was used to clambering out of the cockpit by then. He discarded most of his gear and was glad to see a local rowing-boat cutting through the water towards the sinking machine. That was escape number . . . He had forgotten how many.

Sandwiched between all the other operations were one or two which stood out – such as the day that Barker shot down the Austrian ace Linke. After a large-scale running dogfight, Barker faced the Austrian at 600 feet range. Tracers etched a pattern between the two planes, forcing Linke to dive for his own aerodrome, which lay a mile or two off. But Barker followed him, matching Linke's urgency, and with the Austrian within sight of safety, Barker hit him mortally and his plane crashed in a mass of wind-fanned flames. In the wider sense, the loss of Linke and his leadership had a definite effect on the Austrian offensive begun along this front on 15 June. Here is an account of the battle published shortly afterwards in a Vienna newspaper. The translation conveys the feelings of the Austrians all too well:

In the plain near San Dona and Cap Sile, General Wurm's storm battalions were sent over the Piave River and the canal. From Treviso, General Diaz sent against them the 30th and 27th Corps, and General Croce's corps, newly formed from eighteen-year-old youths. The Austrians thus gallantly won a most important objective; the summit of the Italian hinge position was thrust through by the storming of the Montello. The rolling up of the whole of the Piave front from there appeared possible – indeed, certain.

63

Suddenly airmen appeared. They come down silently from a great height in far-reaching Volplanes. Now their motors hum again and their machine-guns rattle. A hail of steel pelts down on the pontoons, which sink riddled. The guns of the defence bark from the bank and the fragments of their shrapnel endanger the lives of their own men, men whom they wish to protect.

One, two, three of the great Caproni-bombarding planes descend, shot down on the mud of the Montello. A Nieuport comes down like a torch hurled from heaven. The famous airman Major Baracca is a heap of ashes. His list of victories is the same as that of his most victorious Austrian adversary, Captain Brumowsky, who conquered thirty-four opponents.

Lieutenant von Hoffman, in peace time a ministerial official in Vienna, and his band dash against the biplanes. Like raging bull-dogs, the English advance in their furiously swift Sopwiths against our airmen, engineers, artillery and infantry. Nothing, absolutely nothing, avails. The enemy airmen are too numerous, the enemy's shells too many. Like Sisyphus multiplied a hundredfold the bridge-builders work incessantly; they fall and disappear in the flood with a cry; they launch new pontoons; they think out new methods of transport from bank to bank – nothing helps; absolutely nothing avails. Six times are the bridges and footways completed, six times they are destroyed.

But Major Baracca was not a heap of ashes and survived to see the Austrian advance held.

Despite a steadily mounting toll of the enemy, Barker wanted to persuade their best pilots to a decisive combat. Accordingly, he had hundreds of copies of the following notice dropped on enemy aero-dromes:

Major W.G. Barker, D.S.O., M.C., and the officers under his command present their compliments to
  Captain Brumowsky
  Rither von Fiala
  Captain Havratil
and the pilots under the command and request the pleasure and honour of meeting in the air. In order to save Captain Brumowsky, Rither von Fiala and Captain Havratil and gentlemen of his party the inconvenience of searching for them, Major Barker and his

officers will bomb Godega aerodrome at 10 a.m. daily, weather permitting, for the ensuing fortnight.

Barker kept his word but the enemy were singularly disinclined to fight!

The climax of the Barker story now approaches with his return from the Italian to the French front in September 1918. He had the joy of flying one of the latest Sopwith Snipes with a top altitude of 24,000 feet. Barker made merry with this machine for a month, as he could climb higher than any of the new enemy aircraft.

By 27 October, 1918, the Allied armies had advanced across the Somme plains to bring the war within a fortnight of its end – although no one knew it then. Barker had chalked up forty-six official successes, with many more probables. But on that morning of 26 October, he was due to bid farewell to the front, as he was already packed to take up a posting in England at last.

It was the very morning he was due to leave; almost an anti-climax to his career. Or so it seemed.

Barker settled himself in his sparkling new Snipe, ready to fly home. He took off and gained altitude – then he spotted an enemy two-seater flying high over the Allied lines. He could not ignore it. The ace climbed to 21,000 feet north-east of Mormal Forest. It was half past eight in the morning.

Barker let himself in for more than he imagined in that split-second of decision to engage the enemy. He weaved around trying to manoeuvre into an attack at four miles up in the sky. It was an unprecedented altitude.

Within a minute or two, the enemy observer had got in some shattering hits on the Snipe, so Barker decided to try and come up from underneath – which he did. Wheeling away, he returned with twin intentions. First he took meticulous aim at the enemy observer himself and from a range of 200 yards shot him dead. Safe from that source, Barker consolidated. He tore in and squeezed a short burst from his guns at almost zero range. The enemy broke up in the air and Barker saw one of its occupants parachute out of it.

This was the start of the story, not the end.

While he had been busy, a Fokker biplane had started stalling and shooting at him, as soon as it was able to do so. One of the trail of tracers that came at him hit his right thigh. It was an explosive bullet and put that leg out of action. Barker swerved towards the fresh foe and with both of them losing a little height, he hit it.

Falling into a spin for a few seconds, Barker became dimly aware through his pain that the Snipe was surrounded by a formation of about fifteen Fokkers, two of which he attacked.

Turning at once to the dozen or more left, he hugged the tail of one and flew to within ten yards of it before bringing a deadly lead-stream on it. The rest were really focusing fire on the Snipe from all angles. Bullets were bound to hit it, and they did. One hit him, too, wounding him in the left thigh this time. Barker fainted and the plane fell spinning out of control. It must have been the momentary shock, for he came to quickly, as if in a nightmare – which it was.

A fresh formation of twelve to fifteen large enemy aircraft pounced on the poor shattered Snipe. Observers on the ground were watching the whole horrifying scene, powerless to get airborne in time to help him. They put the number of enemy planes now in the battle against Barker as *at least fifty*.

Somehow stung to further action, his instinct got him on the tail of yet another one, which he dispatched to its death from five yards. At this very second, he received a third wound, from a bullet plunging into his left elbow. The enemy machine that inflicted this wound closed to within ten yards of the Snipe. It looked like the end, but it was not.

Barker fainted from loss of blood and the machine spun down thousands of feet to 12,000. All this way, he was quite unconscious and the engine wide open. Some survival power operated again, and Barker became aware of it all once more. Still the same nightmare.

Another complete formation of enemy aircraft was awaiting him here at this lower level. He subconsciously thought it was the end as he saw smoke belching from his machine. Mistakenly imagining it to be on fire, he spotted a Fokker dead ahead and made to ram it. Before he actually did so, he opened fire from two or three yards – and the Fokker fell in flames. His aim even then remained deadly.

His left elbow had been shattered, yet with both his legs useless he manoeuvred the machine by his right arm alone – and shot down a total of four enemy planes.

Still only semi-conscious, Barker decided to dive for the ground when he was once more set on by eight enemy. Although he was as much dead as alive, he wriggled and weaved out of their way, firing a few bursts as he went.

Barker made one final lunge for his own lines, as an enemy shot

William Barker in his Sopwith Snipe being attacked by fifty enemy Fokkers. Somehow he survived to tell the tale.

away his petrol tank from under his seat. It did not catch alight, and as his strength drained off into a daze, his reflexes forced him to switch over to the emergency fuel tank. He could not see where he was going by that time.

Just behind the British lines, plane and ground met. The Snipe somersaulted at speed. Soldiers raced to him to find he had now broken his nose. But he was still alive. Major Barker remained unconscious for a number of days, and the Armistice arrived before he passed the crisis and began to recover. So the First World War was over.

9

HAWKER AND GRIEVE
Attempt on the Atlantic

It was just after three o'clock on the afternoon of Sunday, 18 May 1919. Two Englishmen clambered into the cockpits of their Sopwith biplane at Mount Pearl airfield, St Johns, Newfoundland, hoping to be the first to fly the Atlantic non-stop. Aptly enough their speck of a plane was christened *Atlantic*.

The pilot was Harry Hawker and his navigator Commander Mackenzie Grieve. Hawker had flown throughout the four years of the Great War. For weeks they had been waiting for the weather to improve. Now it seemed perfect.

Hawker had made several last-minute changes in his aeroplane, including replacing the original four-bladed propeller by a more conventional two-bladed one, and planning to take the highly unconventional step of jettisoning the undercarriage on take-off to give the machine maximum lift. To lessen the risk of a crash on landing Hawker fitted small steel skids which he hoped would enable the machine to glide along the ground to a stop.

But the landing was far in the future. Now it was 3.15 p.m. as the two men shook hands and waved the usual farewells to the crowd on the airfield. The sky was blue and the wind blew from the north-west as the little aeroplane jolted off on its long take-off run. It was carrying a huge load of fuel, and the spectators wondered whether it could ever take to the air.

But it did, though to get it up at all, Hawker had to taxi it diagonally across the field for extra length. Finally he managed to coax it into a laborious climb clear of the fence at the edge of the airfield – and they were away.

The sun glinted on the biplane, with its tail wagging slightly as if in pleasure at being airborne. And on that tail was the name Sopwith Aviation Company, Kingston on Thames.

Hawker and Grieve were really on their way, the first men ever to try and fly the Atlantic in a powered aeroplane.

The aircraft ascended steadily to some 2,000 feet and set its nose eastward for Ireland – nearly 2,000 miles off. And they knew that if they couldn't keep airborne all that way, it was a million to one that they would drown.

Wearing a check cap back to front, Hawker flew straight over the city of St Johns and the Quidi Vidi airfield, where rival airmen were actually preparing to take off on this fantastic race to be the first across the Atlantic and win the *Daily Mail* prize of £10,000.

Hawker signalled 'Farewell' to the crowds gathered below, and then just before leaving the land altogether, he jettisoned his undercarriage, and with it the landing wheels. Many people thought him unwise, but he knew that every extra pound must make the flight more difficult and more dangerous.

The signalman at the marine lookout on Newfoundland reported: 'Atlantic plane flying south-easterly out of sight at 8,000 feet and a speed of 80 mph.'

After only ten minutes in the air, though, Hawker and Grieve lost the strong sunshine as the aeroplane faded into the infamous fog banks off Newfoundland. Hawker decided to try and rise above them, and soon succeeded in raising *Atlantic* well over the swirling sea-mists.

This was better in one way, but worse in another – for the fog blanketed all sight of the sea from them. For over an hour they flew blindly on eastward, though a brief break in the mixture of mist and cloud did give Grieve a chance to take bearings.

For four hours they droned on, then they suddenly ran into clusters of cloudbanks, building up with every eastward mile. Their black outlines looked ominous against the oncoming night.

Four or five hundred miles out, the storm started.

Rain raged against the poor little aeroplane, shaking it from propeller to tail, making every yard more of a struggle both for the men and the machine. The squalls seemed to be coming at them almost horizontally.

The silver wings fluttered, quivered, but remained more or less level. This was the weather they had wanted to avoid all those endless days. As night fell they met more great gusts of wind and rain, which roared through the thin struts of the biplane.

It seemed impossible that with everything else coming *down*, the aeroplane could stay *up*.

Grieve tried to take sights with frostbitten hands, as Hawker veered, banked, dived, dodged, to get round those black blots of clouds. Their course became erratic, but they flew on.

Harry Hawker said later:

The trouble did not start until we were five and a half hours out from St Johns.

Then the temperature of the water in the radiator began to rise.

It did not mean a great deal at that moment, but we could see that something was the matter with the water circulation.

They couldn't just stop and cool it off, like a car on a road. They were at 10,000 feet now – two miles over the angry Atlantic. Not many people would be where they were for ten million pounds – let alone ten thousand.

Grieve continued trying to take sights, though they had not seen the water since that moment ten minutes out from St Johns.

Hawker, too, peered outside at the dark facade of sky. He saw cloud peaks towering up to 15,000 feet, making a very bad horizon. The moon had not yet risen, so the whole scene seemed appallingly dark. Yet he said, 'We were very comfortable'!

After the first shock of that rise of the radiator temperature, Hawker glanced down regularly at the dial registering the thermometer level of the cooling system in the engine. At first the water temperature in the radiator read 168 degrees Fahrenheit. Two or three minutes later it showed 176 degrees Fahrenheit – an eight-degree jump. Things were hotting up.

'Only thirty-six degrees to boiling point,' he thought aloud.

But luckily it stayed there for the next couple of hours.

Then it started to creep up again.

Hawker wiggled the lever controlling the shutters on the radiator. These were supposed to vary the temperature – but they didn't. The needle showed another two-degree rise.

Hawker had thought it was as much as he could do to fly the plane through the dark drifts of clouds. Now he had the problem of heat to cope with as well. For the first time he felt slightly worried.

If the water reached boiling point and evaporated, their Rolls-Royce engine would overheat and seize up, and they would fall into the hidden storm-ridden waters below.

He started searching for the cause and came to the conclusion that something must have got into the water filter in the feed pipe from the radiator to the water cock and blocked it. Most probably solder or the like shaken loose in the radiator. Then he tried to remedy the fault.

He throttled down the motor, stopped it altogether, and pointed the nose of the *Atlantic* down towards the ocean. He hoped this would give the system a chance to cool, and also clear anything blocking the filter.

The aeroplane drove down through the rain, with the wind twanging the taut wire struts. Hawker screwed up his eyes to try and see something, but couldn't really, so went by his instruments.

Between 6,000 and 7,000 feet he flattened out in a graceful arc and opened the throttle again. He had done the trick. The filter was clear and the thermometer needle flickered back to a lower level.

'Thank God,' he breathed.

After another hour of ploughing through the fleeting films of clouds, they were about 800 miles out from St Johns. The weather was still stormy, with a northerly gale coming up fast.

Then it happened all over again.

The filter choked, the water got hotter; the needle on the dial moved steadily upwards. The moment of truth was approaching, and so was the point of no return.

Hawker did the only thing he could. He dived again to try and clear it, but it was no use this time. And the climb up afterwards heated the water more rapidly still.

The dial now read 200 degrees Fahrenheit: twelve degrees off boiling point.

The aeroplane staggered up through the stormy clouds, the engine getting hotter all the time. The two men were in a tight corner and they knew it. Midnight had come and gone, but for the fliers it was still the middle of a wild night over the Atlantic – in an aircraft that must soon seize up. They were now 900 miles from St Johns, and nearing the point of no return. No men had ever flown here before.

Hawker tried again to clear the filter by diving, but failed. And after the third attempt the water was boiling fiercely.

The dial read over 212 degrees.

If he went on like this, they would waste all their precious water for cooling the engine, so he climbed to 12,000 feet and they decided to stay at that height for the rest of the way.

They hadn't yet seriously doubted the aeroplane's ability to get across. At two and a half miles up, they were above most of the clouds. Moonlight broke the blackness, and they managed to keep a better course. They discovered that the gale had been blowing them southward, miles out of their course.

By throttling down to a slower speed, Hawker got the water off the boil and back to 200 degrees again. Nursing the controls with all the tenderness he could muster, he kept them flying for the rest of that endless night.

Dawn edged alight ahead of them.

Then, twelve hours out from Newfoundland, they came to clouds again, too dense to fly through and too tall to climb over. And anyway, each time Hawker ascended, the water bubbled and boiled.

'Nothing for it,' he shouted. 'Have to go below them.'

But the cloud base seemed to be non-existent. Hawker took the aeroplane lower and lower. At 6,000 feet the clouds were thicker than ever. Down and down he manoeuvred, praying for a break. At 1,000 feet they suddenly saw the sullen swirling sea. Hawker reacted instantly and opened the throttle.

There was no response.

As the last few hundred yards slipped away, Grieve desperately fiddled with the fuel pump to get the engine going. It looked as if all was lost, when literally yards from the waves, the engine coughed, convulsed, and came back to life.

Up at 1,000 feet again, they were on course as a stormy sunrise loomed red and grey ahead. But even without climbing any higher they could not keep the temperature below boiling. Now they knew the worst – they had passed the point of no return – and they could not hope to reach their goal. It was a grim moment. They could go neither forward nor back.

The water began to boil steadily away, and with it went their hopes. Hawker reckoned he could keep the aeroplane flying for another two or three hours; their expectation of life for, as the Irish coast was still nearly 900 miles off, he knew they could not hope to reach it.

'There's only once chance,' he called to Grieve, 'and that's seeing a ship. We're near the main routes.'

But both of them knew that the chances of spotting a vessel in the vast watery wastes of the Atlantic were extremely small, and to do so before they burned up were virtually nil.

Hawker swung the nose and began to zig-zag across the line of their original route. The minutes, the miles, the fuel and – worst of all – the water, were all being consumed.

Both men craned out of their cramped cockpits, desperately scanning the sea through the scudding clouds. But no ship came in sight. It seemed silly even to hope for one.

This went on for an hour. They had really burned their boats now, and the water went on boiling away. They knew, too, that the chances of setting an aeroplane down on this churning ocean were as slim as sighting a ship.

The *Atlantic* chugged on, back and forth. They had no radio to call for help. The whole world was waiting to hear news of them, but wouldn't begin worrying till they became overdue in Ireland.

Only these two men in the entire world knew of their plight. All they could do now was to keep their aeroplane airborne for as long as they possibly could. For the throb of the motor was virtually their own heartbeat. When one stopped, the other would soon follow.

It was now two hours since Hawker had decided to adopt their zig-zag course. There was still not a sign of a ship. The temperature needle stayed permanently above boiling point as they flew to and fro.

Hawker still had his hands full controlling the plane, for half a gale was whipping the sea and buffeting the frail fuselage. It was as if they were being softened up for a final knock-out. The rollers rose and fell to the gusts of the gale.

Another half-hour passed, and Hawker wondered how much longer they could last. In his heart he knew it was only a matter of minutes.

Through it all the Rolls-Royce engine purred on, but by now all the water had boiled away. The engine was red-hot and growing hotter.

They were at latitude 50°20'N and longitude 29°30'W. St Johns was now 1,100 miles away, and Ireland 800 miles away.

This was when they should have died – but they didn't.

The miracle happened.

'It's a ship! A ship!' Hawker shouted, pointing down for Grieve to see. They nodded to each other, overcome.

She was quite close on the port bow, and came looming out of the low morning mist.

Hawker swooped down to 400 feet, fired three Very distress signals, and then flew across her until he saw some men on deck. The next problem was *landing* on the sea. At any rate he wouldn't miss his wheels.

He went a couple of miles ahead of the little vessel, veered round, and then came down towards the storm-ruffled surface.

Now Harry Hawker had to call on all his reserves of calmness and skill. He saw the sea spread out beneath him like a rippling landscape. At last came the touchdown. With infinite care he set the machine down on top of the waves – and it actually floated on an even keel.

The next step was for the two of them to take to their little emergency boat. Useful as this was, it would not have supported them very long in the restless rollers of the mid-Atlantic.

The waves were running up to twelve feet and breaking right over them and the aeroplane, which slowly started to settle and sink. Soon only its tail remained above the water.

An hour or so later the ship's boat reached them. The rescuers turned out to be the *Mary*, a small Danish steamer bound for the Scottish coast.

The ironic thing was that this 1,824-ton vessel had no wireless, so the world went on waiting for news of the famous fliers. In fact it was a week after their take-off that the *Mary* passed Lloyd's signal station at Butt of Lewis and broke the breathtaking news that the aviators were safe, long after they had been given up for lost.

They were both awarded the Air Force Cross, and the *Daily Mail* gave them a consolation prize of £5,000 for their gallant attempt which took them nearly two-thirds of the way across the Atlantic. So the names of Harry Hawker and Commander Mackenzie Grieve went down in aviation annals as the men who were nearly the first to fly the Atlantic.

And the strange postscript: their plane did *not* sink. The US steamer *Lake Charlotteville* spotted it bobbing up and down and salvaged it.

10

COMMANDER READ

Across the Atlantic in Stages

Who flew the first heavier than air machine across the Atlantic? Most people would say Alcock and Brown, but they would be wrong. It was Lieutenant Commander A.C. Read and his crew of the US flying boat *NC-4*. Alcock and Brown gained the major honour, of course, by being the first to fly non-stop on a transatlantic trip.

It was the American Navy's flying boats that really forced Hawker and Grieve into their hurried take-off on 18 May 1919, for no fewer than three US seaplanes had heaved their loads up from Trepassey Bay, Newfoundland, on the afternoon of 16 May in an attempt to fly the North Atlantic to England in stages.

NC-3 and *NC-4* took off two minutes apart – at 10.03 and 10.05 Greenwich time – and together left Mistaken Point bound for the Azores on the first leg of their southerly route over the ocean. Ten minutes later they sighted *NC-1* several miles behind them and flying higher.

Although their course was in warmer latitudes than Hawker's route, they saw icebergs in the smooth sea below. The whole operation had been planned very thoroughly by the US Navy, which had ships at a whole string of predetermined points to guide the fliers. The flying boats had the advantage of being capable of landing safely on the water if the engines failed at any time, provided that the weather was moderately calm.

The seaplanes were each powered by four 400-horsepower Liberty engines. They could fly for twenty hours, so their complete projected journey from Newfoundland to Plymouth would have to be carried out in three stages: Trepassey to the Azores, 1,381 miles; Azores to Lisbon, 1,094 miles; and Lisbon to Plymouth, 895 miles. The total distance therefore amounted to 3,370 miles. *NC-4* was the newest of the flying boats, with a take-off weight of 22,000 pounds.

They flew at about 800 feet. *NC-4* drew ahead but when it reached the first US destroyer it circled around for *NC-3* to catch up. Then for the next hour they flew on together, until the running lights of NC-3 gradually grew too dim to be distinguished and *NC-4* lost sight of it altogether. From then on *NC-4* proceeded as if alone, with the engines turning well, and both oil and water temperatures correct.

That night their only light at first was the stars showing in a dark sky, but then at midnight the May moon began to rise, somehow comforting the crew of *NC-4*. The air became bumpy, so they climbed to 1,800 feet, but it was no smoother there.

They sighted each destroyer in turn in the positions appointed for them. Star shells, seen from up to forty miles away, first signalled the ship's position, then searchlights and ship's lights guided NC-4 on its well-marked route. All the vessels were brilliantly illuminated; some ships were precisely in position, others less exactly.

So far their average speed had been 104 miles an hour, indicating a fourteen-mile-an-hour favourable wind. At 5.45 a.m. they saw the first smudge of dawn. As it spread into daylight, most of their worries seemed to be past, at any rate for the first leg of the flight. They were half way; the power plant and everything else was functioning perfectly; the radio worked wonderfully. The radio officer had even sent a message to his mother in the United States via Cape Race, then 730 miles off. Messages came in from as far away as 1,300 miles.

Cape Race reported: 'NC-3's radio working poorly'.

By intercepting signals they learned that *NC-3* flew ahead of *NC-1* and both were astern of *NC-4*.

The crew of *NC-4* had a comparatively comfortable time, eating sandwiches and chocolate candy and drinking coffee from the thermos bottles. Lieutenant Commander Read made several inspection trips aft and asked the radio operator and the engineer how things were going.

At 6.55 a.m. they passed over a merchant ship and at 8 a.m. the flying boat coasted through light patches of fog. This soon passed but at 9.27 a.m. they met more fog – dense this time.

The sun faded from an orange outline to nothing at all and they rapidly lost all sense of direction. The spinning compass suggested a steep bank and Read had visions of a possible nose dive. Even the best precautions could not have avoided this. But fortunately it did not last long and the sun suddenly pierced through again and the sky became blue instead of foggy-grey. Read put *NC-4* on an even keel and climbed above the fog and upper limit of the layer of clouds. Their altitude now reached 3,200 feet, still not high though substantial for the weight being borne. The fog remained below them.

At 10.38 a.m. and 10.55 a.m. they sent out radio messages to the nearest destroyer, asking if the fog had lifted near the ship. But the replies were not encouraging, reporting thick fog near the water. Light rain brushed the flying boat but passed like a spring shower. Then at 11.13 a.m. they radioed the destroyer *Corvo* asking about conditions further on and heard the reply: 'Visibility ten miles.'

Cheered up by this promise of better, brighter conditions ahead, *NC-4* thundered on for the Azores.

Suddenly at 11.27 a.m. a hole in the clouds and fog gave them a glimpse of the sea – and what looked like a tide rift on the water. Two minutes later they saw the ragged, irregular outline of rocks. The tide rift was in fact a line of surf along the southern end of Flores Island, the most westerly of the Azores.

'It was the most welcome sight we had ever seen,' said Read afterwards.

This told them, too, that they were forty-five miles off their calculated position, indicating that their speed from the last destroyer sighted had been about ninety-seven miles an hour. The wind was blowing them east and south. They took their bearings from the island and shaped their course for the next destroyer, flying low with a strong following wind. The fog stopped 200 feet above the water.

At noon they looked down on destroyer No. 22 right in her proper place, the first in the chain of destroyers they had seen since No. 16. As visibility had then extended to twelve miles, and they had plenty of petrol and oil, Read decided to keep on for Ponta Delgada, their real goal in the Azores.

But then the fog swirled round them once more, and they completely missed the next destroyer, No. 23. Then the fog really closed down, but they decided to keep to their course until 1.18 p.m. and then make a ninety-degree turn to the right to pick up Fayal or Pico Island. However, at 1.04 p.m. they made out the northern tip of Fayal and felt safe again.

They headed for the shore, the air clearing quickly as they got nearer to the beach. *NC-4* rounded the island and landed in a bight they mistook for Horta. The error did not matter much and they simply took off again, leaving a trail of foam, and rounded the next point. Through the fog the dark blur of a vessel clarified into the USS *Columbia* and *NC-4* landed near her at 1.23 p.m.

The total time since take-off had been fifteen hours eighteen minutes, at an average speed of ninety-four miles an hour.

NC-4 left Horta for Ponta Delgada to take in fuel, and they hoped to make only a brief stay at the island of San Miguel before aiming due eastward for the next destination – Lisbon.

While *NC-4* waited to continue its journey, attention naturally switched to the other two flying boats behind it – *NC-3* and *NC-1*.

The crew of *NC-3* under Commander Towers had a terrifying experience. The failure of the lights on the pilot's instrument panel forced him to fly above the clouds to see the stars for guidance. The last destroyer he sighted was No. 12. He dropped below the heavy clouds at daybreak but missed destroyer No. 14. He assumed that the high velocity of the upper winds had hurled him off course. He laid a parallel course, but at 7.45 a.m. GMT on Saturday, 17 May, he ran into heavy rain squalls. These went on for nearly six hours, when the weather cleared.

Commander Towers said afterwards: 'We then decided to land to make observations, as we had only two hours' fuel left. We discovered a heavy sea running, too late to remain in the air.'

When *NC-3* alighted on the water, the impact slightly damaged the hull and seriously damaged the forward centre engine struts. They could not take off again – and they were still just over 200 miles from Ponta Delgada.

A gale sprang up that evening, but the flying boat rode out the stormy night. The seaplane suffered severely but the crew succeeded in keeping it afloat all through the gale. At 9 a.m. the next morning they lost the port pontoon.

They had to try for Ponta Delgada, but they could not fly, so the only way to get there was on the surface of the sea. Slowly, bumpily, *NC-3* taxied the 205 miles from the point where it came down right to Ponta Delgada. It arrived there at 5.50 p.m. on 19 May, two days later, under its own power. They lost the starboard pontoon just outside the harbour, but they were there – safe.

The fate of the *NC-1* and its crew was even more remarkable.

Like the *NC-4* and *NC-3*, *NC-1* had left Newfoundland just at 10 a.m. GMT on 17 May. Its flight was more or less similar to that of the other two for the rest of that day and night.

With the glow of dawn, everyone in the crew felt confident that they could make Ponta Delgada easily. Then they began to run into thick overcast patches and visibility deteriorated quite dramatically. As they went through one patch, Station Ship No. 16 loomed dead ahead of them. Some of the station ships radioed weather reports to them. They passed No. 17 on the port hand at a range of twelve miles.

They flew on at 600 feet, and then ran into really thick fog. It dimmed the goggles of the crew and misted the glass over their instruments, so that they could scarcely read the dials. The pilots, Barin and Mitscher, brought the seaplane up to 3,000 feet, above the fog, but at this height they could not see the water and so did not know how far they were drifting off course.

They dodged one patch of fog but kept running into more. They side-slipped and turned in an effort to keep on course until at 12.50 p.m. they decided to come down, get their bearings and fly underneath the ceiling.

At seventy-five feet over the water, visibility extended to half a mile, the air was bumpy, and the wind shifted from 350 to 290 magnetic. They changed course to conform to the fresh conditions and sent out radio signals requesting compass bearings.

They decided to land if the fog thickened. It did.

A few minutes afterwards, they ran into a low, frightening fog-belt. Lieutenant Commander P.N.L. Bellinger turned the flying boat about and headed into the wind, landing at 1.10 p.m. after a flying time of fifteen hours.

The water was much too rough for them to try and take off again. The outlook seemed gloomy, even grim. The wind and water both prevented the plane from taxiing over the surface to windward, as NC-3 had done, and they soon found that radio contact between the aeroplane and the ships was erratic and unsatisfactory. They realized they had to wait where they were and hope to be found.

Shortly after they touched down they put over the sea anchor, but the strong swell carried it away almost immediately. Then they rigged up a metal bucket as a sea anchor, which survived and did a lot of good.

The wings and tail, however, went on receiving pounding punishment from the rough sea, so they slit the fabric on the outer and lower wings to help preserve the structure. In a further effort to reduce the damage Bellinger kept one of the centre motors running.

Despite all their efforts, the weather badly buffeted and damaged both wings and the tail. For some time it seemed as if NC-1 would actually capsize, although it was a seaplane and so designed to float. All the men realized the danger, but showed no fear. They waited for hour after hour.

Finally at 5.40 p.m. someone said: 'Look! There's a steamer!'

The seaplane taxied across towards her. The vessel was the *Ionia*, carrying no wireless. She sighted the Americans but before she could get over to them, the fog clamped a curtain of grey between them, and the seaplane vanished. Later the weather lifted and the aircrew saw the ship steaming towards them. The *Ionia* took them in tow. A destroyer came alongside during the night and took charge of the battered *NC-1*, while the crew were later landed safely at Horta in the Azores from the *Ionia*.

Three seaplanes had set out – but now there was only one.

NC-4 took off from Ponta Delgada at 10.18 a.m. on 27 May on the second stage of its flight, from the Azores to Lisbon. Commanding it was the same small, lean, wiry thirty-two-year-old man, Lieutenant Commander Arthur Read. They had 1,094 miles to fly before they could claim to have crossed the Atlantic.

The sea was speckled with waves, and the flying boat had a good following wind. Thick clouds draped the hills of San Miguel as NC-4 gained height to 800 feet.

The Americans had fourteen marker boats out, and the naval seaplane saw them all but one. The whole way to Lisbon was without adverse incident. When they could not spot a ship, they could contact her by radio, so communications remained complete despite the mist which still seemed to be dogging them.

The grey body and yellow wings of NC-4 thrust ever eastward, its high-pitched tail planes detracting from any appearance of grace. No one could really call it beautiful, though that is what it seemed to Read.

The navigator plotted the course, seated in a cockpit forward of the four engines, while the two pilots sat side by side just behind the engines. The engineers were aft with the radio operator.

So the flight went on and they had little to report till they reached Lisbon in nine hours twenty-five minutes, to a great welcome. They had flown the Atlantic.

The speed of NC-4 on the second leg varied from 69 to 104 miles an hour depending on the winds, but not once did it depart far from its direct course to the Portuguese capital. The average speed for the thousand-odd mile hop was 93.7 miles an hour.

So to the final flight: a run of 895 miles north-north-east from Lisbon to Plymouth. *NC-4* rose from Lisbon harbour at 5.29 a.m. GMT on 30 May with a favourable wind behind it but amid squalls. At 7.05 a.m. they discovered a leak in the port engine, so descended for repairs at the mouth of the Mondego river.

From there *NC-4* left at 1.38 p.m. for Ferrol harbour in Spain, which it reached at 4.47 p.m. After an overnight halt to give the crew a badly needed rest, they left Ferrol at 6.27 a.m. the next day, 31 May, sighting only two destroyers en route to England, due to the persistent squalls. They reached Brest about 11 a.m. in showery squalls, typical summer weather for Europe. A headwind did not deter the Americans from the last lap of all – across the English Channel.

Plymouth waited while those two final hours elapsed, and at 1.12 p.m. the crowds spotted the seaplane east of the Sound.

Very lights, sirens, and all the other paraphernalia of welcome made it clear that Britain regarded this as an historic moment in the annals of flying, which it was. The next one came only a fortnight later.

11

ALCOCK AND BROWN
The Atlantic Non-stop

Just under four weeks after Harry Hawker and Mackenzie Grieve had taken off from Newfoundland, Alcock and Brown started on their attempt at the first Atlantic flight. Like Hawker, both Captain John Alcock and Lieutenant Arthur Whitten Brown had gained their experience in the Great War, and in fact they chose a modified bomber for their flight.

This was the Vickers Vimy, a large biplane bomber carrying 865 gallons of petrol, enough to supply the two 375-horsepower Rolls-Royce engines for a journey of 2,440 miles. The actual point-to-point distance between Newfoundland and their Irish destination amounted to about 1,890 miles, so they had fuel for 500 extra miles in reserve. The machine measured forty-three feet and had a wing span of some sixty-nine feet.

Profiting from Hawker's experience, they made certain that the Vimy's water system was working perfectly, and all the water to be used was first filtered, boiled and then strained before entering the tanks. If either of the two engines were to fail after the halfway point, they could carry on to Ireland on the remaining one. If this happened before they had consumed half the fuel, however, the other engine could not support such a load and they would be forced down into the sea.

Alcock and Brown carried Very lights to help meet any emergency like this, and they also had the great advantage of wireless communication. Altogether they seemed to be better prepared than Hawker and Grieve, wearing electrically heated clothing and taking plenty of nourishment, including special sandwiches, chocolate and hot drinks.

The two men sat side by side, but Alcock was to be at the wheel all the way. The Vimy did actually have a driving 'wheel'. Brown said before the flight: 'I suppose I shall be butler and everything, for Alcock will be too busy flying the machine to get the food out.'

It was lucky that the pair were not superstitious, for the date when they finally felt ready was Friday, 13 June 1919!

Alcock's words before the take-off the following day were: 'It's a long flight, but it doesn't worry me any more than the night bombing raids my squadron used to carry out.'

Over their last hurried meal before leaving, Brown added:

With this wind we shall be in Ireland in 12 hours. The air speed indicator shows a ground speed of 42 miles an hour. We can't hope for that all the way, but the winds are favourable, and we might be in sight of land in anything between 19 and 20 hours. I am steering a straight line for Galway Bay.

Brown intended to use the ordinary Mercator chart of the North Atlantic and reckoned to find the position of the aeroplane at any time by observing the height of the sun, or a suitable star, through a sextant, noting the Greenwich time and plotting the result by a special chart showing the curves of equal altitude. He would also take account of the effect of the wind on them by a drift-bearing plate.

The fuel weighed three and a half tons, and the whole aircraft over six tons. Despite the forty-mile-an-hour gale gusting into the airfield, Alcock decided to go ahead. It was 4.13 p.m. GMT on that Saturday afternoon when they started up the two engines. After Alcock had listened to them for a few minutes, he felt satisfied with their behaviour and gave the signal to clear the chocks from the wheels.

The long tapering body of the Vimy vibrated to the gale and the pulsing purr of the engines, like an animal eager to leap. Alcock took the aircraft forward uphill – the field had a fairly steep gradient.

It took nearly a quarter of a mile before the plane eventually left the ground. Nearly all the population of St Johns had climbed to Lester's Field to see the start. Rising steadily the Vimy passed over the town and across the White Hills, at the point where Hawker had set out nearly a month earlier.

Then the crowd had a shock as it appeared that the plane had dipped and disappeared, while it actually flew up a valley. They had to open the engines full out to get up that valley, thrusting the whole power of the Vimy against the force of the funnelled wind.

They crossed Signal Hill, Newfoundland, at precisely 4.28 p.m. GMT, the official time of the start of the flight, and almost from that moment on things began to go badly. It looked like being Hawker and Grieve's experience all over again. The weather was certainly similar.

They put themselves at the mercy, or lack of it, of the elements – fog, ice and wind. In fact, despite all the planning, Brown was able to take only four readings of their position; one from the sun, one of the moon, one from the Pole Star, and one from the star Vega.

They quickly climbed to the agreed initial height of 1,000 feet and at Signal Hill set out a course for the ocean on 124 degrees compass point. The elements then almost took over completely; the strong south-west wind added to their speed, but the fog and clouds closed in all around, blinding them.

Early on Alcock throttled down nicely and let the plane gradually climb. At dusk they had got up to 4,000 feet, and found themselves sandwiched between layers of clouds, and unable to see either sea or sky. The lower level of fog and clouds drifted at about 2,000 feet and the upper at 6,000 feet. Before dark the clouds had hidden the sun altogether. They could not see the sea, and when night came the clouds concealed the moon and the stars. It was all pretty comfortless.

Those first six or seven hours were really bad. The fog hung low over the water, the clouds moved north-east before the wind in the same general direction as the aeroplane. Alcock could only go on trying to fly blindly between the main layers above and below.

Alcock divided his time between straining to see ahead and watching the air-speed indicator and compass. In this way he hoped to keep the Vimy roughly the right way up.

Still struggling forward on their original course, they came to a momentary magic break in the conjunction of cloud and endless, enveloping, Atlantic fog all about them.

Through the crack in the clouds, they saw stars sparkling and twinkling. Alcock took the bomber up towards the gap and called to Brown: 'Now's your chance. Can you get a bearing?'

He could and did, getting a 'cut' on Polaris and Vega as Alcock managed to keep the aeroplane level with the unaccustomed luxury of an actual horizon ahead of him. Rapidly Brown did his calculations and gauged that they were about two degrees south of the course they had set.

'New course 110 degrees compass point,' Brown told Alcock, who adjusted the plane accordingly and flew on.

The clearance of clouds turned out to be brief, so it was lucky they got their bearings when they did. Soon the weather started to thicken again. They were at those darkest hours before dawn, when flying in a clear sky would have been hard enough. But to control a big bomber as it throbbed through blanketing banks of fog was almost too much for Alcock.

'We began to have a very rough time,' admitted Alcock later.

He could not see the sea, the sky, or where they met. The only thing he could rely on was his air-speed indicator. Then it jammed.

Sleet had been falling for the last hour or so and in icy conditions nearly a mile up in the Atlantic night, the sleet had frozen on the indicator. They could also smell smoke.

So whether Alcock opened the throttle or closed it, the air-speed indicator still showed the same reading: ninety miles an hour. Only this device could have told them that they were flying roughly level, for if they rose or fell in altitude, their speed would change provided the throttle remained the same.

Its failure would not have mattered so much in daylight or on a clear night. But to be fogbound, cloudbound, sleetbound, and not know whether they were flying level or not – that could quickly be fatal. Alcock knew it. He concentrated all his supreme skill on keeping the aircraft as steady as he could, and for a time the engines responded with a normal note, but not for very long. It was surprising that he had managed it at all.

It was a terrible sensation, that utter lack of a sense of horizon or gravity, like floating around in a fourth dimension. But they were still very much in a world of three dimensions and if they were not careful they would be in the ocean, drowning.

Now the engine started to shift from the Rolls-Royce whirr to a protesting whine and roar.

'We did some comic stunt,' said Alcock afterwards. 'It was very alarming.'

Through the thick clouds they actually looped the loop in a frantic effort to find some sort of stability. But it was no use. From the loop and ensuing slight climb, the Vimy went into a ponderous but quite steep spiral. Alcock couldn't correct it. He hardly knew what to do. He waited for a few seconds, nerves strung as taut as the wires between the struts.

From 4,000 feet the aeroplane rolled round and down, gathering speed as it fell further through the spiral. Alcock was literally helpless now. It all happened so quickly. He couldn't fight gravity when he still scarcely knew which way it was pulling.

All this took only seconds. The Vimy roared round and round. Their altitude fell to 1,000 feet, with visibility still virtually nil. All Alcock could hope for was to hang on to the wheel and wait.

It seemed impossible that Alcock could ever regain control. Suddenly they came out of the clouds and Alcock spotted the dim suggestion of the sea. It was enough. A faint blur, but a horizon of sorts. He had to act instantly, for they were down to 200 feet already, and still spinning.

Using all his wits and strength, he began to pull the aeroplane out of that alarming angle, but it was already almost on its back.

At 100 feet it was under control again, and at fifty feet it had levelled off.

So they were saved, less than a wing span above the water. It was the closest call Alcock had ever experienced. Only by his instinctive reaction did he manage to right the fall of the heavy aeroplane.

That fall could easily have been their last. It did have one beneficial effect, though, for the air-speed indicator began to work properly again after the shock treatment of that swift dive.

Gradually Alcock and Brown got over the fright of those few seconds. The wind remained more or less behind them. They climbed to 6,000 feet, then they ran into the fog again, even at that altitude. To look into it for long hypnotized the mind and made the eyes watery.

Alcock climbed above the fog twice, only to run into congestions of clouds each time. And in one area one bank of fog lay actually on top of another, lower one. The aeroplane emerged from the gloom once, and the pilot snatched a peep at the moon and surrounding stars. But before Brown could do much about fixing their position, the aeroplane ran straight into a vicious combination of hail, snow and sleet at 11,000 feet.

As far as navigation went, they were trusting to the compass. In any case they had far worse things to worry about as the night wore on than flying off course.

Ice threatened to envelop the whole aircraft. The radiator shutter and water temperature indicator became covered in it, and it put the air-speed indicator out of service once more. They were still amid the fog and cloud. Alcock said suddenly, 'It's jammed the ailerons.'

Alcock knew that the presence of ice on the radiator shutters would sooner or later react on the engine. It seemed as if something must give out before they reached Ireland. However, the most pressing problem was the air-speed indicator, so Brown forced himself up from the cockpit to a position near the centre-section strut. Exposed in this way, the navigator risked falling out of the machine altogether, but he somehow struggled on, to chip off the ice with a knife. This improved the air-speed indicator, but he had to repeat the operation regularly. It gave trouble again later, when it became full of frozen particles.

They never saw the sun rise, but finally after some thirteen hours, the clouds did scatter slightly to let in dim daylight. The wild weather remained with them and so did the ice.

Two or three hours from the Irish coast, Brown took some rough readings, but could not tell where they were with any certainty, so he motioned for Alcock to go down lower, below the clouds. They had communicated by shouts or gestures most of the way, for their inter-com telephones had broken down a quarter of the way across. And as for wireless messages, they never heard so much as a single one!

The pilot tilted the nose of the Vimy and there was almost a rep-etition of the near-disaster back in mid-ocean. Down and down they dived, till they shot out of the low clouds. Alcock was able to straighten up with comparative ease and he kept the Vimy throbbing and thrumming eastward as Brown tried to take any checks he could.

They flew over the sea at a mere 300 feet, as the sun made a fitful, feeble attempt to appear, but was defeated by the miles of clustering clouds.

'It was a terrible trip,' Alcock said afterwards.

Only after another hour at this low level did the frozen particles start to fall off the air-speed indicator, but they did not really need this much now. They followed the horizon at a height of a mere hundred yards. They were not sure where they were, but by time and indicated speed, it seemed that they must soon see land. Any part of the cliff-lined coastline of Ireland would look like paradise itself, but still the water spread out ahead, a mixture of cloud-grey and sea-green.

Those last minutes seemed longer than the rest of the flight put together. Tiredness crept over them as they looked alternately at the instrument panel and the horizon.

'Should be roughly on course,' Brown called above the wind, after another careful check.

They had flown and fought the elements for nearly 1,900 miles. Where was the land?

Then they saw two little islands, Eashal and Turbot. The two men spotted them simultaneously, and a few miles further on they saw the Irish coast itself, at about 8.15 a.m. GMT on Sunday, 15 June.

In no time they were over land and looking down on Ardbear Bay, an inlet of Clifden Bay. When they saw the slender mast of the Clifden wireless station, they knew exactly where they were. They had navigated to the precise point they had aimed at – and there it rose below them in the grey morning. Alcock and Brown exchanged quick glances. They had no need for words.

Alcock circled over the village of Clifden, craning out of the cockpit to spot the likeliest landing place. He saw what looked like a lovely green meadow, and banked to bring the Vimy round for the historic landing. Throttling down, he idled the great Rolls-Royce engines, and positioned for a perfect run-in.

But the meadow was a bog! The moment the four wheels touched down, they started to sink axle deep into the soft mud. The inevitable occurred. The Vimy toppled on to her nose; the tail tipped up at forty-five degrees; the lower wing crunched and crumpled; the propellers dug into the bog; and Alcock and Brown were pitched forwards.

But they weren't hurt and hoisted themselves out to realize that they had become the first men to fly the Atlantic non-stop. They had done it in sixteen hours twelve minutes.

A big broad smile covered John Alcock's ruddy face. Arthur Brown smiled, too, looking slightly more tired. Both men were knighted and received the £10,000 prize from the *Daily Mail*.

Tragically, Alcock was killed just six months later on a routine flight from England to France.

12

ALAN COBHAM
Epic Flight to Cape Town

One of the greatest 'first flights' of all was Alan Cobham's 17,000-mile epic from London to Cape Town and back: only surpassed by his amazing Australia-and-back venture immediately afterwards.

Alan Cobham took with him on the Cape Town trip two other men, A.B. Elliott as engineer, and B.W.G. Emmott, a Gaumont-British photographer who was to make a film of the whole flight.

Their plane was a De Havilland Type 50 biplane. This had a passenger cabin to the rear of the engine, with the pilot's own cockpit situated separately, though Cobham was able to talk to the others. The plane was powered by a 385-horsepower Siddeley-Jaguar engine, strong enough to convey the mass of gear for such a stupendous undertaking.

The three men took off from Stag Lane aerodrome, near Hendon, on 16 November 1925, but only got as far as Paris that day. Next day they flew on to Marseilles, making another overnight stop.

The weather was bad by now, and a surging north-easterly gale swept up and over the southerly Alps. In an attempt to escape the violent air turbulence, Cobham took it up to 6,000 feet, but the turbulence got even worse. He appreciated that he dare not risk these conditions for long, or they would fail before getting further than Europe. So he swung the aeroplane out to sea and skimmed over the choppy Mediterranean towards Pisa and the leaning tower that gave them their bearings.

The next stop was Taranto, at the heel of Italy, and from there they hopped across a stormy sea to Greece, again finding themselves buffeted by wild winds gusting over mountains. Cobham came down low over the water once more, crossing the Gulf of Corinth and making Athens by 20 November. The 480-mile flight south over the Aegean and Mediterranean to Africa was uneventful and they reached Cairo safely and settled in there for a week or so, making several flights over the Pyramids for Emmott to take pictures – quite a novelty at the time.

They resumed their journey and flew on down the course of the Nile over Luxor – more opportunities for filming, this time the Aswan Dam. They were aware that they were witnessing what no one had seen from the air before, the ever-shifting ageless panorama of Africa. The flight became a list of exotic place-names like Wadi Halfa, Atbara, Khartoum. Before getting to this outpost of Kitchener's days, they saw beneath them the junction of the Blue and White Niles.

They spent Christmas at Khartoum, having flown all the way from London. In 1925 that still seemed fantastic, like a Wellsian dream. But to Cobham, it conveyed a glimpse of a realizable future for international airlines.

At Malakal they watched a war dance by the local Shulluk warriors, who even posed before the aeroplane. The contrast between these primitive people, who had never seen an aeroplane, and the machine itself was quite dramatic. They stood with simple dignity, even indifference, before the DH-50 with its markings 'Imperial Airways Air Route Survey' painted beside the enclosed cabin. Then they moved to the beat of tom-toms, brandishing spears and disturbing the dust. It was all extremely strange.

So far the plane had functioned perfectly and Cobham foresaw no problems. The next stage in this pioneering flight was to Mongalla. The direct line lay over the swampy Sud region, which would prove dangerous and even fatal if they were forced to land. Cobham kept to the east of the Nile, which slushed a course through the Sud, and in this way managed to skirt the worst areas of this unknown swampland.

The next point was Jinja, almost on the equator. This place, beside the Victoria Nyanza lake, was several thousand feet higher than the aerodromes Cobham had negotiated so far in Africa – and he nearly had an accident because of this change.

The colourfully clothed natives of Uganda practically filled the whole runway at Jinja as Cobham brought the biplane in to land among them. He was piloting the plane just above a banana plantation, on the edge of the aerodrome, when some of the locals got so excited they ran right across the runway in the path of the machine.

Instinctively, Alan Cobham reacted as he would have done in such an emergency in England and started to land slightly short of them, hoping in this way to avoid any chance of hitting them.

Coming down shorter meant slower, too, but in the rarer air of Uganda, 4,000 feet above sea level, he needed a higher landing speed than he possessed to keep the plane airborne until the actual touchdown.

The De Havilland plummeted no less than ten feet on to the baked Uganda ground and the three men received a sharp jolt. Luckily the undercarriage was equal to the force of impact and did not show signs of damage. Cobham had learned his lesson, however, and did not forget it for the rest of the flight.

At Kisumu, an elderly lady asked them, 'How do you manage to sleep at night?' thinking that they spent several days at a time in the air. She seemed surprised when they told her they landed.

After Tabora in Tanganyika they ran into the rains with a vengeance. The date by then was 18 January 1926.

Cobham found this sector, from the southerly tip of Lake Victoria Nyanza to Palapye Road in Bechuanaland, about the worst of the entire trip. They had to travel over total jungle all the way, with no chance of setting an aeroplane down in the event of engine failure. Cobham knew nothing about what sort of weather to expect, apart from general indications.

They flew on to Abercorn, Northern Rhodesia, and N'Dola, above the vast Lake Bangweolo. The railway line guided them at this stage. The landing grounds here, as at other similar spots, were two runways in the shape of a cross, so that Cobham could come in from any one of four directions, depending on the wind. Knowledge of such things as prevailing winds was sketchy at that time, to say the least.

The next stage of their journey was from N'Dola to Broken Hill, over the railway, and on towards Livingstone, named of course after the explorer. The little wings cast their still smaller shadow over the trees and scrub and railway.

They left Broken Hill soon after breakfast, bound on the 290-mile hop to Livingstone, still following the rails. After a few hours' flying, and with virtually all of that stage behind them, they saw smoke, or what they took to be smoke, on the horizon. Suddenly Cobham realized it was not smoke but *spray*. They were flying towards the legendary Victoria Falls and nearly never flew away from them.

Livingstone spread away beneath them, but they were attracted to the Falls. Cobham flew on the few miles to the scene. They gasped as they gaped down from the cabin at the mile-wide Zambezi. Cobham kept to his course and was soon over the top of the waterfall, that mile and a quarter width of water eternally rolling, roaring, falling beyond the brink and converging on the single sheer chasm.

The Falls suck masses of warm air down the gorge with the water, and this rises later, sending up the spray in liquid mist to 1,000 feet higher than the lip of the falls.

After the two others had taken moving and still photographs, Cobham flew them in close along the line of the brink, for Emmott to film the whole vast expanse of water as it hurled itself over the top. Cobham decided to fly as slowly as he could, without undue risk of stalling.

After the approach at the westward end, he started along the actual brink, fifty feet above it and fifty yards away from it. He hoped to make his pass last a couple of minutes or so.

Suddenly the spray surged briefly up and around them. Globules of water dripped off the wings.

It happened again, and they were lost for a few moments in a fog of fine spray. The plane bumped about. They came out of it all right and headed more steadily for the far side of the Falls, with less than half a mile to go.

Nearly at the end of that great gaping brink, the De Havilland vanished into a thick vaporous spray, just as they were above the chasm.

Cobham was worried. He could not see a thing, but he knew that only feet away on their right rose the gigantic railway suspension bridge spanning the gorge. On the port side, the millions of gallons of the Zambezi went on thundering down. And ahead were rocks and jungle.

Then the engine croaked.

They had flown all the way from London to the Victoria Falls and it had not happened before. It stopped, started, stopped again.

Cobham turned to look at the other two through the dividing window. The trouble was that the air-intake pipes to the carburettor were sucking in spray. Cobham had to try to keep the engine going and the propeller revolving through the fine fog.

The engine went on faltering.

Luckily the engine just managed to fight the spray in the pipes, but Cobham still had to get clear of the Falls. Another serious engine cut-out and they could still speed down into the churning torrent below them.

He hauled back the control lever, and their reserve of power enabled the aeroplane to climb. Continuing to keep the engine full out, Cobham climbed as fast and as far as possible.

The aeroplane responded and rose several hundred feet over the Falls before the pilot started to veer off towards the airfield. They were not out of danger yet, he knew, for the engine was still sputtering. Cobham had to try and get completely clear of that area. It was no use being caught with an engine failure over the forest; that would be as bad as the Falls.

He willed the aeroplane away from that petrifying spray and the great jaws of the gorge. The engine reacted marvellously and bore them back towards the landing ground at Livingstone. Only when Cobham was sure that he could glide down did he feel safe. It had been touch and go. They realized this more fully that afternoon when they visited the foot of the Falls at ground level and were suddenly soaked by the fierce spray storm.

The rest of the route was quite tame after that: Bulawayo, Pretoria, Johannesburg, Kimberley, Bloemfontein, Beaufort West, and finally Cape Town on 17 February, three months, and 8,500 miles, since that foggy day at Stag Lane.

Alan Cobham had made air history in those months but now he wanted to improve on the time taken – to bring Britain and South Africa closer together. He had another incentive to get home quickly, too, for on 26 February, the very day they took off again, the steamship *Windsor Castle* left for Southampton, and a unique race was launched between the liner, which would sail 5,300 miles, and the aircraft, due to cover 8,500 miles.

At the Livingstone–Broken Hill stage they had trouble, but not so serious this time. Cobham had to fly through hours of misty rain over hundreds of miles of utterly uncharted interior. If they came down anywhere there no one would know.

At N'Dola five inches of rain in four hours turned the landing ground into a morass of mud. That put them back a day.

While they were landing at Tabora, one wheel of the plane sank up to its axle into the ground, and it took quite a force of helpers to pull them out. The take-off was worse. As Cobham taxied towards the take-off point, one wheel or the other sank into the soft earth every yard or two. At last they did decide to go ahead and try to get

94

up, but the wheels clogged and clamped them down. All the while it seemed as if the De Havilland must tilt forward, but at the fringe of the field it managed to heave itself a few feet off the ground at a speed scarcely faster than a car. It was one of those nasty moments of the return route.

The next headache proved to be the torrid tropical heat. It was tough on the men but worse for the machine and gear. The lubricating oil started to warm up alarmingly, but they managed to maintain oil pressure. Cobham found that at times he could not look out over the fuselage, as the draught scorched past like an actual flame. Landing was like entering an oven, so airless did the atmosphere seem at ground level.

Cobham and Emmott were doing rather more than Elliott, who had suffered an attack of malaria on the outward stop at Johannesburg and was still convalescing.

In some respects, the return journey was worse than the outward, in spite of the fact that it was so much shorter. They took off from Khartoum amid the after-effects of a sandstorm, and even at heights of 10,000 feet and beyond they still had to fly through clusters of the swirled sand. Visibility was just a word.

Coming down carefully through the sickly-yellow, sand-laden air, they reached Atbara, to be told that the dust was thicker still ahead. But they risked it. Climbing once more to nearly 12,000 feet, Cobham began to find it more and more difficult to follow the course of the Nile, his only reliable guide. The thought of a forced landing in the desolation of the desert haunted him.

Then he suddenly said, 'It's *not* the Nile!'

He realized they were lost in the banks of dust between aeroplane and ground. What he thought had been a river was not. Cobham came down through the two miles and more of dim dusty air, the propeller threshing through the thousands of minute particles. Nothing on the ground gave him a clue as to their position.

Then he saw an old dried-up waterway, followed it, and found the Nile. That extinct river bed may well have saved their lives. He then flew at a height of twenty feet to Wadi Halfa.

After leaving the Nile, Cobham followed the telegraph poles projecting above the straight railway line, keeping as close to it as he could. Elliott was busy checking the engine records. They got in to Wadi Halfa, filled up their tanks, and nosed on for Aswan, which they reached at sundown – glad to be back to comparative civilization.

Reaching Egypt on 7 March they set up the record of the first Cape Town–Cairo flight.

The tail skid broke while they tried to take off from Sollum for Athens, which delayed them for a day. With an extra-heavy fuel load, they struck north over the Mediterranean and Aegean for Greece. Cobham reckoned to pass over Crete, but even if he missed that island, he estimated it to be only a two-hour hop to the Greek coast.

But visibility shut down sharply to a mile. After three hours he still saw no land. Three and a half hours passed and still nothing. Rain streamed off the windscreen, reducing the outlook to a grey blur.

Cobham began to wonder if he had missed Crete and Greece, and was heading for the open Ionian Sea. Their fuel supply drained away with every mile they battled through the murk. Half a dozen times they thought they saw land; then at last they really did. It was not Crete, but the isle of Kythera. Soon the mainland loomed on a dim horizon.

Cobham struck down-draughts again off the mountains. The powerful currents bumped and bounced them all over the sky. Then one tremendous thrust forced the three men and all the gear right up against the roof of the cabin. The petrol in the top tank was poured up against the roof. The fuel was gravity fed, but they were falling faster than gravity could operate, so no fuel got through to the engine and it stopped.

As the aeroplane was pushed towards the sea, it met a sharp up-thrust, the engine began to get fuel, and it re-started. They reached London a couple of days later on 13 March 1926, after a fifteen-day flight from Cape Town. They had beaten the *Windsor Castle*.

13

ALAN COBHAM

To Australia by Seaplane

From England to Australia and back in a seaplane. This was what
Alan Cobham undertook only three and a half months after the
triumphant trip to Cape Town.

With his mechanic, A.B. Elliott, he took off from the slipway of
Short Bros. works at Rochester in Kent, before 5 a.m. on 30 June
1926. The De Havilland Type 50 biplane had been fitted with
seaplane floats instead of the normal undercarriage, and ahead of it
lay a two-way trip totalling 28,000 miles. Apart from four test flights
the week before, Cobham had never flown a seaplane at all! He did
know a lot of the route, however, as he had already made a journey
to Rangoon and back.

The maximum load for the plane was 4,200 pounds, but they were
actually bearing about 5,000 pounds. Despite this extra loading, the
Siddeley-Jaguar engine seemed able to cope quite well, and before
long they were cruising across France at 100 miles an hour. Cobham
had only rather a crude means of working out if he had enough petrol
to take them to any particular destination. It went like this: 'If I can
do 220 miles in so many minutes, how long will it take to do
670 miles, etc.'

His arithmetic proved accurate and they came down on the water
by Marseilles after a non-stop hop of six hours and forty minutes.
Cobham liked the freedom offered by a seaplane: wherever water
existed, he could land. That was the theory.

During the next jump, across to Naples, he made rough measurements of the distance flown by using his fingers on the map! Gliding
gracefully into Naples Bay, he had a nasty jolt. The sun had gone
down and the seaplane base lay on the islet of Nisida, 300 yards off

the mainland. He remembered that telegraph wires spanned this short stretch, but in the fast-fading summer light, he nearly flew into them. In fact, Cobham was pretty tired after his long months of preparation following right on top of his Cape Town epic. He did manage to get across to Athens, however, where he stayed to rest for a day on doctor's advice.

Cobham was still not fully fit, yet went on to the rigid timetable he had set: Athens, 3 July; Alexandretta, 4 July; Baghdad, 5 July.

After they had crossed over from the Tigris to the Euphrates and gone about 150 miles, they ran into a thickening sandstorm. Bringing the seaplane to just a few feet above the river, Cobham hammered on through a blinding bank of choking sand. Finally it got too dense to see safely at the speed he had to travel, and he came down on the river beside a local police hut, beaching the plane on the mudbank nearby. This was the asset of the seaplane; he could set it down anywhere in the world, provided there was water. After a rest during the remaining hours of the morning, they took off to try and reach Basra that day.

After half an hour they met another sandstorm near the vast swamplands above Basra. Cobham did not feel too happy about flying over the murky mixture of mud and sand that merged into one and almost obliterated any sense of horizon. The storm was just as bad as cloying fog. All he could do was to screw up his eyes and strain to see the rushes and weeds growing from the swampy brown lake below.

After passing the town of Suke Shuyuk, Cobham took care to keep to the rather wavy shores of the lake-swamp, marked by the ghostly rushes rising out of it. He was at about fifty feet on a zig-zag course.

Slowly the swamp seemed to come to an end and a sandy coast appeared. Cobham thought they were over the worst of the storm and would soon be at Basra.

Suddenly he heard and felt a fierce explosion. It seemed to come from the cabin.

He shouted through the connecting window, 'What on earth has happened? Are we on fire?'

The only explanation Cobham could think of was that one of their rocket pistol cartridges had gone off, which would have set the plane alight.

Elliott called back feebly, 'Petrol pipe's burst.'

Cobham could hardly hear him. As he was still flying low, he could not switch off the engine and just glide, so as to hear him more clearly. He scribbled a note on his writing pad, ripped the sheet off, and stuffed it through to Elliott.

After a pause, Elliott sent back a message that the petrol pipe from the reserve tank in the cabin to the supply tank on the top wing had burst a few inches from the point where it was joined to the cabin tank, and that he was hit in the arm very badly and was 'bleeding a pot of blood'.

Cobham snatched a glance and saw how terribly pale he looked. Should he land and try to give first aid – or fly for Basra? It was an awful decision to be forced to make, but it was really made for him when he looked below. Once more all he could see were shallow swamp waters, dark, dank and dirty. The heat was terrific and Cobham knew that even if he did land he would run the risk of beaching the machine and not being able to take off again without Elliott's active help.

Against this, he thought, 'Elliott is bleeding and I might be able to stop it'.

But this was the short-term outlook. Elliott obviously needed a doctor and if Cobham got caught in the swamp and the dust storm that still eddied all around them, then they might never get out of that appalling place again. So he decided to try and make Basra at maximum speed.

In a temperature of 110 degrees Fahrenheit in the shade, Cobham raced the seaplane on at fifty feet. He reckoned they were about a hundred miles from the city, so he hoped to get Elliott into medical hands within an hour. The oil got hotter as the plane shuddered full out at 125 miles an hour, still skimming the bank of the lake. At last, thirty miles from Basra, Cobham flew out of the severe storm and the sun broke through scorchingly.

A quarter of an hour later the De Havilland aeroplane was angling for the wide Tigris at Basra. But as Cobham came down over the river, he found that the open bank he needed for beaching the aeroplane did not seem to exist along the heavily built-up riverside. Finally he found a clearing, landed, and beached the aeroplane up on the mud.

The second that Cobham opened the cabin lid, he realized Elliott was in a bad way. The afternoon heat had become unbearable, and Elliott was having difficulty in breathing. Cobham got one or two reluctant locals to help him out of the cabin, but as the pilot had

Elliott in his arms, and was struggling to step down from the lower wing on to the floats, Elliott whispered, 'Turn the oil off'.

Elliott feebly tried to push down the lever close by him.

Cobham gave him some brandy and began a long fight for help. No one would do anything at first, but eventually he did get Elliott away to hospital. Cobham remembered Elliott saying, 'I can't understand how the petrol pipe burst'.

Meanwhile, the pilot returned to the seaplane and supervised its towing down the river into the backwaters of the RAF inland water-transport dock, where they moored it.

That evening Cobham tried to explain to the commanding officer there how the accident had happened, but the engineers insisted that the petrol pipe could not have burst, or even if it had done, could not have caused so much havoc. Cobham heard that Elliott was holding his own. He went to bed that night still wondering about the whole strange episode. Next morning he learned the truth.

'Did you see any natives about when you were flying over the swamp?' the engineer-officer asked Cobham at breakfast.

'No – we couldn't see anything at all for the dust storm.'

Then the officer broke the devastating news that natives must have been there – and shot at the plane.

'A petrol pipe didn't do the damage,' he explained, 'it was a bullet. It entered the machine, pierced the petrol pipe, and hit Elliott.'

So that was it. The officer took Cobham to the seaplane to prove it.

Cobham worked out that they must have actually heard the gun being fired by an Arab. Then the bullet passed between the two floats, pierced the wall of the cabin, shot straight through the petrol pipe inside the cabin, and went on through Elliott's arm and into his side, passing both lobes of his left lung, and finally lodging itself under his right armpit.

Cobham was just about to go to bed that night when a telephone message reached him: 'Tell Cobham that his engineer Elliott had a sudden relapse and died at 11.15 tonight.'

Alan Cobham was utterly stunned and decided to give up the whole project. He had known Elliott for a long time and flown tens of thousands of miles in his company. It was as if he had lost part of himself.

The authorities investigated the crime among the Arabs in the area of the storm and later on an Arab actually confessed.

But before this, Cobham had been persuaded to continue with

100

his plans and so chose an RAF Sergeant, A.H. Ward, to accompany him from Basra. Ward was a cockney with a sense of humour and Cobham certainly needed cheering up after the tragedy that had marred this great venture.

They took off on 14 July and immediately ran into more trouble. While flying over desolate swamp near the head of the Persian Gulf, the engine started to die. The indicator showed a fall of two hundred revolutions. Cobham could not account for it, and fortunately it did not last long, or they might have been marooned in the damp deserted wastelands. That was the only moment the engine faltered during the 28,000-mile flight.

The next panic came an hour or two later when Cobham noticed that the petrol was getting perilously low. He doubted if he could reach Bushire on the fuel left in the tank.

Ward pumped and pumped but still there was no sign of more petrol getting through.

'What's wrong?' Cobham asked.

Then as things began to seem desperate, he suddenly remembered that there was a petrol cock at the bottom of the pump.

'Perhaps it was turned off while we were at Basra,' he called.

Ward nodded and in a second or two that minor crisis was over.

The next crisis occurred when they had to come down on the water at Bandar Abbas while a very heavy sea was running. Cobham managed it. Then as the seaplane was being towed out, one of its wing-tips and one of the tail-tips collided with a launch.

Two days later at Chahbar, they had just refuelled in readiness to push on to Karachi when Ward stepped on a float that was not there and fell into a choppy sea, but he was no worse for his ducking. Another thing that the engineer had to bear in mind when working on a seaplane in the open water was that unless he had a sheet underneath the engine, whatever he dropped he lost!

There were plenty of incidents to keep Cobham's mind from dwelling too much on the tragedy of Elliott. At Bahawalpur, deep inland on the Indus river, they were just taking off when Cobham shouted, 'Look! There's a chap hanging onto the floats!'

Cobham throttled down and shouted to Ward to get out of the cabin and make the man get off. The only way to force him away was for the engineer to tread on his hands until he had to let go. The alternative would have been worse for the Indian, to be dragged up into the air as he would have been in another moment or two. After he splashed into the water, Cobham saw some Indians rescuing him. Ward scrambled aboard again and they were airborne.

They flew on eastward: Delhi, Allahabad, Calcutta, Akyab, Rangoon, which they reached on 27 July. Although they still had some thousands of miles to go, the flight went pretty smoothly from there on, with almost an air of inevitable achievement. By the end of July they were at Singapore, and then they flew on via Muntok, Batavia, Sourabaya and Bima to Kupang, touching down there by 5 August.

The last lap to Port Darwin represented the longest jump over the ocean of the entire flight – 500 miles to the Australian coast. They started out on this long, lonely vigil from Timor to Port Darwin at a height of 100 feet and never rose above it all the way. Timor means fear. They hoped they would have no cause for it.

Cobham flew straight at the south-east trade winds. After about twenty minutes from Kupang they had left these behind and resigned themselves to some four hours' flying towards a horizon devoid of anything save the sea and sky.

Cobham calculated the shortest time this could take, and also the longest. If they had not sighted land when the latter had elapsed, he would have to fly due south in order not to miss the Australian continent. He did not want to career on east towards the Pacific with only a limited fuel supply aboard.

He had heard that visibility in that region might reach the phenomenal figure of 150 miles, and so when he had not sighted land after a reasonable time, he started to get slightly worried. He reasoned to himself, though, that he could not see so far that day, and so persevered on the same course for some miles.

Still no land appeared. This meant that either the headwind was holding them back more than they had realized, or they were drifting north of the island of Melville, and missing Australia altogether. Cobham thought the wind must be to blame. The shadow of the seaplane darkened the coloured coral reefs, but still there was no land. The engine ran perfectly. But time was ticking away ominously and Cobham was concerned by now. He worked out how much longer the fuel would last and then wondered how he would land on the rather rough water.

After what seemed an infinity of miles and hours, Cobham glimpsed a dim kink on the horizon.

'Look! Land!' he shouted through to Ward.

Half an hour later the seaplane sailed over a sandy beach, backed by red cliffs which were topped by a bushy jungle. It was Herd Bay, only five miles from the point they had aimed to hit. A hundred miles and one hour later, they saw the harbour of Port Darwin.

Four fantastic weeks followed, from 8 August to 4 September, as Cobham and Ward flew all around Australia to tumultuous welcomes at each stopping place, large or small: Katherine Station, Newcastle Waters, Brunette Downs, Camooweal, Cloncurry, Longreach, Charleville, Bourke, Sydney, Hay, Melbourne, Adelaide, Oodnadatta, Alice Springs, and back to Katherine Station and Darwin.

Just as Cobham had taken his time on the outward trip to Cape Town and then hurried home, he wanted to try and do the same from Australia and arrive back on 1 October – a dash flight, as he called it. He planned to make two jumps a day, averaging 700–1,000 miles. In Australia, Cobham and Ward had been joined by a third crew member, C. Capel, for the return journey.

They left their twin float trails in the waters of Port Darwin on 4 September, and reached Penang four days later. They left Penang, and suddenly felt the full impact of the monsoon lashing across the Indian Ocean.

The rains slashed at the seaplane, as Cobham desperately dodged the worst deluges for fifty miles and more. Finally he found himself surrounded by storm-centres and forced to go through them. On the outward leg, he had been able to see sixty miles in this area; now he was lucky to see sixty yards.

The faithful plane flew on, buried in the banks of the storm. By now Cobham could scarcely see out at all, and he suddenly sensed a dark mass dead ahead of him. He did a steep vertical bank, just in time to avoid hitting a gaunt rock rising five hundred feet out of the ocean.

Later on he made an emergency landing on an uninhabited island forty miles from the mainland. They eventually got away from the island, only to find that the wooden propeller had been damaged by the downpour, so Cobham had to put down at Tanoon.

Getting as far as Victoria Point, they tried to forge on to make up time, but conditions were against them. The further north they flew the more the monsoon worsened. The force of the rain blinded Cobham, so that to steer on would invite disaster. The cascading rain wiped out all vision through his goggles, so he had to shelter behind his screen and just look out sideways, without getting the full fury of the rain in his face.

They turned back and were pleased to see Victoria Point again. They had to stay there, itching to be airborne, for four days while up to five inches of rain fell daily. They even had to bore holes in the floor of the plane to let the water out.

They saw the back of Victoria Point on 14 September and from then on made steady progress to Karachi. Then they really turned on the pressure, even through the oven-hot Persian Gulf, when the oil emerging from the engine registered seventy-six degrees centigrade.

The flight from Karachi to home took a mere week. When it was nearly over, Cobham was hurrying to keep to his schedule of reaching London on 1 October. During the flight over France to Paris he went down to an altitude of only 100 feet over hill and dale to avoid the strong winds. He knew too well that if the engine failed or a fault occurred just then, they would have no time to find water and it would mean the end of a marvellous plane and perhaps themselves.

At Paris, Cobham collected a telegram asking him to land on the Thames in front of the Houses of Parliament at two o'clock the following afternoon, which he did. As a result of this fantastic flight of 28,000 miles in three months, including the return trip in under a month, he was given a knighthood. No one would deny that he deserved the honour.

1. Wright military aeroplane, 1909. *Left to right:* Lieutenant Benjamin D. Foulais, Wilbur Wright, Lieutenant Frank P. Lahm and Orville Wright.

2. Flight Sub Lieutenant Warneford, VC, RNAS, with his Morane Parasol monoplane from which he bombed and destroyed a German Zeppelin between Ghent and Brussels on 7 June 1915. He was killed ten days later.

3. Captain Albert Ball, VC, DSO, MC.

4. Captain Leefe Robinson, VC.

5. Captain W. Avery Bishop, VC, DSO, MC, with his Nieuport 17 escort.

6. Major William George Barker, VC, DSO, MC.

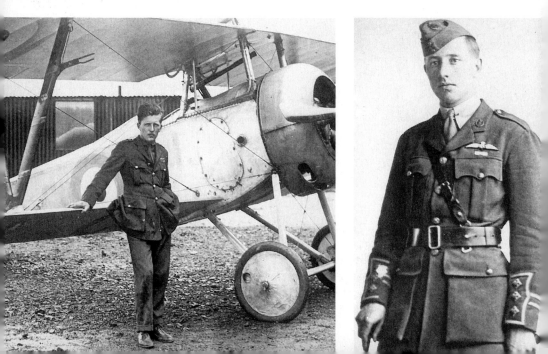

7. *Top:* Sir Alan Cobham's De Havilland DH50 during his flight to Australia, July 1926. The flight engineer, A.B. Elliott, was killed by a Bedouin rifle bullet flying over the desert on their next stage.
8. *Middle:* Charles Lindbergh and the *Spirit of St Louis* in the unlikely setting of RAF Gosport, Hampshire, 31 May 1927.
9. *Bottom: Southern Cross* during Charles Kingsford Smith's conquest of the Pacific.

10. Amy Johnson after a record-breaking flight from Britain to South Africa.

11. Amelia Earhart, the first woman across the Atlantic.

12. *Winnie Mae* – Wiley Post's immortal aeroplane in which he circumnavigated the globe in eight days.

13. Scott and Black talking to the Prince of Wales at Mildenhall before their prize winning flight to Melbourne.

14. Jean Batten arriving to acclaim in New Zealand.

15. Sydney Camm (left), designer of the Hurricane, and its test pilot, Flight Lieutenant Bulman (in plus fours) in front of an antiquated Hawker Cygnet.

16. R. J. Mitchell, designer of the immortal Spitfire.

17. Designer Frank Whittle congratulating test pilot Gerry Sayer on a safe landing.

18. VC10 of RAF Transport Command in the 1960's.

19. Test pilots Brian Trubshaw and John Cochrane on the flight deck of Concorde prototype 002.

14

BYRD AND BENNETT

To the North and South Poles

Admiral R.E. Byrd was the conqueror of both the North and South Poles by air. These flights were fraught with hazards as bad as any in aviation history.

The attempt on the North Pole was made on 9 May 1926, and Byrd was actually only the navigator on this flight. The pilot was another well-known American, Floyd Bennett.

In fact the air conquest of the North Pole developed into a dramatic race between the Americans in an aeroplane and the explorer Amundsen in an airship. The latter had been designed by the notable Italian flier, General Umberto Nobile, and was called *Norge* in honour of Amundsen's country, Norway.

The Americans' machine was a Fokker Type F.VII monoplane, powered by three 230-horsepower Wright engines. They had called it *Josephine Ford*. There could be no doubt that it was a Fokker for the word was painted practically all over the body and wings.

Both parties found themselves at Spitzbergen at the same time in early May, and it was a toss-up which type of flying craft would be ready for the honour of the first shot at the polar flight. The Norwegians and Italians had the harder job of preparing their cumbersome craft, but they laboured right round the clock to try and win the honour for the airship.

Meanwhile Byrd and Floyd Bennett had their own troubles. The Americans had to try and perfect special skis instead of wheels, so that they would stand a better chance of landing safely on ice, if necessary. Wheels would be useless at the polar ice-cap. But every time they tried the vital functions of take-off or landing they had accidents to the skis either on leaving or returning to the ground. Each pair that snapped or otherwise came to grief under the strain shortened not only their supply of skis but also the time available. They could see that the rival group were putting the last touches to their plans for the flight.

The night of May 8–9 proved decisive, for Byrd and Floyd Bennett knew the airship would be ready by next day. It was midnight. They fitted the final pair of skis.

'Let's have a shot at it,' Byrd suggested.

'Okay – I'm game,' came the pilot's response.

So at about 1 a.m. in the Arctic twilight world, the *Josephine Ford* slid forward over the Spitzbergen ice and was airborne. Their rivals were left gaping and could only wait to see if the aeroplane was successful; the machine carried fuel for some twenty hours so they would know by the end of that day one way or the other.

The big sixty-five-feet-span aircraft headed north. In this Arctic realm of no night, the twilight broadened and brightened into day. The two fliers sat muffled up like polar bears as the plane passed over the strange, silent, white world below. They had already gained valuable knowledge of Arctic conditions while flying over Greenland, and it was because of these flights that Byrd had developed some special navigational aids for the region; a bubble sextant and a sun compass.

Now the little huts of Spitzbergen lay far behind, together with the extra signs of civilization such as an odd ship or two, the airship's mooring mast, and wireless masts. Now they were well on their way along the 800-mile line to the Pole, which meant a round trip of 1,600 miles over the pale plains and uplands. The whole landscape seemed to merge into a single flat, white canvas – virgin, isolated, icy.

Byrd took some readings with his special instruments and announced: 'Should be nearing it now.'

Then they discovered in dismay that there was a leak from one of the oil-tanks. As so often happened, the fault at once presented them with a choice; to fly on and hope for the best or to try and land and see if they could plug up the leak. Either way they could be wrong, and to be wrong could so easily mean death.

Byrd bore in mind the trouble they had had so recently which resulted in those pairs of smashed skis. He did not want to risk that again, for they might never be able to get off the ice. But the alternative was not promising either. The leak would not improve by itself and would probably deteriorate, resulting in a forced landing. Whichever option they chose gave the prospect of possible disaster.

'Think we'd better stick it out,' Byrd said. 'no point in landing unless we have to.'

They kept going and the oil-leak dripped away, no better, no worse. Around 9 a.m., eight hours out from Spitzbergen, Byrd double-checked his measurements and reported, 'We've over it.'

While Floyd Bennett wheeled the plane in a steep circle, as if to encompass the hallowed area, Byrd threw out an American flag they had brought for the occasion, to signify the success of this first flight over the North Pole. They did not hang about after that, as they knew that although they had achieved their aim, they were only half way to the total distance which must be flown before regaining the safety of Spitzbergen.

Trouble met them as they headed south. As the aeroplane was tilting at a rather sharp angle, the bubble sextant slid off Byrd's chart table to the floor of the cabin. It was no use to him or anyone after that, but nor was a normal compass so close to the Magnetic North Pole.

The resulting panic was merely momentary, though, for Byrd had his special sun compass, which served as a good substitute. As Floyd Bennett concentrated on the flying, Byrd exerted all his prowess in striving to see that they hit Spitzbergen.

They had been flying non-stop for fifteen and a half hours when the Fokker finally topped one of the white hills around Spitzbergen, a dark dot in a clear sky to the watchers. As it came nearer they could see that its sleekly tapered wings flew dead parallel to the icefield.

Amundsen bore no grudge against Byrd and Floyd Bennett, shaking them sincerely by the hand soon after the plane had landed.

Despite having been beaten, Amundsen went ahead with the *Norge* flight, and instead of making a there-and-back trip like that of Byrd and Floyd Bennett, he determined to become the first to fly right over the roof of the world.

So on 11 May, the *Norge* started its sensational flight from Spitzbergen to Alaska. It had a crew of sixteen and the airship was actually under the command of the Italian General Nobile.

The course to the North Pole was uneventful, but from there on they were over entirely unexplored territory. Then two things happened. Firstly their radio transmitter failed, so that the world had no news of them. Secondly, the great dirigible blundered into a thick bank of freezing Arctic fog, which persisted for ten hours. Soon after they ran into this it started settling on the airship as moisture; the moisture froze into ice on the metal portions of the craft; and it was then sucked into the propellers of the airship in the form of jagged icicles. The revolving propellers spewed these out viciously against the lower part of the actual envelope of the airship. The icicles ripped rent after rent in the vital fabric and gas started to seep out.

The Norwegian and Italian crew had to put patches on as many of these tears as they could. The work was appallingly hard in freezing foggy weather but they managed it, and so the precious gas was conserved and the airship kept aloft.

Right on across the unexplored wastes they floated, all the time nearing Point Barrow, Alaska, their goal. The Beaufort Sea, the loneliest water in the world, drifted away beneath the cigar-shaped craft and eventually they reached Alaska after nearly three days and nights in the *Norge*, which had covered 3,500 miles.

Although airships are really outside the scope of this story, any account of the exploration of the Arctic and Antarctic from the air must include the sequel of the voyage of the *Norge*.

General Nobile wanted to extend Arctic exploration by airship by building a new one that would enable scientists actually to land on the polar regions to collect data and pictures. He interested his government in the idea, and the prompt result was the *Italia* airship, faster and more powerful than the *Norge*.

By the time it was built and had made a long journey from Milan to Spitzbergen, two years had elapsed. The *Italia* reached King's Bay, Spitzbergen, and took on 1,500 gallons of petrol for its three engines, which gave it a speed of seventy miles an hour. One engine was situated towards the rear and the other two in wing cars. Each of the three cars could be reached via the massive keel of the airship. The total volume of the *Italia* was 653,000 cubic feet.

Aboard the 'semi-rigid' now were a Swedish scientist, Professor Malmgrem, and three Italian naval officers, Viglieri, Mariano and Zappi.

They hoped to land at the North Pole, as well as fly over it, but as it turned out, a weird whining wind was sweeping the snow into ominous drifts when they arrived, and so they dared not risk a landing. They dropped a wooden cross down, given to them by the Pope, and with it fluttered the flag of Italy. Their radio sent messages far across to the Mediterranean. They even played music on a gramophone.

That was the high point of the voyage, and after it came tragedy.

Fog suddenly shrouded the airship, the same sort of freezing fog that had threatened the *Norge*. It was also snowing. The fog froze into ice, and the ice stuck to the envelope. The airship got heavier, its controls slower and more sluggish.

They used all its engines throughout that night, but the wind worsened and the ice remained. With morning came only the dim sight of solid ice-packs below and solid fog above. Everyone was tired but at least the airship was still moving. Then the elevators jammed.

The coxswain could not turn the wheel.

They stopped all engines while repairs were being rushed, and the vast volume of gas floated the airship up over the uncharted Arctic snowscape to 3,000 feet.

With the controls working again, they started engines and nosed down through the layer of filmy fog to 1,000 feet. All appeared to be well once more, but it wasn't. The ice on the envelope was forming more and more thickly, thrusting the airship downward at the stern under its deadening weight. It was too late to do anything but wait for the worst to happen.

General Nobile recalled it like this:

The recollection of those last instants is very vivid in my memory. I had scarcely time to reach the spot near the two rudders, between Malmgrem and Zappi, when I saw Malmgrem fling up the wheel, turning his startled eyes on me. Instinctively I grasped the helm, wondering if it were possible to guide the ship on to a snowfield and so lessen the shock . . . Too late! . . . There was the pack, a few yards below, terribly uneven. The masses of ice grew larger, came nearer and nearer . . . A moment later we crashed.

There was a fearful impact. Something hit me on the head, then I was caught and crushed. Clearly, without any pain, I felt some of my limbs snap. Some object falling from a height knocked me down head foremost. Instinctively I shut my eyes, and with perfect lucidity and coolness formulated the thought: 'It's all over!' I almost pronounced the words in my mind. It was 10.33 on May 25.

He was in the control-car of the *Italia*, one of ten men there. The airship struck the ice-pack so hard that the control-car was wrenched off and left sprawling on the jagged ice.

Suddenly lightened by the loss of the car, and ten men, the *Italia* swooped up, shot higher into the air, faded into the fog, and was borne away on the wind higher and higher – with the remainder of the crew. It was a terrible nightmare. Nothing was ever heard of it again.

One of the ten men in the control-car was killed by the crash, and Nobile had been hurt. The radio had been damaged but they were able to repair it and send out distress signals.

They had camping gear and food with them, so things were not yet hopeless; but the ice around them might break up and with it might drift their pitiful little camp, and any hope of rescue. Before this could happen, three of the survivors decided to leave the rest and set out to try and get to the mainland. They were Malmgrem, Mariano and Zappi.

As soon as the radio signals had been received, rescue operations were set in motion. Amundsen himself arranged to be flown in a French seaplane to the area, piloted by Rene Guilbord. Tragedy struck again, for the two men never reached General Nobile and the rest, disappearing to their death at some remote point along the route.

There followed a long, long wait. Many days passed.

Eventually a large flying boat penetrated as far as the marooned men, dropping supplies to them by parachute. The ice was beginning to break up badly then, so the flying boat could not land and rescue them.

After that a Swedish flier landed beside them in a Fokker monoplane specially equipped with floats, but he could only take one man back. The others made Nobile go as he was injured. On the Swede's next trip, his plane became damaged and the rescuer himself was stranded with the others.

Meanwhile, all this time the ice-breaker *Krassin* had been cracking and crashing her way through towards them, complete with aeroplanes. First of all, the *Krassin* reached Mariano and Zappi, two of the three men who had tried to escape on foot.

They were exhausted, starving and all but dead. Malmgrem had collapsed earlier and insisted that they leave him and carry on alone. No one ever traced him.

At length, the *Krassin* forced her way through to the main party of survivors – six weeks after the loss of the *Italia*.

After that episode, Byrd's success over the South Pole the following year came almost as an anticlimax.

He was well equipped for this operation, with four pilots and four aeroplanes, housed at his base in the Bay of Whales, 400 miles from the Pole. Their preliminary survey flights were not devoid of incident and during one of these expeditions three of the men were trapped by an unexpected blizzard that blew their plane over, as if it were a toy model. The storm did not die down for over a week, and all that while the men had to exist flat out amid the scant shelter of the Antarctic mountain. Byrd eventually rescued them in a Fokker monoplane.

They loaded provisions for several months into the Fokker aeroplane, which was powered by three Ford engines. The group comprised Admiral Byrd; Balchen, the pilot; June, the telegraphist and MacKinley, the photographer.

Everything went well. They flew up a huge ravine, to avoid attempting to top the highest peaks in the Queen Maud range, but they had underestimated the extreme concentration of down-draught rushing through the ravine. The aircraft wobbled and wavered. The wind worsened the nearer they got to the top of the ravine. Suddenly Byrd sensed that they could not make it, laden as they were.

So they started to pitch everything possible over the side; food, fuel, stores, the lot. With each load that went overboard, the aeroplane flew a little more easily and rose a few feet higher. They left a strange trail of assorted stores up that ravine, a slope never before seen by man. At last the plane shot over the summit of the pass and they flew over a fantastic plateau.

They surmounted more mountains and all at once the four Americans were actually on top of the snowswept, ice-capped, gale-torn South Pole. The date was 29 November 1929. Byrd had made history twice by flying over both extremities of the earth.

15

CHARLES LINDBERGH

First Atlantic Solo

Lindbergh – the name seems to symbolize the spirit of the great pioneers. Charles Lindbergh was the first man to fly the Atlantic solo, but the Lindbergh story started years before that landmark in his adventurous aviation career.

Flying had always been in his blood. He flew first at the age of twenty in Nebraska and soon afterwards spent most of his time in that state doing 'barnstorming' flights, either giving the public paid flips or daredevil exhibitions. Wing-walking and other such stunts figured among the acts created to bring people to watch him.

It was 1923 when he raked up the money to buy his first aeroplane at a cost of precisely 500 dollars! After more barnstorming and more flights for the public at five dollars a time, the young Lindbergh reviewed his prospects and decided that he would get more aviation experience by becoming a flying cadet in the US Army Air Service. After this top-grade training, he came a second lieutenant in the US Air Corps Reserve of Officers.

But not before he had nearly been killed. Lindbergh had done quite a bit of parachuting during those earlier stunt days, but to qualify for membership of the Caterpillar Club, a man had to show that he had made an unpremeditated jump; in other words in an emergency. Lindbergh could prove that easily – several times over.

Twice during his actual service training, he had to bale out. On 6 March 1925, the aeroplanes of Lindbergh and another pilot collided during a mass dummy diving run on Kelley Field, Texas. Not only did the two aircraft collide, but they interlocked too. Inextricably jammed, they started spinning down with their young pilots. The two men wrestled with their respective controls for an instant or two, but soon saw it was hopeless.

Lindbergh jumped, and the other pilot followed his example, but realized that the planes were liable to hit him if he opened his parachute at once. As soon as Lindbergh felt fairly safe from the risk of the cascading planes, he pulled his ripcord and his free fall was jerked to a sudden stop.

Still tightly together, the spinning aeroplanes carved their way into the Texas soil far below, erupting into fire. Lindbergh watched them and thought how lucky he was not to have gone with them. Skilfully pulling on his parachute lines, he drifted down in a clear spot and saw the other pilot reach earth safely too. That was escape number one.

On 2 June 1925 came number two, while he was still with the Air Corps under training. Trying out a machine at about 2,000 feet, Lindbergh suddenly found the plane careering into a diabolical spin. He knew he had some seconds at that altitude, so did not abandon the aircraft at once. He did all he knew to level off, but nothing stopped the headlong spiral. Lindbergh finally gave up and found he had nearly left it too late to jump at all. He baled out when a mere 100 yards above the ground at St Louis, but his parachute opened in time and he was saved again.

Such incidents were all in the game during those days of early flying. A pilot risked his life all the time. It was a recognized part of the profession, in fact almost an attraction.

When Lindbergh left as a qualified service reserve officer, he went back to barnstorming, but with much more knowledge of the art of aviation. This was only temporary, for he heard he had been accepted as a pilot to fly the early air mails between St Louis and Chicago.

Lindbergh was overjoyed and proceeded to extend his experience still further, with practical routine flying month in, month out. Routine was hardly the word for it, though. Lindbergh had to overcome fog, ice and everything else that the Mid-West weather presented. 'The mail must get through' might have been his slogan. There were at least two occasions when it nearly *didn't*.

He was flying through fog at night on 16 September 1926, when he got lost in mid-air above an invisible town and its aerodrome. Flares and searchlights on the ground could not pierce the foggy layer between the airfield and the flier, whose petrol gauge indicated nearly nil.

Lindbergh went on for a few minutes, hoping for a way round the fog, but there was none. In a last climb, with the final few pints of petrol, he nosed up above the black blanket. Then the fuel ran out. Since he could not hope to land the aeroplane through that total black-out down to ground level he baled out.

As he floated towards the fog, the aeroplane he had just left started spiralling down towards him and actually threatened to hit him. He pulled on his various shrouds and just managed to avoid the spinning aeroplane.

Through the fog-belt they both fell, and Lindbergh landed in Mid-Western corn. Then he went to look for his aircraft and found it with the mail safe. Lindbergh had used all his petrol to avoid any risk of fire when the plane crashed.

The winter was the worst time for flying the mail, as Lindbergh found out during that season in 1926–7. He did not get off to an encouraging start either, for on 3 November 1926, he had to bale out for a fourth time to save his skin.

The temperature had dropped so low that after darkness Lindbergh had to fly through snow falling so thickly through the night sky that it was like three-dimensional flaky fabric. In addition it was misty.

First of all Lindbergh tried to land, but it was hopeless. He and his little mailplane were stormbound; he could not see the landing field and the petrol would not last long.

Lindbergh climbed to the colossal height of two and a half miles, through the wild weather. He jumped. The night air froze him as he fell amid the mixture of snow, sleet and rain. He hoped he would land somewhere soft. He didn't.

The parachute brought him faithfully through the storm-swept air, to come to earth on some barbed wire, but he was not hurt. Lindbergh spotted his tangled mass of a machine from the air the following day. He landed and retrieved the mail undamaged. Both times he had to bale out, the mail got through in the end.

It was during those days and nights on the St Louis–Chicago mail run that Lindbergh first really thought of flying the Atlantic solo. Once he had set his heart on it, he ploughed full ahead, managing to raise the necessary money quite easily from sponsors in St Louis. Hence the name of his monoplane, *Spirit of St Louis*.

He chose a monoplane in preference to a biplane for various reasons, including its ability to carry a greater load per square foot of surface at a higher speed. Lindbergh favoured a single-engine plane since although it was more liable to forced landings than one with three engines, it had much less head resistance and so a greater cruising range.

With the triple-engine aircraft, there was also three times the chance of motor failure – an interesting way of looking at it! If this happened in the early part of the flight, it would not cause a forced landing, but would mean dropping part of the fuel and returning to try again. Lindbergh talked quite blithely about 'landing' though this would probably mean death by drowning, if it occurred over the Atlantic.

He summed up his choice of engine like this:

> The reliability of the modern air-cooled radial engine is so great that the chances of an immediate forced landing due to motor failure with a single motor would, in my opinion, be more than counterbalanced by the longer cruising range and consequent ability to reach the objective in the face of unfavourable conditions.

Lindbergh settled for a Ryan monoplane powered by a Wright Whirlwind engine developing 220 horsepower and having nine cylinders. He took immense trouble over every detail and reckoned that in the worst event the aeroplane would be kept afloat on the Atlantic for a while by air in the fuel tanks. That was his idea, anyway.

The makers took equal trouble over details for this flight, for not only was Lindbergh's attempt to be the first solo crossing of the Atlantic, and the first flight since Alcock and Brown, but it would span some 3,600 miles – nearly double their record-breaking effort eight years earlier. Lindbergh would have to do everything himself, including navigating, and in addition combat the chronic loneliness that must engulf anyone attempting such a desolate undertaking.

In fact, so unlikely did success seem that no one took the flight very seriously beforehand. Some even dubbed him the 'flying fool'. It was strange how a few days changed him from a foolhardy airmail pilot into a worldwide hero, but only typical of public opinion.

The clean-cut twenty-five-year-old American, Charles A. Lindbergh, spent long hours tuning up for the flight. Or rather, for the two flights. For the first 'warm-up' lap was to be across America from San Diego, California, to New York, via St Louis. The plane had been constructed in California by the Ryan firm.

Lindbergh left San Diego at 3.55 p.m. Pacific time on 10 May

1927, flew all night, and touched down next morning at St Louis after a flight of 1,600 miles. After a night's rest, he took off for New York and got there the same afternoon to establish a record for the flight from California to New York. The term 'flying fool' was hardly heard at all now. Even the idea of the totally-enclosed cabin and a periscope for all external vision did not raise so many objections. Lindbergh had already flown some 3,000 miles across America. There was no real reason why he should not do the same over the ocean – though it still seemed quite impossible.

At 7.50 a.m., 20 May, at Roosevelt Field, New York, the real test began. Captain Lindbergh, as he was by then, was called in his hotel about 2 a.m. Outside, rain dripped off the windowsill of his room. But that did not deter him.

Lindbergh took two sandwiches and two bottles of water with him, and crammed himself into the tiny pilot's 'cage' of the Ryan monoplane. *Spirit of St Louis* was painted just fore of the wing.

He grinned goodbye with a boyish wave to the thousands watching him leave. Then the plane gained speed swiftly down the artificial hill runway, but barely cleared the trees at the far end. Its total weight was 4,750 pounds and it carried 448 gallons of petrol. This would last Lindbergh for some time beyond the forty hours estimated by him for the flight.

Reports of his progress started to come in erratically. A wobbling aeroplane at 600 feet went over Rhode Island at 9.15 a.m. By 9.40 a.m. he was over Bryantsville, Massachusetts, flying so low that people could read the markings NX-211 painted on the underside of the wing.

For several hundred miles, the aviator followed his route at an altitude of 100 feet or less over the sea, coming as low as ten feet at times. As *Spirit* sped on across the wide expanse of sea between Cape Cod, USA and Nova Scotia, Canada, Lindbergh ran into worse weather. And quite soon after leaving Nova Scotia, he met rain and even some snow. Taking the plane down to sea level and then up again, he looked in vain for better weather.

The aeroplane was sighted several times before leaving Nova Scotia. It reached Main-a-Dieu at 4 p.m. heading for Newfoundland.

As he flew further across that 300-mile stretch towards Newfoundland, the significance of his isolation could begin to be gauged. For not only was Lindbergh alone, but he had no radio, and no easy way of landing on the sea if he had to.

Furthermore, Lindbergh carried only elementary small-scale maps and a comparatively primitive outfit of instruments. His secret of successful navigation, however, later transpired to be that he had memorized all the definite details of his route – from New York to Newfoundland, and on across to Ireland and France.

The world was already excited about his progress, but as he neared Newfoundland there was bound to be a long gap between there and the next news, from Ireland if all went well.

As he flew north-east over Newfoundland, the weather worsened hourly. He failed to spot the island's coastline at all, obscured as it so often was by the flier's enemy, fog. But he did glimpse the ground inland as he went over, since it was white with snow.

As the telegraph systems of the world whirred with comment and speculation, Lindbergh went on sitting blind in his little cubby-hole, occasionally looking into the periscope.

Just before darkness fell, while he flew low over the ocean, he had the shock of seeing floating ice jolting about beneath him. He thought he had better be careful and not fly so low, in case he flew slap into an iceberg. He did not want to end up the same way as the *Titanic*.

As fog wisped more thickly through the blue-black air, he became increasingly worried about the risk of hitting icebergs and he decided to climb. From just a few feet over the Atlantic, he made a long gradual ascent to the region of 10,000 feet – only to find thick storm clouds instead of the fog. He tried aiming *Spirit* straight through a bank of clouds, but sleet started to appear on the slender wings. He knew what that would mean if it continued so he changed course to try and find better weather, but had to settle for the fog throughout the rest of the night. Fortunately the darkness was fairly short due to the northerly latitude of his course. He spotted the lights of one or two ships far below.

Cramped in his cockpit, he began to find the flight monotonous, though he did admit that it kept him at full stretch, attending to the various jobs apart from the actual flying operation. By dawn Lindbergh had already finished practically all his water.

At daylight the weather took a turn for the better. The remainder of the sleet slipped off the wing. The improvement was short-lived, though, and more fog appeared in front of his periscope. The flier took the aeroplane down low to try and get below it, but couldn't. It was too risky flying so low, and he went higher again, relying only on his instruments for two more hours.

Lindbergh almost lost track of time as the aeroplane plodded on through the patches of fog, which, to his tired eyes, seemed to take on the forms of trees, coasts and other shapes so convincingly that he felt they must really exist.

Once the fog finally cleared, Lindbergh decided to come down as low as he could, ranging from his minimum of ten feet to a maximum of 200 feet. For the rest of that day *Spirit of St Louis* skimmed eastward for Ireland. As he himself said:

During the day I saw a number of porpoises and a few birds, but no ships. The first indication of my approach to the European coast was a small fishing boat. Less than an hour later a rugged and semi-mountainous coastline appeared to the north-east. I had very little doubt it was the south-western end of Ireland. I located Valentia Island and Dingle Bay and then resumed my compass course towards Paris.

In a little over two hours the coast of England appeared. Then across the English Channel, striking France over Cherbourg. The sun went down shortly after passing Cherbourg, and soon beacons along the Paris–London airway became visible. I first saw the lights of Paris a little before 10 pm, and a few minutes later I was circling the Eiffel Tower at an altitude of about four thousand feet.

The lights of Le Bourget were plainly visible, but appeared to be very close to Paris. I had understood that the field was further from the city, so continued out to the north-east into the country for four or five miles, to make sure that there was not another field farther out which might be Le Bourget. Then I returned and spiralled down closer to the lights. Presently I could make out long lines of hangars and the roads appeared to be jammed with cars. I flew low over the field once, then circled round into the wind and landed.

Fantastic crowds of cars and people blocked Le Bourget completely. Drivers clambered on top of their vehicles to get a better view of the night sky, swept by searchlights, shattered by rockets and storm shells. It was some minutes after 10 p.m. when they heard the first faint drone of *Spirit of St Louis*. Lindbergh announced his arrival by dropping a fuse and then after his circling of the airfield, he dipped in for a landing.

118

The plane taxied for a hundred yards or so. The crowd brushed aside the cordon of police and soldiers, smashed the fences and flimsy barricades, and acclaimed their hero: '*Vive* Lindbergh!'

Then they dragged him feet first from the plane. It was the most dangerous moment of the thirty-four hours since take-off.

16

CHARLES KINGSFORD SMITH
Conquering the Pacific

Southern Cross was the perfect name for the plane carrying Captain Charles Kingsford Smith across the Pacific, from Oakland, California, to Brisbane, Australia. It was a Fokker monoplane fitted with three Wright Whirlwind 220-horsepower engines, and it had a wing span of seventy-one feet eight and a half inches. The total petrol capacity amounted to a substantial 1,298 gallons.

With Kingsford Smith were his co-pilot, Charles Ulm, Harry Lyon, navigator and James Warner, radio officer. The trip was planned to be made in three stages; the first, Oakland to Wheeler Field, near Honolulu, the second to Suva, Fiji and the third to Brisbane, in Kingsford Smith's own country.

It was on 31 May 1928 that *Southern Cross* soared into the air from Oakland, San Francisco, for the first hop of 2,400 miles to Honolulu in the Hawaiian Islands. The aeroplane was well prepared for communication and navigation. There were three radio transmitters and two receivers, with a wireless direction finder as well. For navigation they carried two earth inductor compasses, a periodic compass and sextants.

This flight was destined to have its main climax at the end. In fact the first 2,400 miles, flown in twenty-seven hours twenty-seven minutes, was so smooth as to become quite monotonous to the crew of four.

The only excitement came almost at the completion of this initial hop, when *Southern Cross* radioed at 11.43 a.m. on 1 June: 'We are heaving in sight of Oahu. It is going to be a race whether we make land before our fuel is exhausted.'

Before that time, Warner, the radio operator, had notified that his receiving apparatus had broken down and that he thought they were lost. Despite this gloomy guess, *Southern Cross* circled in to Wheeler Field at exactly 12.15 p.m. Pacific Coast time. Five thousand people cheered as they landed and taxied down the field to the front of the reviewing stand. Kingsford Smith emerged with his fellow Australian, Charles Ulm, and announced that their petrol supply had virtually dried up, all but a few gallons.

Southern Cross went on later to Barking Sand, Kauai Island, about a hundred miles from Honolulu, and then in the early morning of 3 June, took off on the second stage of the 7,300-mile epic, to Suva, Fiji.

The aeroplane was once more loaded to capacity with fuel, and Kingsford Smith said that if they went into dangerous winds they would attempt to land on one of the Phoenix Islands. If all went well, though, the Suva landing would be the next, on a 400-yard long cricket field with its fences removed. They were still keeping their smelling salts handy, in case any of them felt sleepy and needed reviving. So *Southern Cross* winged its lonely way for the next 3,200 miles.

The course for Honolulu had been roughly south-west. The route taken now veered nearer south. The weather was worse in the earlier hours of this giant stride of almost a day and a half. Rain beat against the three engines and rolled off the propellers, but the aeroplane throbbed on at an average of nearly 100 miles an hour. Sometimes it had to describe an arc to try and avoid the storms. Its name *Southern Cross* was lettered large on its body, but there was no one now to see it.

Radio messages gave a good idea of the changing conditions as they neared the equator. They had momentary engine troubles, storms, adverse winds.

'You can't stop us smiling', they transmitted rather naively.

'We're dodging about to miss heavy clouds', read another.

'A great game dodging these dark clouds.'

'Motor spitting.'

'All okay', came a little later.

'One generator quit, only three hours out, no chance to charge battery, and headlights also; wireless transmitter, too, has failed, so now using auxiliary light.'

These minor mishaps passed, however, and Kingsford Smith was later able to signal his position as latitude 2 degrees south, longitude

170 degrees 33 minutes west, at an altitude of 1,400 feet. An hour and a half after that, they were over the Phoenix Islands, not needing to land.

Radio silence after that report began to cause apprehension in the small room at La Perouse, Australia, where the messages were being received, but following a two-hour gap, *Southern Cross* transmitted: 'Doing fine. Been expecting to sight land, but none sighted yet. It is not so clear as one would like.'

This was followed by a message giving their position as latitude 5 degrees south, longitude 172 degrees 25 minutes west.

A full tropic moon shone out of a perfect Pacific night at Suva. Then another day dawned. *Southern Cross* radioed that they had been driven west of their course and were then north of Fiji with adverse winds and seven hours' petrol left. They had exceeded their average fuel consumption, but still hoped to make the Albert Park Sports Ground. They did and achieved what was then the longest non-stop ocean flight on record, 3,138 miles in a time of thirty-four and a half hours.

As soon as it became known that *Southern Cross* was about to take off from Naselai Beach, Suva, on 8 June, Australia became agog with excitement. The fliers had covered the first leg of 2,400 miles and the second of 3,200, and now they were poised for the third of 1,700. Could they accomplish this 7,300-mile marathon?

The take-off was at 2.50 p.m. from Naselai Beach. Ten minutes later *Southern Cross* saluted Suva and then struck south-west for Brisbane. And the messages started to pour in as the Australian people grew more and more excited.

Well, here we are, on our way again. Everything okay. In 19 or 20 hours we shall be in dear old Aussie again. The landing at Brisbane will be the culmination of ten months' hard work and the realization of our ambition to be the first to cross the Pacific. After arriving at Brisbane will leave next day for Sydney. Can assure Brisbane public we shall return after couple weeks' rest. Cheerio.

And another message:

Smithy is at the controls with a sandwich in one hand. Ulm is working radio, while alert, loyal, efficient colleagues are a few feet behind us. When we started the flight we wondered whether

Australia would want to kiss or kick us on arrival, in view of so much adverse criticism against our undertaking, but we've been so overwhelmed with kind congratulatory cablegrams and wireless reports that we feel our fellow-Australians now agree that we were right in sticking it, completing our self-appointed task. We had a long but narrow strip of beach to take off from at Naselai, with fairly strong cross wind, but, comparatively speaking, only light load, 880 gallons petrol, 32 gallons oil.

At 5.25 p.m.: 'Since leaving Naselai we have had trouble with one compass; nothing to worry about, cheerio, one generator bad.'

At 5.50 p.m.: 'Cheerio everybody. Won't be too long now. There's possibility of dirty weather tonight. Ulm has relieved Smithy, so may be better rest for tonight. We're happy as Larry up here, cooee!'

At 6.30 p.m.: 'Will spare batteries, only one generator.'

At 7.12: 'Did not wish to worry anyone before while going through a storm, but now it is almost passed will admit that the last two hours we have been battling with the worst weather of the whole flight.'

At 7.20 p.m.: 'Encountering exceptionally heavy rain. Bumps in air pockets, frequently dropping 400 feet. Smith and Ulm wet through. Cold, no gloves. As soon as the moon comes out and blind flying ends for the night we will eat and have a spot of our emergency whisky rations. Too cold to write more.'

They were not happy as Larry any longer. The distance to Brisbane still measured a thousand miles. And the storm still raged around them.

That troublesome compass was really right out of service, so they had to trust the magnetic steering compasses. The moon did not come out. Smithy had to try and get above the dangerous combination of wind and rain, but at 6,000 and then 7,000 feet things were no better, in fact the reverse.

The wind-lashed torrent had torn through the windscreens of *Southern Cross*, shattering the glass over the cockpit. Water flowed inside. Kingsford Smith was no longer resting. He coaxed a climb out of the monoplane, but the weather went right up behind their ceiling, and the higher they went the colder they felt.

This was a night they would never forget. After the smooth flying for the first 6,000 miles, it seemed as if they might be beaten in the last straight.

An electrical storm sparked off all around them.

123

Fierce flashes of fork lightning exposed the night wastes of the ocean in grotesque light. *Southern Cross* was the only object in the sky. All the time they half-feared they might attract one of those fatal flashes, for the plane seemed to be flying right through the storm centre. This was something they had not expected.

They were frightened that flooding might cause the magnetos to fail at any time. They saw blue flames sparking across the leads of the three engines, through the soaking insulation.

Kingsford Smith felt his hands getting increasingly numb, while the rest of the crew became just as icy. The rain still streamed in through the smashed screens, directly under the wing.

Those air pockets were awful. There were sudden sheer falls of 300 or 400 feet through the wildness of the night, the crew never knowing when they would come, or whether the plane would ever stop the descent once it did start.

At 11.16 p.m. they reported briefly: '700 miles to go.'

At 1 a.m.: '600 miles.'

But between 6.15 p.m. and 3.20 a.m., nine nerve-racking hours, Ulm only made one entry in the log of *Southern Cross*. That was how bad it was.

The nightmare of fireworks and sickening drops passed.

At 6 a.m. they estimated that they were 250 miles from Brisbane, but it was not until 10.13 a.m. that *Southern Cross* finally fought its way there.

The career of Kingsford Smith cannot be left there, though, for he had many more successes, and failures too, as one of the pioneers in those early days of worldwide flying.

After several successful Australasian flights during the rest of that year, Kingsford Smith and Ulm set out for a flight to England on 31 March 1929, which was destined to fail. They had H.A. Litchfield and T.H. McWilliams with them.

Soon after leaving Richmond, Australia, they lost their longwave aerial, so that they could not receive radio messages, although they could still send them. This turned out to be merely the first in a chain of mishaps, for as a direct result of it they did not hear warnings broadcast to them of a sudden storm in central Australia. They flew straight into it.

Somehow they survived the night, but the storm did not die at daylight. Kingsford Smith intended to fly round Cape Londonderry to reach Wyndham. They tried to get their bearings by dropping a message to local natives in a habitation below, but due to a misunderstanding they were directed the wrong way for Wyndham.

Kingsford Smith realized that the petrol was bound to run out before they could reach Wyndham, but there was little to be done but to try to plod on. An hour later the engine gave its first signs of fuel shortage and the pilot knew he must come down somewhere very soon. McWilliams went on sending messages giving their position as far as they knew it, and then he told Sydney that *Southern Cross* was making a forced landing.

Smithy looked doubtfully at the inhospitable landscape, lying wild and uncharted below them. He brought the aeroplane down as best he could, but the surface he had chosen was mud made wet by the recent storm.

At once the wheels sank into the squelching swamp and the aircraft was trapped. So were they, for dense jungle enclosed the mud-ridden ground, not to mention waterways alive with alligators.

It seemed silly, but there was nothing for them to do but wait. It would not have been a good idea to leave the area, for at least their radio signals were being received and search parties would be beginning to look for them from the air.

Then the next blow fell in the chapter of strange accidents, when they looked for their emergency rations – there weren't any. Their main nourishment would have to be the quantity of special baby food on board which was to be delivered to Wyndham. Their only food was small amounts of coffee, brandy, glycerine and snails. Starvation looked a likely prospect, failing rescue. They found a source of water nearby, though it was not very wholesome.

Though the plane was stuck solid, they explored the immediate zone and managed to kindle a fire on a nearby hillock. The rescuers would have to be quick to be in time.

In the overpowering, humid heat of the interior, the men began to weaken as early as the second day after landing. Two days later they were nearly too exhausted to keep the fire alight.

Meanwhile the rescuers were doing all they could to trace them. The stranded airmen had evidence of this. They saw three aeroplanes at various times, but for some reason the searchers did not spot either *Southern Cross* or the fire. This was the last straw, but worse was to follow before their luck changed.

Weaker each day, they could only wait while the ceaseless struggle to find them went on. Two of their flying friends, Keith Anderson and H.S. Hitchcock, had joined in the hunt – and vanished as well.

At long last, on 12 April, the thirteenth day after the start of the ill-starred flight, a De Havilland 66 Canberra biplane spied them, just in time. Circling overhead, the pilot made an accurate drop of food for them. For four days this went on, with daily drops of supplies, and they began to feel better. Then on 15 April a light aeroplane landed on the sun-baked mud. Two more planes brought petrol on the following day. On 18 April *Southern Cross* itself was able to rise again from the hardened mud-swamp and carry on to Wyndham.

The tragic sequel to the story was that in trying to find them, Anderson and Hitchcock had themselves been forced down in a dry desert and perished.

The rest of the career of Kingsford Smith was full of ups and downs, including a number of triumphant first flights. He pioneered England–Australia air mail flights when a colleague in his own airways company took off from Sydney with the Christmas mail for England. The aeroplane crashed five days later, but Kingsford Smith at once flew to the scene of the crash, transferred the huge batch of mail to his machine and forged on for England.

The weather was cruel to him, but despite fog and snow he touched down at Croydon airport on 16 December, just in time for Christmas delivery. This flight in less than a fortnight and at a moment's notice was one of his major successes. Another came in 1933 when he flew from Lympne, Kent, to Australia in the remarkable record time of one week, or to be more precise seven days, four hours, forty-three minutes.

Then in the autumn of 1934, Sir Charles Kingsford Smith, as he now was, and Captain P.G. Taylor tackled the reverse run across the Pacific, from Brisbane to Oakland, California. Flying a Lockheed, they accomplished this by 4 November in the short flying time of some forty hours.

Kingsford Smith's final, fatal year was 1935. His first setback was when *Southern Cross* took off from Sydney at 12.30 on the night of 15 May to fly to New Zealand with special Jubilee mail and other cargo.

About 7 a.m. the next morning, in the middle of the Tasman Sea, a fragment of exhaust pipe snapped off from the middle engine, and shattered a blade of the right-hand propeller. Smithy took immediate action to avoid disaster and then wheeled round to head home for Australia on two engines.

Southern Cross had to face a fierce headwind and the left-hand engine started to overheat. Captain Taylor crawled out of the cabin and along the wing with the thermos flask, removed oil from the right-hand engine and took it over to damp down the left-hand one.

He did this a total of six separate times.

He succeeded. They had to ditch fuel, freight, a large proportion of the precious mail, but they limped back to Sydney alive.

Kingsford Smith's last flight of all began on 6 November, when he was trying to beat the record for the flight from England to Australia. In a Lockheed Altair two-seater, with Pethybridge, he got as far as India – and then vanished over the Bay of Bengal.

17

AMY JOHNSON
Solo to Australia

The first and most famous long-distance flight by Amy Johnson was her solo trip to Australia in May 1930. She had taken up flying in her spare time and had later given up her office job. She then raked up the £600 for a second-hand Gipsy Moth light plane and calmly announced that she was going to try and fly from England to Australia and beat the existing solo record for the flight, Hinkler's fifteen and a half days.

At the age of twenty-two Amy was not only a qualified pilot but also the only woman to hold an Air Ministry licence as a ground engineer.

She took off from Stag Lane aerodrome, near Hendon, where she had first been attracted to aeroplanes when passing in a bus! Five light aircraft of her club escorted her across to Croydon, the official starting point for all record attempts, and from there she ascended at 7.45 a.m. on 5 May. Normally a two-seater, the Gipsy Moth had had its second seat removed to make room for extra fuel tanks. Amy would need all the petrol she could carry on her 13,000-mile flight.

She had christened the plane *Jason's Quest*. She left the Surrey suburbs behind with fuel for a range of over a thousand miles. Amy's first scheduled stop was the Aspern aerodrome, near Vienna, 780 miles away. She got there by 5.15 p.m. the same day, after nine and a half hours in the air.

The flight was not yet attracting headline attention in the press; there was just a brief note that she reached San Stefano aerodrome, Constantinople, at exactly the same time, 5.15 p.m., the following afternoon. So far the flight had been without incident, but then things got hectic for a day or two.

Crossing the Taurus Mountains on 7 May, at a height of 8,000 feet, Amy found she could not get as much altitude as she wanted, so she clung to the railway line through the narrow pass amid very poor visibility.

From Aleppo to Baghdad on 8 May she had a nerve-racking spell. Midway between these two remote places, the little Gipsy Moth was tossed about in the grip of a gale. It might almost have been a shuttlecock; it certainly dropped like one, from 7,000 feet to 300 feet in ten minutes. Sand swirled all around her and she decided to land.

She brought *Jason's Quest* down in the face of a fifty-mile-an-hour gale, but it would not stay still once it was actually on the desert. Amy lugged out her tool boxes and luggage and with sand-dust stinging her eyes, she shoved it against the wheels of the machine as chocks to stop it being blown away altogether and leaving her stranded an unknown distance from Baghdad.

She struggled to cover the exposed engine, too, so that sand should not penetrate and damage it. Alone there in the desert, she heard the eerie barking of dogs but saw nothing.

Two hours later the weather relented a little and she was able to take off again. She spotted the Tigris, the surface choppy from the storm and was able to follow its course. Atmospheric conditions then worsened so much that she missed Baghdad completely. The junction of the Tigris and Diala told her that she had overshot her target. Amy swung the little aeroplane around and later set it down neatly on the Imperial Airways aerodrome. When she bobbed out of the open cockpit, she was covered from hair to shoes with a thick coating of sand; evidence of the ordeal she had endured.

Amy flew on for Bandar Abbas, where landing was less easy, and she felt glad to get away from the fantastic heat of the Persian Gulf. Another lap of 720 miles took her to Karachi, where she arrived after six days, ahead of Hinkler's time for the flight to this first point of India. Now people started to take increasing interest in the young Englishwoman's exploit. She spent that night at Government House.

The public now learned that the Gipsy Moth had already done service on long flights well before Amy bought it. Captain Hope had used it to follow the Prince of Wales on his recent Africa tour, and it had since been flown by an air taxi concern. Its mileage had exceeded 35,000 before Amy left home in it.

She found herself short of petrol on the way to Allahabad, so spent the night at Jhansi. Landing there in the strange Indian dusk, she struck a post with a wing of the plane, which was damaged. An Indian carpenter managed to repair it promptly, however, and she proceeded to Allahabad and thence to Calcutta, which she reached on 12 May. She was still well ahead of Hinkler's time.

She made a 7 a.m. start on 13 May from the Dum Dum aerodrome, Calcutta, for Rangoon. Before leaving Amy made the modest statement, 'This is just an ordinary flight, except that it is longer. Every woman will be doing this in five years' time.'

She added that as she had to overhaul the machine herself at various stages of the journey, she had only managed to average three hours' sleep a day since leaving London.

She seemed to be unlucky in her landings. When she was about nine miles north of Rangoon, she mistook the playing fields at Insein for the Rangoon racecourse, her appointed field. This only happened because of bad visibility and forced her to fly at 200 feet or less, brushing the treetops with the exhaust of the plane.

She made a perfect landing at Insein, but as her machine taxied across the playing fields it ran into a concealed ditch which slightly damaged the wings, wheels and propeller. Amy did not intend to let a little mishap like that delay her, but she did, as it turned out, have to wait an extra day or two there, for the weather was misty and windy and the wings and fuselage needed repairs after the jolt in the ditch.

Amid blinding monsoon rain, 16 May dawned, yet Amy had set her heart on taking off for Bangkok – so she did. She left Rangoon behind at 10.45 a.m., knowing that the delay had cost her all reasonable chance of breaking the record. There was still plenty to fly for, however, apart from the mere fact of finishing what she had started.

Amy set the nose of *Jason's Quest* south-east heading for Moulmein, but the vital pass through the mountains eluded her, being hidden by the dense monsoon clouds. Try as she might, she could not find a passage, so she dragged the laden aeroplane up to 9,000 feet to cross the mountains blind. With this kind of manoeuvre, the risk always existed of miscalculating either the height of the mountains or of the aeroplane. Either would have been instantaneously fatal. Amy just kept to her course through the swirling skyscape. Looking out, it was as if the aeroplane were a toy lost in a grey world of fluffy, floating cloud-base.

Eventually she staggered out into clear weather again, only to have the shock of realizing she was still on the Burmese side of the mountains. She made another, more frantic, shot at finding the Moulmein, still totally invisible, and this time she did come out on the Siamese side of the heights.

She was not out of trouble yet. For three more weary hours, fighting sleep all the time, she could pick up no landmarks at all, roaming on and on through the layers of storm clouds. Then she espied a railway junction and all was well.

For six hours she had been lost in a fabulous world of monsoon-racked mountain tops between Burma and Siam.

Amy touched down amid the quaint curving temples of Bangkok at 5.45 p.m. on 16 May, dead beat but still game.

Two days later she got to Singapore. Between Bangkok and Singora, Amy had run into bad weather once more, and for the whole of the hop from Singora to Singapore, she had to fly at under 1,000 feet. Two seaplanes met her seventy miles out, escorting her to the aerodrome at Selegar on Singapore Island. Amy landed at 1.50 p.m. grinning at the cheers of the Malays, British, Chinese and other nationalities there.

As the 13,000 miles gradually reeled off, the flight assumed proportionately greater interest to the world at large. To succeed would be wonderful; to fail now, awful. Amy Johnson; the name was on everyone's lips in every tongue.

She left Singapore on the morning of 19 May bound for Sourabaya. But she was destined to have a dreadful time over the desolate Java Sea south of Singapore.

The rain literally hosed her off her course towards Sumatra and she had to fly over the miles of thick jungle which covered that huge wild island. Towards Banka, a large island off the mainland of Sumatra, she veered out to try and find better conditions over the sea.

Torrents of tropic rainfall soaked her and swept her down to mere feet off the whipped-up sea surface. She only had to lose a little more height and hit that water once for it to be all over.

'I really thought this was the end,' she said later, 'but somehow I reached the coast of Java and followed the coastline till I ran out of fuel.'

It was just one thing after another.

The heavy weather resulted in her using too much petrol – and too much time. She was virtually out of fuel and *Jason's Quest* was still almost an hour from Sourabaya.

Amy scoured below for somewhere to land, failed to notice a

military emergency landing ground in the neighbourhood, but did see a small clearing. It was that or nothing.

Reappearing over Tegal, which she had passed a little while earlier, she circled several times before deciding that this piece of ground recently cleared for building a new house for the local sugar estate manager, was in fact long enough.

Amy deposited the aeroplane and herself on its short strip of 250 yards – the usual minimum was 300 yards – and accepted an invitation to stay the night there in the middle of Java as casually as if she were back at home with her parents in Hull.

Amy discovered the wings of her aeroplane were perforated in five places. Bamboo poles supporting young fruit trees had causes these rents as she had come in to land. The holes were only small but the slightest flaws could be fatal. So the holes were patched up temporarily with sticking plaster!

Next morning, with a small supply of fuel to carry her on, she prepared to take off for Semarang. It was going to be touch and go getting airborne, however, from the wet, short clearing, so the estate manager kindly took part of her baggage to an emergency landing field five miles away, where she could pick it up en route.

Jason's Quest just succeeded in skimming the ricefields surrounding the Tjomal estate, and Amy was on her way again. The biplane reverberated on for Semarang and fresh fuel.

These delays were of course inevitable in an epic journey on such a scale. The miracle was that she had got that far at all in a Gipsy Moth costing £600!

At 11.30 a.m. Amy left Semarang for Sourabaya. But before she did so, she said in a tired tone, 'I want so very much to rest.'

By the time she reached Sourabaya, the strain was starting to tell not only on her but on the faithful *Jason's Quest* as well. After a trial run in the afternoon shortly after getting there, she did not feel happy about the state of the machine and so organized repairs to the engine late that night.

By dawn it was running sweetly and at 6 a.m. on 22 May she winged up from Sourabaya into a blue sky. She intended to fly for Atambua on the north-west coast of Timor Island, but bore in mind Bima on Sumbawa as a possible interim landing place.

The suspense by this stage was growing unbearable. Would she do it? Could the machine last out?

She had told spectators that the blue sky was a happy omen for her flight, and she was still waving to them several hundred feet overhead. Then she was gone, bound for Atambua, 750 miles off. It was a nasty spin, mostly over the sea.

At 11.30 a.m. she passed over Bima, but did not land. She was due to arrive at Atambua about 4.30 p.m. the same day.

The wireless station of Kupang on the island of Timor was kept open until 11 p.m. but then reported no news of her.

The whole world held its breath.

Surely she couldn't fail now?

Next day the news filtered through; 'Amy Johnson landed at the village of Halilulik, on the island of Timor, and went from there by motor car to Atambua, her original destination, which is about 12 miles away.'

The village had no telephone link with the outside world, which accounted for the delay in the news of her safety. She managed to send news of her arrival from Atambua in time to stop a naval aeroplane leaving Sourabaya in search of her.

It was not until later that she told how when she had landed on Timor she was met by 200 natives. They crowded round the aeroplane but she could not communicate with them. One of them took her hand and led her three miles through the jungle to a church, where she met the local parson. After that she was soon bumping over a twisting track to Atambua.

Then there remained the last and most hazardous hop of all. Amy Johnson had flown her *Jason's Quest* from Croydon to Timor. Ahead of her lay the 500 miles of sea separating that island from Australia. She had done over ninety per cent of the trip.

The 100-horsepower engine of the Gipsy Moth had brought her to the very edge of everlasting fame.

Amy took off from Timor, and set her course roughly south-east across the empty, liquid miles. She was utterly exhausted and cut off from the world.

Second after second passed, minute after minute, and hour after hour, with nothing below but water in all directions.

Amy flew on for Australia, across the sea of fear – Timor – as other fliers had done before and would do again. But until now no woman had ever done it alone.

It was at 3.50 p.m. on 24 May, Empire Day, that *Jason's Quest* formed a dark dot in the sky over Fanny Bay aerodrome, near Darwin.

133

Amy saw land and shouted for the sheer joy of it.

At 3.57 p.m. she was down. Cheers came in waves over the hot afternoon air; cameras clicked; she'd done it.

Dressed in khaki shorts, puttees, and a green sun helmet, and looking sunburnt and tired, Amy said: 'Don't call me Miss Johnson. Just plain Johnnie will do. That's what my English friends call me.'

So Amy Johnson became the first woman to fly alone to Australia. Her time of twenty days was made in spite of two forced landings and an ignition fault corrected at Sourabaya.

As soon as her arrival was known in England, King George V sent the following message to the Governor General of Australia: 'The Queen and I are thankful and delighted to know of Miss Johnson's safe arrival in Australia and heartily congratulate her upon her wonderful and courageous achievement: George R.I.'

JIM MOLLISON

Greatest Solo ever Flown

The greatest solo flight ever made; this is how Jim Mollison's epic east–west Atlantic crossing has been described more than once.

G-ABXY were the letters painted on the body of the small mono-plane, which bore its name immediately beneath the cabin window, *The Heart's Content*. Jim Mollison's little silver streak of a plane was a De Havilland Puss Moth, measuring a mere twenty-five feet in length and with a wing span of thirty-six and three-quarter feet. Its other vital statistics were: petrol capacity 162 gallons, cruising speed 110 miles an hour, powered by a 102-horsepower Gipsy engine.

When fully loaded with petrol, no suitable airfield could be found in England, so early in August 1932, Jim Mollison took his little Puss Moth out of its hangar at the Stag Lane aerodrome and with only a nominal volume of fuel, flew it across to Portmarnock Strand, Co. Dublin, where there were several miles of flat beach at his disposal for a take-off with a full fuel load.

The weather was bad for early August and he had to endure day after day of waiting for it to break. The full moon came and went in the middle of the month. Then a heatwave hit London and the Irish and Atlantic weather got better, too. The temperature leaped to ninety-six degrees in London.

Mollison had married Amy Johnson shortly before the flight and she was there to see him take off at about 11.30 a.m. on 18 August. He had been waiting all this while for the surface winds over the Atlantic to lessen below twenty miles an hour, for these meant head-winds of twice that strength at the altitude he would be keeping.

He carried no wireless and he reckoned his fuel would last for a maximum of thirty-three hours. He felt sure this would be long enough as he expected to reach Harbour Grace, Newfoundland, within twenty-four hours. But he had to be careful about those head-winds, which could cut the actual aeroplane speed fatally.

His two compasses would not be affected by the magnetic distur-bance off the Newfoundland coast if he maintained a minimum height of 1,000 feet. His total rations comprised some chicken sandwiches, a flask of coffee and some sticks of barley sugar for energy.

In fact the flight was intended to form the outward leg of a two-way ocean crossing within three days, later abandoned.

Navigation seemed to be the main difficulty and danger for Mollison. A pilot could not afford to make much of an error or be forced far off course by elements such as fog, cloud or wind. Apart from direction, there was always the question of pilot fatigue. To keep awake and alert for twenty-four hours is never easy and to fall asleep would be the surest way to die.

The Gipsy III engine was being tested just as severely as Mollison and if it succeeded it would prove itself fit for anything, since the east–west transatlantic crossing was much more difficult due to the necessity of flying against the prevailing south-westerly winds.

If Mollison made it, he would be the first person to fly solo west-ward across the Atlantic.

Loaded with its 162 gallons, the slender silver monoplane pressed its wheels hard into the mixture of sand and shingle as it gathered speed and finally rose from Portmarnock Strand.

The crowd stood dotted across the shore, cars intermingled with the people. A lot of spectators ran after the plane, as if helping it on its way. Then it shrank to a speck, vanishing over the sandhills in the direction of Malahide and the west. Soon after midday Mollison was reported over Galway at 1,000 feet. Then there was silence.

He was in an aeroplane of lower power than any which had previously attempted the ocean flight. Mollison's plan was to fly close to the water in daylight and rise only to a moderate height at night. He wanted to avoid blind flying if he could, although he had the usual instruments of those days.

Keeping low by day, his outlook was scarcely any more than that of a ship's captain from the bridge. With all these restrictions, it was clear that the weather could play considerable tricks with the course he hoped to keep. Just a small angle of error or drift through head-winds could fan out and amount to a substantial mileage at the end of the ocean journey of 2,000 miles. In fact Mollison's drift amounted to less than ten per cent.

The last ship to report seeing Mollison overhead was some 800 miles out from the west coast of Ireland. Then darkness spread rapidly behind him, chasing him from the west, and he was entirely on his own.

The drift south from his correct course had begun, caused by variations in the strength and direction of the wind. The great danger as always remained that of being swept too far south into the wider wastes of the central Atlantic and then for the plane to run out of petrol before sighting land. Even if the conditions were perfect, having to navigate as well as fly was bound to make the trip an exacting business.

Mollison left the ship behind and headed into the afterglow of sunset. This was the worst stretch, night-time in mid-ocean.

With darkness his horizon clouded so that after the first twelve hours of comparative comfort, things really became trying. As he passed the half-way mark and flew on, mist cast a net over the night. At daylight the situation had not improved and Mollison started to fear that he was not making the 100-miles-an-hour average speed he had reckoned as reasonable. He knew he must be nearing Newfoundland, but nothing more. His original aim had been to fly from Dublin to New York via Newfoundland, yet here he was in the dim morning of 19 August and for all he knew he might be over the St Lawrence or anywhere.

Now the infamous Newfoundland fog-belt really lived up – or down – to its name, blanking out the entire horizon, the seascape and skyscape. Not only seamen but aviators, too, had learned to hate this fearful fog, especially since it cloaked the ocean in the very area where a flier could begin to congratulate himself that he was near to attaining the goal of his flight.

Mollison groped, peered, swore, through the wispy vapours that by their very nature sent a shiver of unreality through anyone in their midst. He scanned the sealine for a break in the fog or the shape of land. He found neither. He reckoned he must have just about reached the coast but he simply dared not descend to water level without being sure. Firstly, he might make a mistake and sink to a watery grave. Secondly he knew enough about that craggy coastline to appreciate that unless he actually saw land he might easily strike on the frequent peaks pointing up from the island's shore. So he strained to see something, anything, and to avoid flying into a rock face at nearly 100 miles an hour.

Finally he found Harbour Grace, Newfoundland, but decided not to refuel there as he had originally contemplated. Instead he circled the aerodrome, headed west once more, and gave the islanders the sight of the *Heart's Content* plunging into a thick fog over the Bay of Fundy. In fact, Mollison had nearly missed Newfoundland altogether by his southerly drift.

Next came that awkward sea stretch before he would be over Canadian soil and more or less safe. He made Halifax, Nova Scotia, all right, however, and had now been aloft and awake for approaching thirty hours. The mist was even veiling the land.

'How long can he keep it up?' everyone was asking.

On he flew over New Brunswick. He had used 152 gallons of petrol. He had ten gallons left, just about equivalent to a tank-full in a big car, and he was dog tired. The time was coming up to 12.45 p.m. New York daylight time, 5.45 p.m. British Summer Time. He had been up for thirty hours fifteen minutes. That was long enough, he reckoned.

Jim Mollison thought he had insufficient fuel to reach New York, so he decided he might as well land wherever he saw a good spot. It came at Pennfield Ridge, New Brunswick, where the little Puss Moth fluttered down through the mist in a meadow.

At once he telephoned to St John, fifty miles away, where a message was relayed to his wife Amy, then awaiting news back in London.

This may have been the most outstanding of all Mollison's flights, but it was not the most eventful. He had several spills throughout his career, none worse than the joint trip by Jim and Amy Mollison across the Atlantic. But before this, Jim chalked up yet another amazing record, becoming the first person ever to fly from England across the South Atlantic to South America. The flight also marked the first solo success from east to west across the South Atlantic. Mollison used the same aeroplane as he had for his North Atlantic triumph.

He was still hankering after that non-stop flight from London to New York, having the foresight to realize that the air traffic of the future must flow between these two great cities.

De Havilland's built a big airliner for the venture, a Dragon twin-engine machine capable of seating ten passengers. For this flight, however, these seats were not included, cylindrical fuel tanks being installed instead to give the aircraft a petrol loading of 600 gallons and a range of 7,000 miles – unheard of for those days. Mollison had visions of longer journeys than merely the London–New York run, though for the time being this was the first object.

Jim and Amy christened their new plane the *Seafarer* and together they set off from Croydon in July 1933. The airliner had travelled two hundred yards along that famous early runway nestling amid the built-up environs, when suddenly its undercarriage collapsed – and that was the end of that.

Neither of the Mollisons had been hurt by the mishap and they felt impatient to try again. By August *Seafarer* was fit to fly but they preferred a sandy start rather than the Croydon field. Accordingly they conveyed the plane down to Pendine Sands, South Wales, which presented a seven-mile expanse of firm sand for the take-off. Jim remembered the successful ascent from Portmarnock and so felt happy that they would get away well this time, too.

Eventually the weather cleared enough to justify their departure. They had cut down the petrol to some three-quarters of the maximum possible, to lessen the aircraft's weight, but this 450-gallon capacity still allowed them ample for a transatlantic trip, or should have done.

Furlong after furlong *Seafarer* sped over the hard Welsh sands, while the cliffs rose in oppressive shadow to the land side. Half a mile passed and they were still on the beach. At last, after 1,000 yards, they got up and away. Then they nearly hit one of those rocky cliffs which loomed out of the sea-mist.

Anyone flying westward across the ocean was almost bound to encounter headwinds, and they were no exceptions. The wind slapped them the whole way over and made the forty hour ordeal even more exhausting. They had actually rigged up a simple bed in the airliner, but although there were two of them to share the work neither slept for an instant. They did take turns at the controls, but there was always something to be done even when not flying the aeroplane.

The climax came at the other end. Even now the danger in flying is mainly on take-off and landing. At their first shot from Croydon, the take-off had failed. Now they were due for a disastrous landing just as they seemed assured of success.

For some forty hours, without a snatch of sleep, Jim and Amy had kept *Seafarer* on its route, determined to reach New York. But as they reached the United States and started flying over the New England countryside dozing below them, they suddenly knew that the few gallons of petrol left would not be enough. The headwinds had done their work.

They were only twenty minutes short of New York when they ran right out of petrol.

Bridgeport aerodrome lay beneath them and Jim started to coast and go into a glide for it. Lower and lower they sank, but it became clear to the group of onlookers that *Seafarer* would just miss the actual airfield. There was nothing Jim could do but put it down wherever he could.

The aeroplane struck a swamp adjoining the airfield, it swung over in two terrible somersaults and spreadeagled into a wreck.

Glass splinters ripped into Amy. Jim catapulted through the glass windscreen and pitched head-first into the slimy swamp. Extensively cut by flying fragments, he fell unconscious.

They were both hurried to hospital, where Jim Mollison needed a hundred stitches in his scattered wounds.

They had proved their point by all but twenty minutes. It was possible to fly from Britain to New York. Next time they would take more petrol.

19

AMELIA EARHART

First Woman Across the Atlantic

Tall, slender, softly-spoken and gentle-mannered, Amelia Earhart made several flights that rank among the finest flying achievements of all time.

She was the first woman ever to cross the Atlantic by air, but this was hardly one of her major deeds, since she merely sat in as a passenger helping with navigation on that memorable flight. It still had its interest, however, for the final few minutes.

Amelia had learned to fly several years earlier, though she did not take the controls on this trip, which was her first experience over the ocean.

She accompanied Commander Wilmer Stultz, the pilot, and Lew Gordon, acting as mechanic. They chose a Fokker seaplane with three 200-horsepower Wright Whirlwind engines. The machine was a monoplane with floats fitted.

They took off from Trepassey, Newfoundland, on 17 June 1928, and the *Friendship*, as the aeroplane was called, commenced the long flight. The details of the flight do not form part of this story. After hours of fog, the morning of 18 June brought clearer conditions.

Stultz saw a large vessel below on an approximately south–north route, which puzzled the three of them considerably.

'Where on earth are we?' Stultz asked.

Where, indeed, after nineteen and a half hours in the air?

Then minutes later another liner loomed over the horizon. They tried to contact her by radio without success. The mystery remained. Ships of this size did not steam on that course just off the west coast of Ireland, where the aviators reckoned they must be. But perhaps the very recent fog had literally clouded their calculations. After all they had not seen a thing until this last hour.

Then while they were still wondering where they were and what to do, they spied the dim outline of land on the easterly horizon ahead of them. They realized that it couldn't be Ireland.

In the long fog-belt, they had flown right over Ireland – the coast-line threading in and out before their eyes was Wales.

Half an hour later the seaplane slowly scored twin ski trails in the waters of Carmarthen Bay and they had done it, but better than planned in fact.

Amelia Earhart had to wait nearly four more years before she could fulfil her real ambition: to fly the Atlantic alone and so become the first woman ever to do so. She would also be only the third person to accomplish it solo after Lindbergh and Hinkler.

Amelia looked a fragile figure as she climbed into her Lockheed Vega monoplane that evening of 20 May 1932, at Harbour Grace, Newfoundland. In reality her frailness concealed capability and courage of an extraordinary order. She was now the wife of an American publisher and so really Mrs Putnam, but the world will always remember her as Amelia Earhart – gallant, graceful, the epitome of an era of flying forever gone.

Some flights seem destined to be smooth, others rough, and this was one of the latter. It was as if she had to be tested to the extremes of endurance.

Amelia revved up her 420-horsepower Wasp engine, opened the throttle wide, and almost before the crowd knew it, she was off, winging into the void at 7.30 p.m. on that mild May evening.

Three hours fled by and Amelia still felt fairly fresh. Then, about four hours out from Newfoundland, several things happened almost at once. Any one of them would have been enough to worry her, but together they seemed to spell destruction.

One section of the heavy exhaust manifold on the powerful Wasp engine fractured slightly, began to leak, and let hot gases pass through. Tongues of flame licked momentarily over the cowling. By day Amelia would not have thought too much of this, but at midnight it was frightening, the blaze of the gases adding to the general fantasy of night over the ocean.

This alone was bad enough, but then she realized her petrol gauge must be leaking, and she could not remedy it. Fault number two.

The scarlet-painted Vega, its slim lines matching Amelia's own elegance, flew on and straight into foul weather. She began five long lonely hours of blind flying through the moonless night, with the aircraft leaving a trail of gas behind it. If Amelia shuddered, she would have been forgiven by anyone. Why was she here? She scarcely had a chance to think about that, which was just as well.

The thick, throttling clouds seemed to press in on the plane, uncanny and claustrophobic.

Then, to add to the flaming exhaust, the steady leak of fuel, and the five hours of flying blind in wind-whipped rain clouds – her altimeter failed.

'For the first time in ten years of flying', she said.

So now was added to her existing troubles the hazard of not knowing how high she was flying, or whether she was level.

Flying blind without an altimeter was dangerous, she knew. She did not intend to run the risk of finding the plane diving into the stormy sea, the sea that might be any distance beneath her.

She had no choice but to climb right into the thick of those oppressive layers of clouds. She continued to climb until the tachometer – the engine revolutions counter – froze from the drop in air temperature, and then at least she knew she could not possibly be near the sea. This was all very well, but the extreme chill did more than merely freeze the tachometer, it started to ice the wings of the Vega. This new development could also be fatal but she had to stay at this height.

The clouds were too thick for the aeroplane to penetrate them, so she did her best to pierce a path above them, not only for the simple benefit of finding and flying in clear weather, but to be able to check her course by the stars. The night was still upon her, seemingly lengthened far beyond its normal span.

She guessed that she was up to 12,000 feet. The ice worsened on her wings and the clouds still showed no signs of thinning. She thought of Hinkler, who had found himself in similar conditions and had done more or less the same as she, and ploughed on through clouds so concentrated that they appeared to be solid.

Then lightning started shooting through the clouds. The leak in the exhaust manifold worsened, as the intense heat at the leaky joint began to burn away the metal. No longer did the burning flecks of gases flicker away into night.

'I looked over at it,' said Amelia, 'and saw the flames coming out, and I wished afterwards I hadn't looked, because it worried me all night.'

143

As the flame-flecked plane proceeded, this trouble naturally grew worse. A piece of the manifold became detached and fell into the sea. Other parts of it began to work loose and serious vibration was set up, which could be felt throughout the structure of the whole machine.

The overheating of the manifold also started to affect the engine and it began running rough. She did not feel any easier knowing that petrol was leaking steadily into the cockpit from the faulty fuel gauge. She feared the petrol fumes would reach the manifold and be exploded by the flames pouring from the gap in it. Amelia had been in a variety of tight corners, but never one as bad as this. Fire was the flier's ultimate enemy.

Early that morning she flew over a ship which sounded its siren at her in greeting. She never saw another one. It did not occur to her to give up.

Now she had passed the half-way mark and daylight had brought its renewal of hope. She went on, doubtful that her navigation could have been accurate during her imprisonment in the clouds. She did some mental calculations and reckoned that she should soon reach land.

After some thirteen hours airborne, Amelia saw the conjunction of clouds and hills, but without an altimeter she could not be sure that she could go high enough through the clouds to clear the hills ahead.

She made landfall in Donegal, though she did not know it, and as she wanted to ascertain her position more certainly, as well as find a safe landing place, she veered north and followed the little railway track she spotted until she reached the misty green hills that came sweeping down to the river mouth west of Londonderry.

Amelia came to earth in a field at Culmore, Derry, after a crossing lasting only thirteen and a half hours. The petrol would have lasted another hour or two, but would the aeroplane? She was not to know the answer to that, yet she felt pretty thankful to be out of the air, much as she loved it.

I had not the faintest notion where I was. I circled around your city awhile in the hope of locating an aerodrome, but finding none I decided to make for the pastures and land on the nearest suitable field.

My flight is finished and my ambition is realized. I have crossed the Atlantic alone, and that is what I set out to do. I did it really for fun, not to set up any records or anything like that.

In fact the flight broke two records. Apart from becoming the first woman to fly the Atlantic solo, Amelia had set up a new fastest time for the near-2,000-mile journey.

President Hoover telegraphed his own and America's congratulations.

Amelia Earhart remained what she had always been, cultured and modest, through her triumphs in the air and the adulation they brought her.

Amelia did not stop there. She had had an urge to outdo the record long-distance flight by a woman, at that time held by Ruth Nicholls with a cross-continent flight in the United States.

So she took a Lockheed Vega, similar to the one in which she had crossed the Atlantic three months earlier, and started from Los Angeles on 24 August 1932. Her aim was a non-stop trip right across the changing landscape of the States, with its mountains and wildernesses, to Newark, New Jersey, the nearest convenient point for New York.

She covered over 2,500 miles in slightly over nineteen hours. Together with her transatlantic triumph, her two flights demonstrated more than any others just what the future held for civil aviation. And the fact that a woman had proved it was possible to get from Los Angeles to London in less than two days underlined its bright future.

On 11–12 January 1935, she undertook a flight which had cost many airmen their lives, from Honolulu to Oakland, California. The distance was 2,408 miles. She flew solo in a Lockheed Vega with a Pratt and Whitney Wasp engine, and touched down at Oakland just eighteen hours sixteen minutes after leaving the Polynesian world of the Hawaiian Islands.

The last and most ambitious flight that Amelia Earhart attempted was to encircle the globe at the equator. She set out with Captain Fred Noonan on this round-the-world challenge. But on 2 July 1937, their aeroplane was lost in the Pacific Ocean between British New Guinea and Howland Island.

Amelia Earhart will never be forgotten.

20

COLONEL BLACKER

Looking Down on Everest

Many men had dreamed of looking down on Everest before the first flight over it was achieved in 1933, and many men had lost their lives attempting to conquer it by air.

Throughout the ages, men had stood and stared at the tallest peak in the world, wondering how it could be tamed. Only with the advent of aviation did the dream of seeing its summit from close quarters really begin to become a possibility.

Until the 1930s no aircraft engine existed capable of carrying the necessary load to a height of nearly six miles above sea level. Of course this height had been exceeded by ten thousand feet before 1933, but only with the minimum load and in the best possible weather conditions. Neither of these factors would apply to any projected flight over Everest.

Yet man was bound to try and surmount this, the tallest of all peaks. It followed naturally after the crossing of the Atlantic and Pacific and reaching the Poles. Everest was one of the shrinking number of unconquered goals. Its conquest was inevitable; it was just a matter of time.

The development of the Bristol Pegasus engine was what tipped the scales in favour of success. It was a definite advance on any other aeroplane engine previously produced. This nine-cylinder, air-cooled radial engine was supercharged and so was powerful even at high altitudes. It was also wonderfully light for its power. Now it only needed someone to take up the idea of flying over Everest.

Lieutenant Colonel L.V.S. Blacker conceived the plan early in 1932, but it took over a year of continuous effort to bring it to fruition. As with so many other pioneering ventures, faultless preparation would go a long way toward success. Many people and bodies assisted in their own way. One of the early decisions to be made was the choice of the likeliest aircraft for the job. Two aeroplanes were selected: the Westland PV-3, subsequently called the Houston-Westland, and the Westland Wallace. These were twin-seater biplanes with high undercarriages. Their broad wings gave good climbing qualities and, most important, they could both be adapted to take the new Pegasus engine.

Despite the fantastically low temperatures expected over Everest, the planners decided quite rightly to plump for open cockpits with windshields. The observer's cockpit in each case, however, was panelled above and fitted with side windows for photography.

Oxygen would be supplied to enable the pilots to breathe as easily as possible in the rarefied atmosphere. As photography would be an important purpose of the flight, too, both survey and ciné cameras were fitted for maximum operational convenience.

In addition to the supply of oxygen in pressurized steel cylinders, complete with face masks and flexible tubing, the fliers were to have the benefit of electrically heated clothing. So much special power gear was needed one way or another that the planes incorporated extra dynamos. The pilot and observer in each of the two aeroplanes would wear goggles against the glare produced by the combination of sun and snow that was the climate around Everest.

When these and all the other fittings had been successfully tested and included, the pilots' cockpits looked like the control panels of an advanced airliner instead of a two-seater biplane.

Apart from gauges indicating air-speed, height, revolutions per minute, pressure, petrol, oil, time, and so on, the pilot had valves and regulators for the oxygen supply, a tail incidence wheel, throttle and mixture control – and the main control column.

Three light Moth aeroplanes were flown out to India to aid in the work of conveying films and other records to Calcutta for processing. The two precious Westlands travelled in a more leisurely manner by sea. Blacker chose Purnea as the base for the attempt on the mountain 150 miles away to the north. At Delhi he met the three other principals of the venture, Lord Clydesdale, Flight Lieutenant D.F. McIntyre and Air Commodore P.F.M. Fellowes.

They flew from there to Purnea in two of the little Moths, and on the way they rounded a lower mountain to get their first glimpse of Everest. It was like the largest gem in a set of three, the others being

Kanchenjunga and Makalu. Bejewelled in brilliant whiteness, they looked radiant yet remote. The thought of flying over them seemed almost blasphemous.

This was only a preliminary survey to see how the airfield and hangars were progressing at Purnea. As things seemed to be going ahead well, they started back to Karachi to collect the two Westland aircraft. At Allahabad, however, a strong storm blew up in the night while they were asleep and smashed the little parked Moth aeroplanes to pieces. They completed the trip back rather ignominiously by train and then in a borrowed aeroplane! That was the only incident at this stage, though, and the four men and their two large Westlands were soon safely back at Purnea.

From then on it was a question of making the final test flights, and of waiting for the weather to improve. They let up balloons to trace the course and speed of the winds over the upper slopes, but these were swept up and away at speeds well above the maximum safe level decreed. Often the wind was twice as fast as the thirty–forty miles an hour regarded as reasonable in the circumstances. It seemed as if they would be marooned at Purnea for ever, waiting for the wind to drop.

The little Moths made daily survey flights to report on the current conditions, and finally came word that visibility was as clear as it ever would be, though the wind was still too high at fifty-seven miles an hour.

'It's no good waiting any longer', Clydesdale said. 'Let's have a shot tomorrow.'

The whole outfit had to work like madmen to make the elaborate last-minute preparations: film, oxygen, fuel, instruments tested, telephones between pilot and observer. Everything had to work. There would be no chance of a successful forced landing where they were going, not near the top anyway.

The two Westlands took off on the morning of 3 April 1933. Piloting the Houston-Westland was Lord Clydesdale, with Blacker acting as observer, Flight Lieutenant McIntyre flew the Westland Wallace, with an air cameraman of Gaumont-British, Mr S.R. Bonnett, filming the flight.

The accuracy of the comparison between the control panel of the biplanes and that of an airliner can be judged as true when one learns that Blacker had to make no fewer than forty-six checks on take-off.

They flew on and up through the inevitable Himalayan haze that lay over everything between 6,000 and 19,000 feet. They rose out of

148

this like a swimmer suddenly breaking surface. Now the haze was a white carpet below them tempting them to try and land on it.

Kanchenjunga soared up to the right. Then they saw Everest itself, with Makalu on its right. The trio of proud peaks rose sheer from the haze which the clear sky seemed to tint pale purple. Billowing like bunting or white smoke from the crest of Everest was the famous rafale, indicating strong winds over the top. The aviators hardly needed the evidence of this snowstream to tell them of the violent air currents around them.

They were aware that no one had seen the glaciers below. On the two biplanes bumped, with Everest their goal. Suddenly the first aircraft was drawn down in a down-draught. Clydesdale and Blacker fell 2,000 feet in what seemed the click of a camera shutter, as if the gods were angry at these mere mortals' daring.

The Houston-Westland approached the gaunt crags of the South Col of Everest. They had watched those weather balloons buffeted about over the glaciers like lost souls and now they were in the same situation. Could the powerful Pegasus engine resist the surging airstream? There was a brief battle between the elements and the engine. The Pegasus gradually got the upper hand and they regained the lost height, but the incident had shaken them.

Soon they were sweeping around the ragged arc that traced the summit. They were literally on top of the world. So close did the Westland sneak to the summit that Blacker stopped taking pictures to wonder whether the tail skid would in fact foul the mountain. Then he went on with his photography.

They were up there all right, but the next problem would be to get down. Clydesdale headed the aeroplane into the face of the wildcat wind as it streamed snow off the summit. The aeroplane had a nominal speed of 120 miles an hour. The speed of the wind must have been as much because for a moment stalemate reigned.

Then the aeroplane ran the whole gauntlet of the plume – that trail torn from the top of the world. Ice crackled into the open cockpit so savagely that it cracked the windows.

They had seen enough of the roof of the world for one day, so after a rapid circuit or two of the peak, they aimed back to Purnea, landing shortly before half past eleven, after three and a half hours of the most unusual flying ever known to man. There had been one or two snags with the machines but nothing that could not be corrected.

They set their hearts on a second shot at Everest, although they had conquered it. Meanwhile the immediate idea was for a flight over the next most majestic of the Himalayas, Kanchenjunga. This was to test the vertical cameras again, as the Everest snowdust haze had marred some plates taken the first time. This secondary trip would also allow them to perfect the rest of the complicated gear of all kinds.

They made the flight the following day, the aeroplanes coming clear of the haze exactly as before at around 19,000 feet. Now only the gaunt shapes of the Himalayan giants broke the infinity of sky and space.

On Kanchenjunga, as throughout the range, they saw the strange contrast between the snow-stacked side and the darker, rocky side where the wind had blown everything off the steep slopes.

When they got to about 28,000 feet, the summit was shrouded in cloud, rather an unnerving outlook. They flew on and then the leading aircraft suffered a series of sudden shocks. It tilted, twisted, shuddered and spun till they felt they must dive downward, but then the pilot regained control and all was well.

They hesitated and then decided not to try and cross the summit, so they veered off for Purnea, rather like a fighter breaking off a dogfight.

They got away from the mountain but then the unexpected occurred, as it so often did in those early days of flying. They had to make two forced landings. The second one was at Dinajpur, where within ten minutes a throng of thousands of locals had encircled the plane, which had run out of petrol. Most of the people had never seen an aeroplane before that moment.

When the photographs of both flights had been processed, they found that the 19,000-foot high haze had in fact blotted out most of the vertical shots, so confirming the need for another flight of Everest. The aviators did not really need an excuse for it, but were glad they could definitely justify the trip.

McIntyre meanwhile had thought of a good way of utilizing the weather. This involved a different approach to the mountain, by taking advantage of the favourable east wind up to 18,000 or 19,000 feet. Then they could swing up to the summit.

This second flight over Everest took place on 19 April. The estimate of the wind force at 24,000 feet was eighty-eight miles an hour, and up to 100 miles an hour around the summit. In other words, nearly the speed of the aeroplane. Despite this disquieting report, they took off that morning.

A hundred miles from Makalu they took a clear infra-red picture of the peak, though at that stage the summit of Everest still lurked behind a bank of cumulus clouds. They felt in a world apart, here with their heads in the clouds. It was a dizzy, dramatic experience.

Blacker concentrated on his vertical photographs for almost an hour. This brought them immediately in front of Everest, some twenty miles ahead.

Then some strange things happened. The electric plug in Clydesdale's oxygen heater suddenly started vibrating. He grappled with the pins to try and tighten the plug, and had no sooner got it right again than a clamping screw attached to the survey camera began to be affected by the intense cold.

One or two other items all gave signs of stress at that increasing altitude and decreasing temperature. Just as long as nothing vital breaks, thought Blacker. He was taking oblique-angle shots of some of the unexplored ridges in the range south-west from Everest. This was exciting stuff. They soared towards Everest, now twelve miles distant.

The long raked rafale lay ahead, visible in a clear deep blue sky through the framework of struts and wires of their little mechanical world. The rafale blew off the summit like the smoke from a funnel of some celestial liner. Away to their right, behind the rear wing strut, Makalu looked almost as high as Everest.

Now they were only two miles away. The crags of the South Col looked like irregular pyramids.

They were over the summit almost before they realized it. Blacker went on juggling with the three cameras in his control: the vertical survey camera, the oblique still camera for pictures from the side, and the ciné camera. He used up all his plates as the aeroplane pounded around the crest quite happily. The whole string of connected peaks in the huge Himalayan range reminded them of a host of rocky islands strung in a cloudy sea.

This blanket base of cloud really insulated the fliers from all external influences. Their world at that moment was the uninhabited, unknown, unspoilt Himalayas, but conquered at last – at least from the air.

On they went over Makalu, gasping with wonder as the Khumbu glacier and Arun gorge unfolded below.

The other aircraft took a slightly different course because the cloud blanket blotted out their environs almost to the foot of Everest. But from both aeroplanes they got good vertical survey pictures, over-lapping to form a valuable series of this totally unmapped region. Here was a forerunner of the future: the limitless scope of surveying from the air. Some of these photos revealed a strange patch on the ice-surfaced face of Everest. Like so much else that they had flown over, no one had ever seen this before.

21

WILEY POST

Around the World in Eight Days

Around the world in eighty days – that might have been good enough for Jules Verne but Wiley Post had other ideas. He flew around the world in *eight* days or, to be more precise, eight days, fifteen hours and fifty-one minutes.

Wiley Post and Harold Gatty did this 15,474-mile marathon in a Lockheed Vega with a Pratt and Whitney Wasp engine. The aeroplane was christened *Winnie Mae of Oklahoma* and they followed this route: America, England, Germany, Russia, Alaska, Canada, America.

Wiley Post was an amazing man. He had only one eye and came of Indian blood. After a spell as a parachutist, he graduated to flying, becoming the pilot of an American oil tycoon named F.C. Hall. It was after Mr Hall's daughter that the plane was in fact named.

So these were the ingredients for the flight; a stocky, one-eyed American with a small moustache, Wiley Post; a handsome Tasmanian navigator with special knowledge of many of the air and land conditions along the route, Harold Gatty and of course the faithful *Winnie Mae* monoplane, emblazoned with the words 'Pathé News, Winnie Mae Round the World Flight'.

The plane had a 450-horsepower engine capable of a maximum speed of 180 miles an hour and it could fly for 3,000 miles without refuelling. This high-wing cantilever plane could normally carry six people and was twenty-seven feet seven and a half inches long with a wing span of forty-one feet. Wiley Post's seat was up in the nose of the aeroplane, while Gatty had to be content with a very cramped spot that gave him just one or two feet in which to shuffle or stretch. Not ideal for flying around the world.

The two of them underwent more protracted training for this flight than any fliers so far in the history of long-distance records. Among the things Post practised were keeping alert for long periods without falling asleep, and also sleeping at order in short cat-naps. They made their equipment as reliable as possible and included an artificial horizon, blind-flying gear and a special instrument indicating the amount of bank and turn.

Eventually they reckoned they were ready. At the dawn of 23 June 1931, 4.55 a.m. New York summer time, they posed for photographers in the misty morning air and then left Roosevelt Field behind them on the first leg of this ambitious attempt.

Their first goal was Harbour Grace, Newfoundland. The *Winnie Mae* ran into midsummer clouds much of the way, but six and three-quarter hours after leaving the magic metropolitan skyline, Gatty told Post, 'Ought to be over Woonsocket in a minute or two'.

The clouds parted as if on cue and the pilot saw the ground, an aerodrome, and a roof bearing the name 'Woonsocket'. Not bad for 1931. So they were poised at Harbour Grace ready for the next little obstacle, the Atlantic Ocean. After a three and three-quarter hour halt for fuel and food, the two round-the-worlders winged effortlessly out over the ocean with a pleasant wind behind them. The plane soon got up to a cruising speed of 170 miles an hour which it maintained with an accuracy equal to Gatty's impeccable course keeping.

But before they could get too excited about their progress, the weather closed in on them and the monoplane met moist vaporous air. Post ascended to 1,800 feet hoping for a break but found none. This was a good initial blooding for their blind-flying equipment, which combined with Gatty's navigation to preserve a remarkable freedom from drift. The navigator was rewarded with a glimpse of the sun as it went down behind them, confirming the course.

For the three hours or so of deepest night, they were once more flying entirely on instruments. With the dawn came the rain. A dreary morning of warm summer rain dulled their senses slightly, though Gatty managed to remain aware of exactly where they were the whole time.

Soon after 11 a.m. Greenwich time, they both noticed a small slit in the rain clouds, like a little ragged hole in a length of grey fabric. Post took the aeroplane through the thick stratum of 'blinding whiteness' and suddenly saw a 'rugged coastline'. It was North Wales, slightly over a quarter of a mile below them.

The next thing they viewed was an RAF aerodrome at Sealand, outside Chester. The time was 11.42 GMT. When they landed Post and Gatty both found they were suffering from temporary deafness, brought on by the incessant noise of the engine, but that was their only complaint. While the RAF filled up their tanks, the two men also replenished their stomachs. They took off again within an hour and a half.

On across England, the Norfolk Broads and the North Sea, to Hanover, Germany. This stop was extra to their schedule, and they only stayed while the tanks were topped up to take them on to Berlin. From the moment they touched down at Tempelhof airport, they were besieged by well-wishers and got fewer hours' sleep than they had hoped.

Early next day they started on the thousand-mile stage to Moscow. The weather forecast was good, but the actual weather they encountered was not and they had a nasty time. At 2,000 feet Post ran into bulging, bursting clouds, so swung down to half that height. The sky still seemed leaden with clouds as they crossed into Poland, East Prussia and finally Russia.

The rain really lashed down and clouds of steam rose off the scalding exhaust pipes. When Post dived low in an effort to outdistance the storm, and to enable Gatty to check their position, he found that more than once the *Winnie Mae* had to dodge the tops of tall chimneys in industrial sectors.

The minarets of Moscow gave them the first inkling of the Orient: this capital that was the halfway house between the West and Far East. They had been flying for nearly three days now and were quite tired, but Post and Gatty had no option but to become the guests of the Ossoaviakhim – the Society for Aviation and Chemical Defence. By the time the two men had consumed vodka and heard toasts drunk to their continued success, only two or three hours were left for the sleep they so badly needed.

A strange error delayed their departure from Moscow. The Russians filled the tanks with the requisite number of gallons of petrol, but they went by the Imperial gallon instead of the smaller American one. The difference between the two measures, multiplied by the gallons loaded, made the *Winnie Mae* too heavy. Eventually the Russians drained off the excess fuel and the aviators ascended on one of the trickiest stages of the whole flight, right across to Novosibirsk in Siberia.

Mid-way between Moscow and this next stop, the Ural Mountains cut their course at right angles. There was no evading them. Things went swimmingly and the smooth sound of the engine lulled them. The altimeter reported 4,500 feet. The colossal crumpled peaks of the Urals rolled away below, melting into the clouds to the far north.

'We'd be for it if anything happened now', Post joked.

He had hardly finished speaking when the Wasp engine gave a gulp as if expostulating. The choking protest stammered on. Post reacted promptly and switched the fuel flow to a fresh source. The engine gave a last protest, followed by a purr. It was being fed again. The panic was past.

Losing height roughly parallel to the eastern sides of the Urals they passed Chelyabinsk, the rail junction between Moscow and Siberia, and actually used the legendary Trans-Siberian Railway as a guide. Several hours over the twin rails brought them to Omsk, which they reached at an average speed for the day so far of 176 miles an hour – pretty good going. They had already been in the air for nine hours, but kept on for the remaining two and a half hours to bring them to Novosibirsk well ahead of their scheduled time. The landing ground was so cut off, however, that they just had to sit and wait for the reception party to drive up by car more than an hour later!

From Novosibirsk eastward, the fliers utilized the Trans-Siberian line again as long as visibility allowed. The rail route passed through a kaleidoscopic landscape of hills, forest and wilderness, which would have been dangerous to them in the event of an accident.

They lost track of the railway below sprays of rain, and Post had to carry out his regular manoeuvre of angling up to 9,000 feet to try and top the clouds. He couldn't, so resigned himself to instrument flying back at the familiar 1,500 feet. After yet another cloudburst, the air seemed to clear a little and Post came down low to tag along above the railway to Irkutsk. By now they found it so straightforward to navigate that Gatty could sink down his allotted couple of feet and doze for a time. They clocked up six hours five minutes from Novosibirsk to Irkutsk.

Another little problem of communication greeted them at Irkutsk. They could not find anyone who understood English – let alone American! Finally a sixteen-year-old girl stepped out of the motley crowd of Asiatic onlookers and managed to act as their interpreter. Food, petrol and oil – that was all they wanted. She saw that they got it.

Post and Gatty had calculated in advance that Irkutsk represented the half-way mark, as near as made no odds. They were still doing well and *Winnie Mae of Oklahoma* was holding up marvellously. Irkutsk could hardly have been further from home. But this proved to be the quiet half of the global trip. From then on things began to get awkward.

Whether they could achieve the ten-day time limit they had set remained to be seen.

They set out again after only a couple of hours on the ground. Having flown for so long over land it was strange to find nothing but water beneath them as they cruised comfortably over the great Lake Baikal. It took them an hour to negotiate the lake during which they actually lost sight of land for a few minutes at the centre.

Their goal was Blagovestchensk. They traversed the remote Yablonoi Mountains and flew on for two or three hundred miles over the stark steppes devoid of any sign of life. It was like being on some strange planet.

By the time they had spanned the Amur river, which was to guide them to their destination, daylight had died. Flares flickered around the aerodrome but the locality had suffered severe rains and the land-ing ground was so waterlogged that the lights transformed the surface into a single shining pool. Post could have been excused for thinking he had overshot by a few hundred miles and was looking down on a Pacific bay.

He nosed down towards the sodden ground.

The aeroplane had been flying at its usual brisk 170 miles an hour. Now Post had slowed it to eighty miles an hour. It touched the mixture of mud and water. The mud clung in the space between the wheels and the special protective spats, while the water sprayed and splashed as the wheels squelched to a halt. As the aeroplane lost speed and stopped, one wheel sank into a morass of mud. This was not the mud of a ploughed field, for when Post and Gatty got out, they immediately went knee-deep in the mire. They tried to move, but looked like two characters in a slow-motion film. Much more serious, though, was the plight of the aeroplane. Just at that moment it seemed highly unlikely that it could be salvaged from the mud in time for them to beat their self-imposed time-limit.

While Post and Gatty got away, attempts were started to haul the aeroplane out of its predicament. Unless something was done quickly it would sink further. Men floundered frantically about the waterlogged aerodrome, eventually linking a car to the aeroplane to try and tow it out. The driver put the vehicle in gear and let out the clutch. The spinning wheels simply hurled up a dirty spray. Post and Gatty restarted the engines on the aeroplane, but instead of getting out of the mess, it merely sank further into the ooze.

While they awaited a promised tractor, the fliers fell asleep from sheer exhaustion, so the time was not really wasted. When they woke the surface seemed to be drying out a bit. As the tractor had not turned up, they tried again to tow it out with the means they had – manual labour plus a couple of horses. The combined strength of all concerned at last managed to drag the aeroplane free of the suction of the mud and on to a firm strip of soil.

The clock had made a complete revolution between their landing and departure from Blagovestchensk, but they were not discouraged; it might have been immeasurably worse. The next hop was to Khabarovask, 363 miles further east, which represented another vital milestone: the vaulting point for the vast 2,000-mile step across the Bering Sea to Alaska and the American continent. They knew this to be the key part of the rest of the journey. If they did it, the worst should be over. They reached Khabarovask easily and prepared for the next leg.

Wiley Post checked everything he could before taking off. He was not too happy about the sparking plugs and so changed them.

They had another wide sea stretch to bridge before the Bering. This was the Sea of Okhotsk. They flew over it at a height of precisely seventy-five feet to cut down the power of the appalling winds.

They ran into rain, gales and hail as *Winnie Mae* skimmed north-east. The hail peppered against the fuselage, like bullets from some offensive fighter plane, and then bounced off and plopped into the froth-filled sea.

Post had to drop even lower than seventy-five feet, yet still the gales threatened to engulf them. The aeroplane touched the wave tops once. The only thing to do was to go right up into the clouds and fly blind, and this he did.

There they got the full fury of the rain, so they rose still higher to 6,000 feet. Later on Gatty said, 'Should be over Kamchatka any minute now'.

They soon were, spotting savage-looking mountains not indicated on any maps. The peninsula of Kamchatka, separating the two seas, was the only land between them and Alaska. Post did not have to look twice at it to see that they really had no choice but to keep right on for the north-west tip of America.

They sped on over the snow-hatted heads of mountains, until they ran into blue sky and blinding sun. They followed the Russian coast as far as they could, and then branched off across the Bering Sea, cutting the actual water crossing to a minimum. Then they crossed the International Date Line, flew into fog, saw St Lawrence Island in the middle of the Bering Sea and finally grounded at Alaska.

Then another accident happened.

As they taxied along the runway, the wheels started to sink in sand. Post throttled to get lift, but the machine tilted on to its nose. The propeller threshed into the sand and bent the tips of both its blades. The two men soon borrowed a hammer and straightened the bends, but when they had refitted the repaired propeller to the aeroplane and Gatty was swinging it, the engine suddenly spat in a vicious backfire. The propeller hit him hard on the shoulder, knocked him out for a minute, and bruised his head. Gatty waved aside any assistance, however, and got aboard at once. They picked up a fresh airscrew when they landed at Fairbanks.

They flew another 1,300 miles to Edmonton, Canada, across the Canadian Rockies. Post and Gatty were pretty exhausted by now after a week of concentrated flying.

After that ordeal came another. They came in to land at Edmonton on a flooded flying ground. Post had to half-fly, half-taxi *Winnie Mae* over to the huddle of hangars, where welcoming crowds surged to meet them.

Neither of the two fliers fancied trying to take-off from that aerodrome, reminiscent as it was of the waterlogged Russian field.

'How about using the highway?' suggested a bright official.

The wide main road ran straight for two miles or more. The only snag was to keep it clear, but the police saw to that. Post and Gatty cruised along the Canadian highway at some sixty miles an hour, to the cheers of the local residents. *Winnie Mae* calmly rose clear of the concrete and was gone. Like everything else, she took this in her stride.

And so they pressed on, over Alberta, Saskatchewan, Manitoba, the Great Lakes, Michigan, Pontiac and Detroit to Cleveland, where they refuelled. Finally, there ahead was the famous New York skyline. They had left it when they headed east and were returning to it from the west.

Aeroplanes paraded on all sides. Wiley Post and Harold Gatty had done it, in eight days, fifteen hours and fifty-one minutes.

There is a small postscript to this astounding story. On 15–22 June, 1933, Wiley Post did it all over again – *alone*! To girdle the globe solo was impossible, friends told him. He smiled at them and set off. He is quoted as taking with him in the same aeroplane as before a quart of tomato juice, a quart of water, three packets of chewing gum, and a packet of rusk biscuits.

Post flew straight from New York to Berlin this time, the first man ever to achieve this, and then on to Moscow and across Russia. Without a navigator it was all many times more difficult and tiring, but he survived somehow. Once he slumped asleep at the control column. Finally he triumphed over the treachery of fog to cross the Bering Sea and strike Alaska on the home stretch.

The world heard he was overdue at Fairbanks. America was aghast.

Then they learned that he had landed at another airport and damaged his propeller. One was rushed up from Fairbanks by aeroplane and Post fitted it to *Winnie Mae* for the last long voyage across the American continent.

He reached New York in the startlingly short time of seven days eighteen hours forty-nine and a half minutes, nearly a day shorter than his previous record with Gatty.

On 15 August 1935, Wiley Post and the comedian Will Rogers were flying a seaplane on a survey trip over Alaska, when fog forced them to land on a river near Point Barrow. As they were taking off, the engine of the seaplane suddenly failed, the machine plunged into the river bank, and both Wiley Post and Will Rogers were killed.

22

SCOTT AND BLACK

The Melbourne Air Race

Mildenhall to Melbourne was the fantastic flight conceived for the first worldwide air race. This England–Australia contest was made possible by the prizes offered by Sir MacPherson Robertson. The prizes were £10,000, £1,500 and £500 for the first, second and third places. The money was to be paid in Australian currency so would be worth about three-quarters of its sterling value. Nevertheless, £7,500 was big enough bait, apart from the prestige attaching to victory.

The total distance was 11,333 miles and to win the race crews would have to be prepared to fly at night for as much of the way as they could. The route to be taken was Mildenhall, Baghdad, Allahabad, Singapore, Darwin, Melbourne.

Stated simply like that, it did not sound as formidable as it really was. From Baghdad onward, for instance, the obstacles became increasingly severe. The white-fringed Persian mountains topped 10,000 feet, while in the Kandahar area before Allahabad, another range rose to 7,000 feet. There was also to be a handicap race over a slightly different course, but the prime interest lay in the speed race itself.

Twenty machines from a number of countries lined up for the start. Apart from British aeroplanes, there were American, Dutch and other nationalities represented, so the event promised to be a truly international epic.

Who would win it? That was the big question at Mildenhall around dawn on Saturday, 20 October 1934.

Despite the early hour, thousands of people from counties far beyond Suffolk fringed the airfield and actually threatened the start altogether. Despite difficulties, the departure time arrived and the exodus began. The starter's Union Jack dropped as a signal for the first aeroplane to roll forward.

Jim and Amy Mollison were in it, needless to say, and to them went the honour of leading the longest flight of aeroplanes ever assembled for a race. Towards the orange-tinged clouds the Mollisons' De Havilland Comet rose firmly. Its twin Gipsy Six engines bore the machine aloft with its 260 gallons of fuel, sufficient to take it across Europe to the first stopping place. *Black Magic* was the name the Mollisons had chosen for their Comet, one of three similar planes entered.

The second of this trio of Comets was piloted by Cathcart-Jones and Waller. The excitement started there and then as it careered a couple of hundred yards over the Mildenhall grass and then suddenly swung round in the direction of the hangars, and some spectators – as if loath to leave at all.

Flecks of flame from the port engine identified the source of the trouble. The crowd could not help wondering how wise it was for the fliers to go ahead and take off again only two minutes after such a moment.

But with so much going on, they did not have much time to dwell on each individual sortie. A lumbering great American Boeing transport monoplane had risen before the first Cathcart-Jones attempt, piloted by Roscoe Turner and C. Pangborn. On its body it bore the name *Warner Bros.*, and on its tail the racing number five. This was bound to be among the possible winners, as the Americans usually did things thoroughly on occasions of this nature.

Stack and Turner in their Airspeed Victory taxied along the runway at their allotted forty-five-second interval, and then stopped, turned, and took off nearly a quarter of an hour later. The reason was that they wanted to collect films of the start of the race and felt this justified the time lost.

Another serious contender among the giants took to the air next. It was the large Douglas DC2 flown by Parmentier and Moll.

So the succession of aircraft headed out from East Anglia towards the Low Countries or France. One of the lesser known machines and entries was the Granville Gee Bee monoplane piloted by Wesley Smith and Jacqueline Cochran. The plane took off as if pregnant with petrol! But it got away; that was the main thing.

Davies and Hill in a Fairey IIIF checked out, but a Fairey Fox with Baines and Gilman did not. It seemed that the engine would not start;

not a good sign at the outset of 11,000-odd miles. It did get away a little later, after it had missed its turn.

Meanwhile all the others of the twenty had risen safely, including the third of the DH Comets with C.W.A. Scott and Thomas Campbell Black. Like the others, their machine was powered by a pair of Gipsy Six engines. Both these men had long aeronautical experience, Scott having beaten the record between England and Australia three times in 1931–2, while Black had piloted from London to Nairobi thirteen times. In 1931 he had rescued a German flier stranded on the unlikely locale of an island in the Upper Nile. They were two strong favourites for the race.

These were the twenty machines and their fliers:

Airspeed Courier, Stodart and Stodart
Airspeed Victory, Stack and Turner
Boeing Transport, Roscoe Turner and Pangborn
Desoutter, Hansen and Jensen
DH Comet, Cathcart-Jones and Waller
DH Comet, Jim and Amy Mollison
DH Comet, Scott and Black
DH Dragon, Hewett and Kay
Douglas DC2, Parmentier and Moll
Fairey Fox, Baines and Gilman
Fairey Fox, Parer and Hemsworth
Fairey III, Davies and Hill
Granville Gee Bee, Wesley Smith and Jacqueline Cochran
Klemm Eagle, Shaw
Lockheed Vega, Woods and Bennett
Miles Falcon, Brook
Miles Hawk, MacGregor and Walker
Monocoupe, Wright and Polando
Panderjager, Geysendorfer and Asjes
Puss Moth, Melrose

One of the most fascinating facts of the race was that the new 200 mile-an-hour Douglas DC2 flown by Parmentier and Moll was actually carrying three paying passengers and air mail. This American-designed plane was run by Royal Dutch Air Lines and it represented the result of several years' aviation development and a taste of the future to the air-minded onlookers of 1934.

163

Some planes had radio transmitters; others didn't. So news was spasmodic, even sparse, considering that twenty machines were in the air and would continue to be all day unless or until something happened to any of them.

The first trouble reported was when the Airspeed Victory came down at Abbeville. Stack and Turner did manage to get through to Le Bourget at 3.22 p.m., but that kind of time would not put them in the forefront, certainly not of the speed race, anyway. It seemed that fog coupled with internal installation faults had caused the delay.

Another casualty over France was the Fairey Fox with Parer and Hemsworth, a leaking radiator forcing them down in the Boulogne area. They were not expected to resume until the following day, Sunday.

The weather was not kind. Brook in his Miles Falcon landed at Plesses, near Paris, while two other machines also grounded 'somewhere in France'; the Fairey III south of the capital through lack of fuel, and the DH Dragon also near Boulogne. Five temporary casualties already out of a total of twenty aeroplanes. In a race like this, it would not be easy to make good any serious setbacks. Someone was bound to get through more or less flawlessly.

What was happening up among the leaders? The Mollisons looked as if they might add to their illustrious careers with a win. Whether or not they could keep it up, they certainly clocked in first at Baghdad, closely followed by another of the DH Comets, flown by Scott and Black. So British aircraft were well to the fore 2,530 miles from Mildenhall. Could they sustain such a pulverizing pace? The answer would be known in another two days. Meanwhile the third Comet had not yet arrived at Baghdad, but was expected fairly soon.

Right up there among the giants, as anticipated, was the Douglas DC2 airliner, which touched down at 11.10 p.m. GMT. Parmentier and Moll in the Douglas DC2 had averaged about 170 miles an hour despite three stops so far.

It was at 11.55 p.m., three-quarters of an hour later, that the fourth place was filled by the Panderjager. Spurred on by this arrival, Parmentier and Moll took the Douglas DC2 up again at precisely midnight GMT.

The big Boeing turned up next, refuelled in half an hour, and pressed on for Karachi. The only snag that Roscoe Turner and Pangborn seemed to have experienced was a failure to contact Baghdad by radio, but they could hardly grumble at that. A technical note: the engine cowlings bore not a single speck of oil.

The third Comet did eventually arrive at the airport an hour after the Middle East dawn had given shape and substance to the alien skyline of Baghdad's buildings.

'Are you all right?' came anxious enquiries of Cathcart-Jones and Waller, for it was widely known that since the Comets had speed they also had a restricted flying time – and this last one of them was overdue by fuel consumption.

Like every competitor in the race, they had an intriguing yarn to tell of their adventures to date.

They had been airborne at 17,000 feet for much of the earlier part of the flight, keeping course by their instruments. Across Hungary and Romania, the weather had been bad, and they only made out the ground beneath them an hour before the Comet flew over the Black Sea. That sojourn over the inland sea was just one more awkward stretch on an outward leg full of unfriendly hazards.

Then they overshot Baghdad!

They actually managed to put down safely 100 miles or so beyond the check point and decided to wait for first light to head back to find it. They touched down at Baghdad with precisely two gallons of petrol left!

Cathcart-Jones and Waller maintained this record of mishaps by taking off from Baghdad at 5.57 a.m. – and landing there again at 6 a.m! The starboard engine was registering nil oil pressure. The lubrication fault behind this resulted in a partial engine seizure, which involved changing a cylinder and piston. Six hours elapsed before they finally got away again, into gathering clouds.

As the leaders raced across the border into India, the Mollisons were still ahead of Scott and Black. Jim Mollison was taking the more southerly, coastal route of the two to Allahabad, and the husband-and-wife team set up a record run to Karachi.

But for the bulk of the field, things went less smoothly, the casualties continuing remorselessly. Woods and Bennett brought their Lockheed Vega in for a landing at Aleppo, Syria. They had already had trouble at Athens and perhaps as a result of this, the plane crash-landed at Aleppo, turned right over on its back, and they were forced to give up all hope of continuing.

Stack and Turner in the Airspeed Victory were also out of the real race, though they were still flying the course. Baines and Gilman in the Fairey Fox, and Shaw in the Klemm Eagle, reached Rome.

The Desoutter had checked in at Aleppo, with the DH Dragon and the Puss Moth en route for that point. So the field was stretched out across thousands of miles already.

Everyone was doing their best, but the spotlight swung inevitably to the east, where a change was about to take place in the leadership.

The Mollisons stayed only an hour at Karachi, anxious to hang on to their lead. But less than half an hour further on, towards the next intermediate point of Jodhpur, they realized that they could not continue. Their undercarriage had sustained a heavy knock when landing earlier on, and now it refused to retract. The Mollisons discussed the situation and decided to be prudent and head back to Karachi, the nearest airport, for they knew that the Comet's engines were liable to overheat if the wheels could not be brought up.

They managed to carry out a makeshift repair on the undercarriage, but then fog enveloped Karachi and they lost more hours before they were finally able to get away. They felt particularly frustrated after having set up such a startling time from England to India.

Meanwhile the second Comet took advantage of the Mollisons' mishap to drone eastward on the 2,300-mile hop from Baghdad to Allahabad at an average of 190 miles an hour. They clocked this speed despite a detour.

So now Scott and Black took over the lead. The interminable delay for the Mollisons also meant that the next contenders picked up a place.

For Scott and Black the third leg of the five-stage flight would take them to Singapore. The trim Comet took off from Allahabad, on the 2,210-mile ordeal to Singapore. They chose the direct route, instead of the overland one via Rangoon and Bangkok. So Scott and Black headed south-east, left India behind, and commenced that long, agonizing span across the Bay of Bengal – graveyard for fliers throughout the century.

The Douglas DC2 landed as scheduled at Jask near the mouth of the Persian Gulf; at Karachi; and then Allahabad. Reports said that it had even returned to Allahabad a few minutes after take-off to collect a passenger missing at the time of departure; a combination of service with speed. By the time the Douglas DC2 touched down at Allahabad, Scott and Black were in the vicinity of the Andaman Islands, flying east of them across the gigantic bay. They had a clear lead of a thousand miles or more, but fortunes could change dramatically in a race of this length, like the sudden switch of the aeroplanes occupying third and fourth places. The Dutch Panderjager was now on the air lane to Allahabad, flying in third position. They had left Karachi a long way behind. As they came down to land at Allahabad, something went wrong with the landing gear and the heavy craft actually struck the ground with a wing-tip and an airscrew blade. For a few seconds the machine made frantic vacillations and then the pilot expertly brought it to a safe halt. But the undercarriage failure put them out of the running. It was all the more galling as they were then under two hours behind the tail of their compatriots in the Dutch Douglas DC2. But that was the luck of the race. The aeroplane with fewest faults would probably win.

Roscoe Turner and Pangborn were glad of this good luck, but they had some bad fortune to offset it. They left Karachi in the big Boeing, but due to a breakdown in radio contact with Allahabad they found themselves flying off course. Fuel and time were both getting short when they at last located Allahabad and got down to earth almost at the last gasp from the fuelless engine. After a hasty fill-up, the Americans were off after the leaders, glad to have a full tank and to be flying third now.

Spread across the Asiatic skies, the survivors of this gruelling cross-continental race roared on. The Comet was really living up to its name, searing for Singapore in a trail of glory. Could anyone catch it?

Despite thick weather over the Bay of Bengal, they made landfall at Alor Star and headed on for Singapore.

They got there at 10.23 p.m. GMT on Sunday. They had flown a phenomenal 7,040 miles in under forty hours. They had made the two controlled halts at Baghdad and Allahabad, one unscheduled stop, and here they were at Singapore, still a clear thousand miles ahead of the field. Their overall average was about 176 miles an hour.

Scott and Black stayed only an hour at the British colony, before the fourth and possibly the worst of the five stages in the race – from Singapore to Darwin.

This 2,084-mile hurdle could be flown in a straight line or over more land via Batavia, Rambang and Kupang. They set the Comet's course direct for Darwin and hoped for the best. At 9.30 a.m. GMT they had covered three-quarters of the distance which left the Timor Sea stretch. After that, of course, they had to fly right across the burning heat of Australia, so the race was far from won. As they aimed out over the sea, they were some eight hours in the lead, by time reckoning.

What was happening behind them? Ill-luck had put the Mollisons out of the 'placed' aeroplanes. They had been troubled by the wind shifts between Karachi and Allahabad and had put down at Jubbulpore, after hobbling along for part of the way on a single engine. They found out there that they had two cracked pistons.

The leaders' only other two possible rivals were chasing them east.

At 7.30 a.m. GMT Parmentier and Moll in the Douglas DC2 were still second as they left Singapore. They passed Batavia, on Java, three hours later at 10.30 a.m., having made the 570-mile leap at an average of 190 miles an hour.

Now, with Rangoon to the rear and Singapore a long way ahead, the Boeing was still running third behind the Dutch airliner.

Fourth at this moment, as they entered into the third day of the race, was the Comet piloted by Cathcart-Jones and Waller.

So the four planes lay in a rough line somewhere between Rangoon and Darwin.

First was Scott and Black's Comet, second the Douglas DC2, third the Boeing and fourth Cathcart-Jones' Comet.

As they progressed, none of those behind the leader could know how near they were to advancing a place. Scott and Black were in trouble over the Timor Sea.

For the whole of that last watery spell, and even earlier, the Comet was flying on one engine. The second engine seized up somewhere before Timor itself. Mile after changeless mile came before their eyes in a hypnotic nothingness of sea and sky. Their remaining Gipsy Six engine held out.

At 11.08 a.m. GMT Scott and Black reached Darwin, having taken two days four and a half hours for the trip.

Now they knew they were being followed relentlessly. The Douglas DC2 was between Batavia and Rambang. The Boeing had left Alor Star for Singapore. The leaders lost two and a half hours at Darwin seeing to the engine trouble, before they could go on to Charleville. It would be too cruel to lose now, but they were all too aware that it was no use having reached Australia in record time. The race was still on. It was like a jockey assuming he would win when he was in the lead at Tattenham Corner.

Meanwhile many notable times were being put up by the slower planes. The Miles Hawk had passed Karachi; the DH Dragon was on its way there; the Airspeed Courier was bound for Baghdad. Parer and Hemsworth gave up in their Fairey Fox.

Further back still, the other Fairey Fox took off from Rome but crashed in Apulia and caught fire. Both Baines and Gilman were killed.

Now the news focused on the finish.

At 10.40 p.m. GMT Scott and Black scorched south-east across the Aboriginal winds of northern Australia at an average speed of 154 miles an hour to reach Charleville, 1,389 miles from Darwin.

The Douglas DC2 had not closed up and 1,000 miles and more still separated them from Scott and Black. In fact, the Boeing was gaining ground on the Dutchmen. Roscoe Turner and Pangborn in the Boeing left Singapore eight hours behind the Douglas DC2, but they were going to try and cut the gap by flying direct to Darwin. Cathcart-Jones and Waller in the second Comet had been placed somewhere between Allahabad and Singapore.

MacGregor and Walker in the Miles Hawk had got to Jodhpur.

But back in Australia, the excitement was passing fever-point. Scott and Black were on the last straight run, the 787 miles from Charleville to Melbourne.

Still flying steadily on one engine for much of the way, they covered those final miles efficiently, effortlessly – or so it seemed.

At 5.30 a.m. GMT, Monday, 23 October 1934, the De Havilland Comet 34 appeared over the Flemington Racecourse, Melbourne, the official finish of the great race. They made the regulation two circuits, landed at Essenden, were brought back to Flemington, and it was all over – bar the fantastic reception.

So Scott and Black had flown from Mildenhall to Melbourne in less than three days: two days, twenty-two hours and fifty-nine minutes.

After that it was simply a matter of waiting to see who would come second and third. The Douglas DC2 reached Charleville several hours after Scott and Black had won, but then the race took a dramatic turn. After leaving Charleville, they started going off course across the desert hinterland of Australia, and finally they had to make a forced landing at Albury racetrack. The Boeing was already heading for Charleville, but a long way behind.

The Dutch decided to play safe and wait for daylight. Then they faced the climax of their whole flight. They had to take off from the confined space of Albury racecourse, knowing that the race depended on it. Could the great Douglas DC2 do it? They were only an hour or so away from Melbourne – but if they failed they might as well still be at Mildenhall.

They got up safely from the short straight track and reached Melbourne second, with a Boeing coming in third.

What a race!

23

JEAN BATTEN
Four Famous Flights

Pretty and petite Jean Batten made not one but four famous flights. Perhaps more than any other pioneer, she sums up the spirit of those great, golden days.

Her first success was a flight to Australia, which nearly never took place at all. She had originally set out from Lympne airfield on 22 April 1934, but ran clean out of fuel over Italy. She had to come down in complete darkness near Rome and was lucky to get away without injury. That would have deterred many people, but not Jean.

A fortnight later, on 8 May 1934, this young New Zealander left Brooklands airfield at dawn to attempt to fly solo to Australia. She reached Rome safely this time but only rated a four-line paragraph in the papers to record the event.

Brindisi, Athens, Nicosia, Damascus, Baghdad, Karachi, Allahabad, Calcutta, Rangoon, Singapore, Batavia – these were the bare facts of her progress. Sandstorms around Baghdad had put her back a bit. It was only when she reached Batavia that public interest began to quicken. She arrived there in thirteen days and had six and a half days left to beat Amy Mollison's record for the flight of nineteen and a half days.

Next day she had got to Kupang. By then her clothes were very grimy as she had had to carry out her own repairs to the Gipsy Moth aeroplane at Kupang and Rambang.

This was in fact the same sort of aeroplane Amy Mollison used, Jean having the small added advantage of a turn and bank indicator. Apart from that, she had to endure the same extremes of fatigue and concentration. She saw the coast near Darwin after another couple of days from Kupang, chalking up the record time for a flight by a woman to Australia of fifteen days – four and a half days less than Amy Mollison.

Jean flew on down to Sydney and later visited her home in New Zealand. Then on 8 April 1935, she left Sydney in her little machine, named *Mascot*, to fly back to Britain, hoping to become the first woman to achieve the two-way trip.

Jean wanted to better her own time, of course, and seemed likely to do it for much of the return route, despite heavy headwinds the whole way after crossing the equator.

Her metal Gipsy Moth aeroplane had a Gipsy One engine of 100 horsepower, capable of cruising at a steady ninety miles an hour. In its open cockpit, Jean was exposed to the dust and heat of the tropics and to the cold at all heights over about 4,000 feet. She carried no radio, but navigated with her usual meticulous care across the Timor Sea.

When this veteran Gipsy Moth G-AARB was 250 miles out over the Timor Sea, flying at 6,000 feet, the engine suddenly stopped.

This was what fliers feared most. She was roughly half way across the gap between Australia and Timor, at the point of no return, and it didn't look as if she would be able to go forward or back – only down.

Jean kept her head and did a long, laboured glide down 4,000 feet. Only at 2,000 feet did the engine get going again. Jean did not recall breathing during that dramatic descent.

Tropical thunder and rain were the next items to vary the monotony of the flight. And the day after that, headwinds held her speed down to sixty miles an hour, a dangerously low air-speed.

Over the deserts of India and Iraq the heat was unbearable. Pumping the petrol began to blister her hands badly, and they got progressively worse.

Finally, she reached Littorio airport, Rome, on the afternoon of 25 April, having been forced to land for a short time while at Foggia because of engine trouble. This was the same trouble she had suffered at Athens before bridging the Adriatic.

Her time from Darwin was still ahead of her outward flight, but to better it she had to reach England before the following night of 26 April.

She was unlucky. Jean landed at Marignane, near Marseilles, about noon on 26 April, but was once more delayed, not only through engine trouble this time, but sheer bad luck. One of her tyres was cut by a piece of glass on the runway, putting her back still further. Even the weather took a hand, preventing a flight through the Rhone valley. She realized she could not take off from the Riviera that day, and so resigned herself to failing to outdo her own record of fifteen days.

Foul conditions around Dijon delayed her yet again, and she had to make an unscheduled stop at Abbeville.

Finally she crossed the Channel and jogged to a halt on the same runway which she had left nearly a year earlier. The flight had taken seventeen days fifteen hours and fifteen minutes.

Her hands were a mass of blisters and sores. She was glad it was over.

Jean's next quest was the record for the South Atlantic flight from West Africa to Port Natal, Brazil. Even before she began, she had to fly from England to Dakar. She left England on Armistice Day.

She took off from Port Thies, near Dakar, around dawn on 13 November 1935, in drizzling rain. It was far from tropical weather from that moment on. In fact, so dreary was the dawn that she had to invoke the aid of headlamps from two cars to illuminate the remote West African runway.

Flying a Percival Gull with a 200-horsepower Gipsy Six engine, Jean left the comfort of the coast behind her and headed out westward across the South Atlantic. This stretch of ocean seemed much more isolated than the busier northern route of the Atlantic. She knew she had to do it in a day: 13 November 1935 would be her day of triumph or death.

Flying at times as low as 600 feet, Jean ran slap into appalling air conditions. The Doldrums did not live up to their name that day. The storms seemed to start as soon as she was in them, and never let up for the rest of the long way west. The odd break did occur, but before she could take advantage of it, another one of the endless succession of storms hit her.

The little light aeroplane rattled and battled on. Jean began to wonder whether she had taken on just a bit more than she could cope with this time.

Despite her preoccupation with the weather, she had time to realize that she had never, could never, feel lonelier. She felt more on her own than she believed it was possible for anyone ever to imagine. She was the only human being over this million square miles of sea. If the plane faltered now . . .

Her spirits at the lowest ebb, Jean found herself flying as if blind-folded through one of the major disruptions. The storm was so savage that she fell lower than 600 feet, and then lower still.

Suddenly the only compass she had started to go haywire.

The needle swivelled senselessly through 180 degrees. She felt all was lost without its guidance.

If she could not rely on that, what could she do? She wrestled with the facts. All her mental and physical faculties were being extended to the extreme. It was worse than anything on either of the Australian flights. Almost always when over land there was some hope of a successful forced descent, but here landing would mean certain death.

Jean just had to trust her other instruments and fly on; to try to weather the blows being fisted at her. Finally she came out of the most violent gale and rain, and the compass gradually swung back to normal of its own accord. She breathed a soul-felt sigh of relief. The only explanation she could think of was that some electrical disturbances in the Doldrums must have played havoc with the balance of the compass. Anyway, it was over and she flew on.

Jean Batten landed at Port Natal, Brazil, thirteen hours and fifteen minutes after taking off through that West African drizzle. She had beaten the previous best solo time by three-and-a-quarter hours.

From there she flew on to Rio, but had not arrived by the evening of 14 November. A ghastly few hours passed before news came of her. Could she be lost after having succeeded in her transatlantic flight? That was the kind of irony that so commonly cut down famous pilots: they survived the worst ordeals to perish in some minor mishap.

A Brazilian military plane was sent to search for her near the city, and the Pan-American *Puerto Rican Clipper* made a detour to try and trace her. This was wild country.

That morning of 14 November, Jean left Port Natal on schedule but ran right out of fuel when still 175 miles north-east of Rio de Janeiro. Hugging the coast, she came down low near the town of Araruama, and force-landed in a steaming swamp.

She did not fancy staying on this doubtful ground, so tried to taxi to what she thought would be a safer spot. In making this manoeuvre, the airscrew struck a heap of sand and became bent, so that Jean could not take off at all. That evening she telephoned to Rio to report that she was well, and she spent the night at a fisherman's hut. She

174

was picked up next day, looking smart in her white flying suit, by a military machine.

So her flight set up three new records. The crossing was the fastest for the South Atlantic; she was the first woman ever to fly across it; and her time from Lympne to Port Natal also represented a record.

She was the victim of another minor mishap in a straightforward flight soon after this. Jean had taken delivery of her aeroplane when it was landed by boat at Southampton from South America and set out to fly to London.

On her flight on 29 December she experienced coil trouble and had to make a hurried forced landing near the South Downs. Aiming for a field at Bepton, near Midhurst, Jean just managed to clear a wood, but struck the top of a low hedge bordering the field.

Fortunately the hedge gave way, but as she came down the under-carriage was damaged. The impact of landing gave her concussion and shock, and she had to receive treatment. Her injuries were not serious, but the incident serves to illustrate how easily an accident can happen.

On 5 October 1936, Jean Batten left Lympne, Kent, on her longest flight – to her home in New Zealand. She was also aiming to beat Broadbent's record for the solo flight from England to Australia.

At Kupang, the final stop before Darwin, she was over a day ahead of this record, allowing an average time for her to cross the Timor Sea. But then a dramatic fault threatened to delay her. There were no spare parts at Kupang, so if an aeroplane sustained damage that could not be repaired, the stoppage could last for days.

As Jean was taking off, a tail tyre suddenly punctured. The split was a serious one, not capable of being patched like an inner tube of a car tyre.

'What on earth can I do?' Jean wondered aloud to the aerodrome officials.

Then one of them had a brainwave, and successfully stuffed a collection of face sponges into the hole!

Jean took off again, complete with the sponges, crossed the Timor Sea, and got to Darwin in the record solo time of five days twenty-one hours and three minutes. Broadbent had taken six days twenty-one hours and nineteen minutes. So she had beaten the record by a clear day.

But that wasn't the end of it. Despite concern in Australia at her idea of flying the Tasman Sea in a single-engine plane, Jean still signified her intention to go ahead with the original plan to reach New Zealand. With that in mind she headed on for Charleville and Sydney, reaching the latter on 13 October.

The local air authorities still said the Tasman Sea venture was 'over-hazardous'; Jean still said she was going to do it, though she did concede that she should have her engine thoroughly overhauled first. Jean could also expect compass trouble between Australia and New Zealand, due to notable magnetic disturbances. She remembered her recent South Atlantic worries over this question. There always seemed to be problems with the compass over the sea.

Jean took off from Richmond, forty miles out of Sydney, on 16 October, hoping to land in her home country in about eight hours or so. The forecasted westerly winds would help her if they materialized.

She made it. Her actual time for crossing the Tasman Sea was nine and a half hours, and the total time from Richmond to Mangere aerodrome, Auckland, was ten-and-a-half hours. She had beaten the previous best time for the Tasman Sea crossing. Her overall time from England to New Zealand was eleven days fifty-six minutes. She had achieved the first direct flight from England to New Zealand. It seemed especially appropriate that a New Zealander had done it. Jean was also the first woman to fly the Tasman Sea.

It seemed that Jean had learned a lot from her former misfortunes. Before her long-distance triumphs, Jean was known more by her failures. She had once pancaked precariously into a farm, and on another occasion she had been rescued ingloriously by camels in Baluchistan!

Yet now, in October 1936, she had completed the crossing of the lonely Tasman Sea to bring Britain into direct air contact with her furthermost dominion.

Jean Batten deserved every honour that was accorded her after her four famous flights.

24

BERYL MARKHAM
Crash Landing in Nova Scotia

Storms raged above the dark Atlantic as the slim silver and peacock-blue monoplane droned due westward. Suddenly its engine spluttered, coughed – and died. Only 2,000 feet of air separated blonde Beryl Markham from the inky-black ocean below.

She glanced at her watch. It was 10.35 p.m. She knew that the cabin petrol tank should have lasted four hours, and that she had taken off only three hours and forty minutes earlier, but the tank was empty.

She had made up her mind to be the first person to fly the Atlantic westward, from England to North America, alone. Only Jim Mollison had done it before – and he had started from Ireland. He had given Beryl his watch before she took off with the warning: 'Don't get it wet!' She hoped she wouldn't.

Apart from Jim's watch, she had a sprig of heather for luck. The only other personal things she carried were three vacuum flasks filled with black coffee, some cold chicken, a bag of fruit and nuts and some notepaper.

Beryl had taken off at 6.55 p.m. on 4 September 1936 in her Percival Vega Gull aeroplane *Messenger*. Its Gipsy engine would fly it at 150 miles an hour without headwinds. She chose Abingdon aerodrome in Berkshire for her take-off, as it had one of the longest runways in the country.

Watched by a crowd of reporters and photographers, the propeller of the little plane spun. The evening sun flashed on the fuselage as it jolted over the runway. Weighed down with a massive load of petrol, the aeroplane taxied towards the trees fringing the aerodrome.

'She'll never get up', someone whispered.

But she did, clearing the silhouetted trees by only a few feet. The great volume of fuel was calculated to last a full twenty-four hours. Whether that would be enough to carry Beryl across the Atlantic depended on the strength of the winds she met.

The crossing from east to west was a very different matter from flying the Atlantic the other way – from North America to England – when the pilot normally had tail winds.

Now Beryl was all alone, flying into the sunset. Her cramped cabin would be the limits of her world for the next night and day.

She was aiming for New York, 3,000 miles away. Almost before she had realized it, Beryl had left England, Wales and the Irish Sea behind her.

Broken clouds were scattering drizzle down on Ireland. Through the rainy dusk, she saw the blurred lights of Cork. Then, as the moon dodged behind the thickening cloud, night closed in. She saw Berehaven lighthouse – the very last link with land this side of the Atlantic.

Beryl flew on blind through the wind, the rain and the night, relying on her altimeter and artificial horizon to keep her level at 2,000 feet.

She had no such refinements as radar or radio, yet she was no longer afraid, as she had been during those long days of waiting for the right weather. Not that this was good flying weather. She was heading straight into a forty-mile-an-hour wind which cut down her speed.

At 10.35 p.m. the engine died. The wings quivered in the wind, and as the engine cut out, the wind was all Beryl could hear. The absence of the comforting drone of the engine jerked her to life.

When an aeroplane stalls, the natural reaction is to pull back the stick to try to climb, but this is wrong. Beryl dipped the nose of the little Gull towards the unseen waterline, and in a few seconds her altitude dropped from 2,000 to 1,000 feet.

She knew she had to reach the cock of the reserve petrol tank to feed fresh fuel to the engine before it was too late. But before she could turn the cock, she had to find a torch. Beryl groped around in the gloom of the cabin. Her fingers closed around the metal torch and switched it on. She quickly flashed the beam around to locate the cock. The altimeter read 300 feet. Each second it was moving nearer to zero.

At 200 feet she found the cock and turned it.

Only 150 feet above the swirling sea, the petrol flooded through and the motor choked, croaked and exploded into life again, like a

178

man who has just won a battle for breath. Muttering a prayer of thanks, she climbed up into the raging storm again, up to 2,000 feet: she had survived the first crisis.

She flew on, through the miles and the hours of watery darkness. Buffeting headwinds drove the rain straight at the frail-looking cabin. Beryl sat with her hands on the stick, battling to keep the aeroplane level.

With her free hand, she tried to pour out the last flask of coffee into a jug balanced on the floor, but a sudden jerk overturned the jug and the coffee was spilt. That depressed her more than anything else on the flight.

Hour after hour, she watched the needle on the luminous dial of the altimeter flickering like some erratic pulse. The point of no return came and went. Beryl thought of her seven-year-old son, Gerald, asleep in his bed at home.

The storm stayed. Then came dawn, lazing up behind her as the plane droned on westward. Nothing much more happened during the morning. She nibbled some fruit and nuts, all she had left to eat. The tiny cabin allowed her to move her long legs only a matter of inches, and she began to feel twinges of cramp, a hazard she had not bargained for.

At 1 p.m. on 5 September, an officer on the Holland-America liner, *Spaarndam*, pointed to the sky. 'Look – Mrs Markham', he said to the man at his side.

They reported by radio that they had seen the speck of her aeroplane about 220 miles east of St Johns, Newfoundland.

She had been flying blind for virtually the whole of her trip. After seventeen hours alone in her cabin she felt frozen and her limbs refused to react promptly. The cold, cramp and petrol fumes were nearly overpowering her. She had to fight off unconsciousness.

Her eyelids started to droop but she jerked herself awake again, shivering. Sleep meant death. Although exhausted and icy cold, she had to go on if she wanted to live.

Ice filmed over the glass of the cabin, adding another hazard.

At 2.04 p.m., the Swedish liner *Kungsholm* reported to the world: 'Plane sighted 60 miles east of Cape Race, Newfoundland.'

So the 2,000-mile stretch over the Atlantic was nearly over when she ran into the fog.

That, and the iced-up glass cut Beryl off entirely from the world outside her cabin. She could not distinguish between the fog and the sea as she peered at the misty banks below. At 2.30 p.m., she was straining her eyes to see land. She reckoned that the Newfoundland coast must be visible soon – and then she spotted it through a gap in the fog. But a moment later it had gone.

For endless minutes she saw nothing more till she began to wonder if she had imagined those ghostly cliffs etched on the shrouded skyline.

At 2.35 p.m. they spotted her over St Johns.

She had reached Newfoundland in nineteen hours forty minutes.

St Johns lay below like a ghost town. She adjusted her course accordingly: first, south to Cape Race, then west to Sydney, on Cape Breton Island.

This was 1936, so Beryl had to work out her course by protractor, compass and map. Somehow she managed to juggle these navigation instruments on her lap, at the same time keeping the stick steady and sparing an eye for the control panel.

Despite the weather and her fatigue, she suddenly felt better. On a southerly course, she passed over Renews, forty-five miles south of St Johns, a quarter of an hour later.

Through the notorious Newfoundland mists she glimpsed the Cape Race lighthouse. An hour after being reported over St Johns, she was out among the Atlantic rollers again, ten miles off Cape Race.

Beryl Markham had one more long hop to fly, the 300-odd miles across the vast jaws of the St Lawrence to Sydney.

After that, she would have land beneath her nearly all the way and it would be fairly plain flying – or so she hoped. As if to add to her sense of well-being, a following wind arose, and the drone of the engine was soothing.

Suddenly, the engine shuddered.

She was still nearly 100 miles from Cape Breton Island. The faithful Gipsy engine belched black exhaust, ominous against the blue-grey and white sea.

Beryl thought urgently: 'Must be an airlock.' She tried to clear it, frantically turning all the cocks on and off, on and off. They had sharp handles, which cut her hands. Slowly the needle on the altimeter fell as Beryl wrestled with the stick and coaxed the controls to try to keep the Gull airborne.

But the aeroplane was falling fast. In fact, the last petrol tank was nearly empty.

The engine was cutting out and restarting continuously now. It barely managed to support the aeroplane over the water. It struggled on for nearly half an hour, getting more erratic all the time.

Could this be the end? It would be heartbreaking for her to fail now, for suddenly she spotted Cape Breton Island, forty miles ahead.

She reckoned all tanks were about empty now, and she prayed that there was enough fuel in the pipes to take her those last miles.

Time was punctuated by the engine's faltering, knocking notes as, desperately slowly, she drew nearer and nearer to the land.

'I never felt closer to death than when I looked down on Cape Breton coastline barely keeping itself airborne.' Then, like a seabird which has sought and found a place to die, its engine gave a last convulsive cough – and died. Beryl had to land. But all she could see was a wild landscape of black ground broken by huge boulders.

The island swelled up at her as she struggled to twist the aeroplane free of the strange coastline below. Amid the ragged rocks, she saw what looked like a field. She had no choice, the Gull had to ground there. And moments later it crash-landed.

Beryl held her breath as the plane hit. The 'field' was a boulder-strewn swamp and the Gull's nose ploughed forty feet through the mud.

The propeller snapped off and the port wing sank into the bog. The engine was shattered. The aeroplane juddered to a stop with its tail reared in the air. Beryl hit her forehead on the windscreen and blood gushed down her face.

As her aeroplane began to sink slowly into the bog at Baleine Cove, Beryl somehow stumbled clear of the wrecked cabin and collapsed.

An hour later, three fishermen found her waist-deep in mud, holding her face in her hands, just 150 yards from the booming Atlantic breakers.

It was still less than twenty-four hours since she had taken off from Abingdon. She had succeeded in flying the Atlantic alone.

Jim Mollison's watch was still ticking.

'Don't get it wet', he had told her. She hadn't.

25

SCOTT AND GUTHRIE

The Johannesburg Air Race

The thrill of an air race is undeniable. One of the most imaginative in the years between the wars was the Portsmouth–Johannesburg £10,000 Schlesinger African Air Race.

Nine aircraft eventually started the race, which was to be handicapped. As it turned out, this levelling device was not necessary to determine the result. The idea was for the aeroplanes all to take off virtually together, or at one-minute intervals, and for the time adjustments to be made when they reached Cairo. The length of the flight was 6,150 miles.

These were the nine entrants:

BA Eagle, Alington and Booth
Double Eagle, Rose
Envoy, Findlay and Waller
Hawk Six, Clouston
Mew Gull, Halse
Mew Gull, Miller
Sparrow Hawk, Smith
Vega Gull, Llewellyn
Vega Gull, Scott and Guthrie

At 6.30 a.m. on 29 September 1936, just three years before the war, the first of the nine machines started to shudder across Portsmouth airport in the clear coastal light. As dawn edged brighter over Langstone Harbour and Hayling Island, the mutter of many engines disturbed the morning air and Findlay and Waller's large Envoy aeroplane led the way into the turquoise sky.

182

But out of these nine aeroplanes competing for the £10,000 prize, only one actually completed the course to Johannesburg.

Once they had faded south-eastward, people could only wait for news from the first checkpoint, Belgrade. The handicaps, incidentally, ranged from the scratch allowance of Halse in his Mew Gull to Alington and Booth's twenty-one hours fifty-eight minutes twelve seconds. The former plane had a formula speed of 200.86 miles an hour, the latter only 116.93 miles an hour. The rest lay between these extremes, with Miller's Mew Gull rated at almost exactly the same scratch figure as Halse.

The first real news of the nine came when Flight Lieutenant Tommy Rose had some fuel feed difficulties and had to lose time by landing his Double Eagle at Linz to put it right. The delay did not set him back too much and he was reported at Vienna a little later.

Yugoslavia was as excited as Britain at the prospect of being on the route of the remarkable race. Belgrade airport was humming with activity all morning waiting for the first aeroplane to show up out of the north-west sky. Which would it be? The weather was still fine and clear, though the prospects indicated rain as the day wore on.

By noon the atmosphere had become electric. Then at 12.08 p.m. a Mew Gull winged overhead. As both of the Mew Gulls in the race were capable of 200 miles an hour it was not surprising that one led the field at this stage. The brilliant red tone of the body identified it as Halse's machine. While the petrol flowed into his tank he gulped down coffee and munched sandwiches, answering questions between bites.

At 12.32 p.m., just twenty-four minutes after landing, Halse took off again with a useful lead. He felt especially pleased that Miller had not landed in the other Mew Gull by the time he had left. Already people were beginning to wonder where Miller had got to.

At 12.42 p.m. Clouston touched down in his Hawk Six, and took off again in the staggeringly short time of twelve minutes. He was not away, though, before the third of the aeroplanes appeared.

'Still not Miller', people were saying.

It was Findlay and Waller in the large Envoy that had left Portsmouth first. This aeroplane was carrying a crew of four, which gave the crew the chance of streamlining the various duties both in the air and on the ground. Despite this asset, they were set back ten minutes by a minor fault in the starboard engine. At 1.16 p.m. Waller was satisfied and they were off.

Meanwhile in the lull while waiting for the next arrivals, Belgrade airport heard from Vienna that both Tommy Rose in his Double Eagle and Llewellyn flying one of the two Vega Gulls had come and gone.

Forty-eight minutes ticked on as the spectators scanned an empty sky, now filling with clouds. Only five aeroplanes had been accounted for, and two of these had yet to reach Belgrade. The main worry was for Miller in the other Mew Gull, which would have more or less used all its fuel by this time.

Victor Smith in his Sparrow Hawk landed at 2.04 p.m., looking frozen from his hours in an exposed cockpit. He was not even wearing an overcoat or extra flying jacket. Someone lent him a leather jacket at Belgrade, which saved the situation for him.

C.W.A. Scott and Giles Guthrie checked in at 2.08 p.m. with the first of the Vega Gulls.

By 2.15 p.m. the weather had broken, with rain soaking into the airfield, spattering off the runway. It was then that they saw Tommy Rose overhead in his Double Eagle. He had arranged to circle the aerodrome to report his presence there and then fly straight on to Athens. He did this, but a minute or two later he reappeared over Belgrade, having decided to get the weather forecast for further down the Balkans.

Just before Scott and Guthrie left, the other Vega Gull landed through the rain to bring Llewellyn in to report at 2.23 p.m. It was just a couple of minutes after this, in fact, that not only Scott and Guthrie but Victor Smith also took off for Athens.

Since the Scott and Guthrie team and Llewellyn were both in machines carrying a comfortable handicap, they were well placed. It seemed that the race might develop into a scrap between them. Llewellyn cut his time on the ground to a mere thirteen minutes and so when he wobbled up into a fresh crosswind, he was only eleven minutes behind his rivals. Rose, meanwhile, received his weather forecast, decided he had plenty of petrol, and continued in the Double Eagle.

So now seven aeroplanes had reported and two were still adrift. During the long afternoon at Belgrade, the organizers got word that the aeroplane having the advantage of the biggest handicap, the BA Eagle flown by Alington and Booth, had had to make a forced landing in the wilds of Bavaria near Regensburg. In doing so, the clatter over the broken ground damaged the undercarriage and they were out of the race.

The last of the competitors unaccounted for one way or another was still Miller. Belgrade knew nothing, nor did London. He should have been in Yugoslavia hours earlier than this in his fast Mew Gull. All afternoon they searched the sky, now completely covered in cloud, for the white-painted plane.

Finally at 4.24 p.m. it calmly came in from the west.

'What happened to you?' came the chorus of questions to Miller as soon as he had got out of the cockpit. They were all relieved but anxious to learn what on earth had delayed a 200-mile-an-hour machine for this time. All the others still in the race were well on their way to Athens, or had already got there.

The answer was simple and sad. Miller had flown to within thirty miles or so of Belgrade airport and then been forced to ground as he had run right out of fuel. As this was Yugoslavia, no telephone existed in the outlying area he had chosen. Miller had been mortified to see three rival aeroplanes passing quite low over his fuelless machine and although he waved feverishly no one spotted him.

The wait was a long one, too, for it took him over four hours to get a dozen gallons of petrol to take him on to the check point. Between noon and 4.15 p.m. he had been begging the Yugoslavs for petrol and when it appeared it could not be described as high-octane by any stretch of the imagination. Ten minutes later he was at Belgrade airport telling his sorry story. The sadder ending was that Miller withdrew from the race as the Mew Gull seemed to be using much more fuel than he had expected, and he might run out repeatedly.

On they flew past Athens to Almaza airport, Cairo. Here the order was still the same as when the leading three left Belgrade.

Halse brought the scarlet Mew Gull down on African soil at 7.07 p.m. Clouston was a fraction over half an hour later at 7.39 p.m. Findlay and Waller brought up the third place another half hour behind that, at 8.08 p.m.

So a mere hour separated the three leaders after the Portsmouth–Belgrade–Cairo stage of 2,249 miles. Halse in his Mew Gull had spanned this considerable distance in something like twelve-and-a-half hours, averaging around 180 miles an hour. Little wonder the Mew Gull was scratch in the handicap ratings.

Three hours after Findlay and Waller, Scott and Guthrie clocked in just four minutes ahead of Llewellyn. So the Vega Gull rivalry had hotted up to an amazing degree, especially as Llewellyn had a thirteen-minute handicap advantage over his colleagues in their sister machine.

So five had got to Cairo, two were out of it, and two remained to reach Cairo. The hop across the Mediterranean might have meant disaster. Until news came, no one could tell. Tommy Rose had not left his troubles at Linz. His Double Eagle was having a harrowing time and so was he. A succession of air locks in the fuel system threatened all across Europe to finish his part in the race. He had landed at a small string of unscheduled stops since setting out that morning. Already the dawn take-off seemed weeks distant.

Finally Tommy Rose coddled the Double Eagle over the sea to reach Almaza. He signalled to his co-flier, Bagshaw, in the other cockpit, and they came down to land at Cairo airport. As the machine taxied across the Egyptian field, one of its undercarriage legs crumpled and collapsed.

Rose brought the aeroplane to a halt all right, but the damage would take time to rectify, and time was what Rose could not spare, so he gave up, never imagining that in fact he might still have had a chance however long it took to repair.

There were six competitors left.

Victor Smith had had to come down at Skopje, between Belgrade and Salonika, with oil tank trouble. Much later he made Cairo safely, but was losing a lot of ground he would be unlikely to recover – especially with a persistent fault.

Meanwhile the five leaders forged south for Khartoum. Still scarcely an hour parted the first three, Halse, Clouston, Findlay and Waller.

The pace was gruelling. Something had to give, and at Khartoum it did. The engine of Clouston's Hawk Six seized up. It was not an unsurmountable accident, but the time delay would probably forfeit him any chance of victory.

Halse seemed to be drawing away from the field now. He had got to Khartoum under an hour ahead of Clouston, who flew much the slower aeroplane. So Captain S.S. Halse was in the lead and Clouston had come to grief, or at least his engine had.

Who would take over second and third places now?

It was like some gigantic horse race run over a 6,150-mile

course, a Grand National of the air with half the hurdles already covered.

Llewellyn touched down a mere two minutes ahead of Scott and Guthrie. The two Vega Gulls were neck and neck. Attention still naturally focused on the first aeroplane, though, and Halse continued to set a scorching rate southward. It seemed almost a formality that he would win. But as with horse races, the result was always in doubt right until the winning post.

Findlay and Waller ran into trouble 300 miles north of Khartoum, necessitating a forced landing for fuel in the inhospitable region between Wadi Halfa and Kareima. They reported at Khartoum that night, though, a while after dark.

Halse left Kisumu about 8 a.m. on the second day.

The rivals in their respective Vega Gull aircraft were still slogging it out, only a few miles apart.

By midday on the second day, Halse was still comfortably ahead, having passed Mbeya, in Tanganyika. He seemed certain to win, or at least arrive first.

Meanwhile Victor Smith was still dogged by the bad luck of the oil-tank trouble and he fumed at Salonika, with his engine practically choked with oil. Clouston, too, was still delayed at Khartoum awaiting a sparc piston. Victor Smith did eventually get as far as Khartoum, a remarkable achievement in the circumstances, but as far as the race was concerned he was virtually out of it.

The toll was mounting all the time. Next followed one of the shocks of the race. Halse was getting tired by the time he approached Salisbury. Twenty miles short of the town, he started trying to identify the airfield, but smoke from veldfires was camouflaging the landscape and the air was very bumpy. He decided to come down in a field at Bomboshaw.

The light was ebbing fast now and he wanted to land quickly. As the aeroplane touched down, it tumbled over on to its back. Halse dislocated his shoulder and received other minor knocks. The aeroplane was badly hit, however, and he had to abandon any idea of finishing the flight.

Scott and Guthrie had leaped from fourth to first place in a matter of hours. While Halse was meeting disaster, they had flown from Khartoum to Kisumu. The other Vega Gull, however, had taken the more conventional and less dangerous route to Juba west of their course.

Scott and Guthrie left Kisumu at 1.30 p.m. that second afternoon and got to Abercorn some six hours later.

The other Vega Gull refuelled on schedule at Juba, flew over Entebbe at 2.15 p.m. and was not reported again for a long time. Findlay and Waller were still in the race with the remarkable Envoy, reaching Entebbe by the end of that day.

On the third day Scott and Guthrie left Abercorn at 3.45 p.m. for the final long hop down to the Rand Airport, Germiston, Johannesburg. The sun rose as they sped southward. By 8.30 a.m. the population of Bulawayo saw the Vega Gull winging on its way with only 450 miles to go to the finish. The race had more shocks in store yet, though.

Llewellyn and his colleague came down low trying to find Abercorn aerodrome, with their fuel almost all expended. The combination of bad weather and lack of fuel forced them into an emergency – and the second Vega Gull crash-landed.

There were three aeroplanes left in the race; Scott and Guthrie in the other Vega Gull, Findlay and Waller flying the Envoy and Clouston still at Khartoum.

Clouston did in fact later fit his spare piston and fly on gamely to Entebbe, 2,300 miles from the start. Then he took off with the prospect of bad weather ahead and was overdue for quite a time before they found him some 150 miles south of Salisbury with the wreckage of his Hawk Six. He was still smiling, perhaps simply glad to be alive.

So to the dramatic finale, between the remaining two competitors.

As Scott and Guthrie battled on south beyond Bulawayo, Findlay and Waller had left Entebbe at 5.41 a.m. for Abercorn, Northern Rhodesia. They landed there safely in miserable misty cloud.

The wind veered so that if they wanted to fly straight on they would have to take off up a slope towards a cluster of trees. The Envoy made the run uphill but failed to get enough lift. It caught the tops of the trees and crashed.

Captain Max Findlay and Mr A.H. Morgan, the wireless operator, were killed. Ken Waller and their passenger, Derek Peachey, were slightly injured.

So then there was one.

Scott and Guthrie sailed supremely on, landing at Germiston at 11.34 a.m. They had done the 6,150-mile flight in two days four hours fifty-seven minutes. This represented a flying average of 156.3 miles an hour and an overall average of about 116 miles an hour.

So C.W.A. Scott had won not only the Melbourne Air Race, but the Johannesburg one as well. It was a wonderful triumph.

26

SYDNEY CAMM

Birth of the Hurricane

The Hurricane story began in 1933, only six years before the war and seven before the Battle of Britain. The Royal Air Force then was equipped with just thirteen fighter squadrons – eight with Bristol Bulldogs, three with Hawker Furies and two with Hawker Demons. All were biplanes, with fixed propellers and undercarriages.

Monoplanes were not unknown during the 1920s. Sydney Camm – the Hurricane's designer – had evolved one, which was never built. The idea of the Hurricane was born in August 1933, when Camm talked to government officials about the way fighter design might develop; in particular, the idea of the Hawker Fury in monoplane form. At that stage, Camm could not present any drawings of his scheme, but by October 1933 he had submitted a first design to the Air Ministry. This early Fury Monoplane conception incorporated a Goshawk engine, but by January 1934 it was superseded by a Rolls Royce PV12. Further design improvements incorporated a retractable undercarriage.

By May 1934, the Interceptor Monoplane, as it was now known, was designed in detail, with loaded weight assessed at 4,600 pounds. Armament consisted of a couple of wing-mounted Browning guns and two fuselage-mounted Vickers guns.

As Nazi Germany rearmed, a weapon took shape that would help thwart Hitler's plans. A one-tenth scale model of the Hurricane was constructed in June 1934 and like so many other inventions before and since, it went to Teddington for trials at the National Physical Laboratory. The vital basic aerodynamic qualities were confirmed to be in order by August in a series of wind-tunnel tests providing the equivalent of speeds up to 350 mph.

A government specification emerged at the end of August. It stipulated a single-seat interceptor fighter with a top speed of 320 mph in level flight at 15,000 feet.

Though all concerned had moved fast, time was still vital. By December 1934 a wooden mock-up of the F36/34 single-seat fighter high-speed monoplane was in existence. The next significant date was 21 February 1935, when the Air Ministry received its initial performance details. The specification had been met. The monoplane could reach a top speed of 330 mph in level flight at 15,000 feet, with a flying weight calculated at 4,480 pounds. The altitude provision was for a 32,500 feet service ceiling and 34,800 feet absolute maximum. The landing speed was just over seventy mph. At this stage, further investigation was to be undertaken into the possibility of providing metal stressed-skin wings and also stepping up the armament. It was to be wartime before production aircraft actually incorporated the metal wing.

In August 1935 the first prototype was under way, with a new PV12 Merlin engine. An increase to eight guns meant that the flying weight rose to 5,200 pounds. Hawkers had an assembly shed at Brooklands racing car track in Surrey. Here the prototype pieces were taken on 23 October 1935 and assembled.

The necessary ground tests were carried out; undercarriage retraction, engine running, taxi trials. In aircraft design, no one can ever be quite sure how the actual centre of gravity will compare with the calculations, but it turned out that Sydney Camm's had been accurate to within half an inch.

On 6 November 1935, Flight Lieutenant P.W.S. Bulman, chief test pilot of Hawkers at the time, closed the cockpit of the prototype. A closed cockpit was itself an invention, previous fighters being equipped with open ones. The small silver monoplane took off for the first fight, climbing off a grass strip that was surrounded by the banked curves of the racing car track. No one in Britain realized then the significance of this date: the first flight of the Hurricane.

All went well on the early tests, and on 7 February 1936 Bulman was able to recommend the fighter as being ready for Royal Air Force evaluation, three months and one day after the maiden flight. This was a tribute to Sydney Camm's design.

The two other pilots involved in the early flight programme were Philip Lucas, who flew some of the experimental work, and John Hindmarsh, who later conducted the firm's production flight trials.

This first prototype went to the RAF Experimental Establishment, Martlesham Heath in Suffolk.

On 3 June 1936, Hawkers accepted a contract to construct 600 aircraft. Not a day was wasted, and within a week they had issued fuselage manufacturing drawings. Soon after this, the Hurricane received official approval from the Air Ministry. Never before had such a sizeable order been given in peacetime. It might be said that this order, rather than the Battle of Britain itself, was the turning point in history.

In the course of production, the firm had to provide for a number of modifications. As a result of rigorous tests by the RAF of the original prototype, several snags had appeared. During these 1937 flights simulating high-speed combat duties, canopies were actually lost on five occasions. This trouble was cured by the following spring.

The first production model, now with a Merlin II engine, made its maiden flight on 12 October 1937. Seven weeks later, seven were in the air. Production was increasing to the rate of thirty a month. The Merlin II engine change had put the overall production programme back. This scheme had originally envisaged 500 Hurricanes and 300 Spitfires in service by March 1939.

The first four Hurricanes for the Royal Air Force reached 11 Squadron at Northolt during December 1937 and a dozen more came in January and February 1938. The British public became dramatically aware of their new super-fighter, the Hurricane, when Squadron Leader J. Gillan, commanding officer of 111 Squadron, took off on 10 February 1938 from Turnhouse, Edinburgh, just after five o'clock on a gloomy and wild winter dusk. Gillan ascended to an altitude of 17,000 feet and flew over the clouds without the aid of oxygen. An eighty mph wind whistled him southwards at a great speed. About forty minutes later, he dipped his Hurricane into a dive, registering an airspeed of 380 mph. Once below the cloud, he made out Northolt airport in the early night darkness – 'startled at the realisation that the ground speed was likely to be in the region of 450 m.p.h.' The statistics for the flight were: 327 miles from Turnhouse to Northolt in forty-eight minutes at an average ground speed of 408.75 mph.

The Hurricane far outstripped anything that came before it. And as the international situation became more menacing, the British people derived reassurance from these squat but effective-looking shapes snarling above them through the skies.

By the spring of 1938, Kenley was the second RAF station to see Hurricanes, when 3 Squadron got its quota of eighteen. The strength of a squadron in the air was twelve, its total strength eighteen. The six extra aircraft were known as IR or Immediate Reserve – held as instant replacements for unserviceable aircraft. When production increased, the IR numbered nine, giving a total squadron strength of twenty-one aircraft.

By September 1938 – the time of the Munich crisis – five RAF squadrons had received Hurricane fighters. Deliveries of the Spitfire were only just starting. Perhaps it was as well for the future that the war did not break out then instead of 1939. From the point of view of Britain's air power, the extra respite given by Chamberlain's appeasement of Hitler at Munich was vital. The intervening year enabled the Royal Air Force to double the Fighter Command strength. From the total of nearly 500 Hurricanes actually delivered to squadrons and to the reserve, about three-quarters had been built in that crucial year. When war started on 3 September 1939, eighteen squadrons of RAF Fighter Command were equipped with Hurricanes.

27

R.J. MITCHELL
Birth of the Spitfire

The Spitfire was descended from a famous dynasty of seaplanes. These were competitors in the Schneider Trophy, the international contest for the aeroplane with the fastest average speed over a set course. Any country winning three times in a row would keep the trophy.

The direct ancestor of the Spitfire made an inauspicious debut. R.J. Mitchell was Supermarine's designer. He invented the S.4 monoplane seaplane for the 1926 competition and it quickly captured the world speed record at 226.75 mph before the actual contest. Hopes were high for the trophy but the S.4 crashed in advance of the competition taking place.

The Schneider Trophy was now the focus of intense international interest and considerable national prestige was attached to it. However, the costs of preparing for it were well beyond the resources of a commercial company. The result was that the British government decided to finance the country's 1927 effort.

In September 1927, Royal Air Force personnel formed the British Schneider Trophy team. This time the contest was to be held at Venice. The British set out with three S.5 seaplanes, developed from the S.4. Two of these were the only competitors to finish the course – and win the Trophy for Britain at speeds of 281.656 and 273.47 mph respectively.

The next Schneider Trophy year was 1929. By that time, Vickers (Aviation) Ltd had taken over R.J. Mitchell's original firm of Supermarine – and he went with it. With the endorsement of the Air Ministry for the Schneider Trophy, the S.6 went into design and production. These early seaplanes certainly had an ephemeral life, being born, flying, and dying often in a matter of months.

Mitchell made a change to Rolls Royce engines for his new project, giving the famous makers only six months for the job. This S.6 design followed the lines of the S.5 but with the new make of engine.

The venue for the eleventh Schneider Trophy event was Spithead, off the Hampshire coast, on 7 September 1929. The British entry looked like being two S.6 models and a couple of Gloster VI seaplanes but both the Gloster monoplane designs had to be withdrawn due to development trouble. So the two S.6s designed by Mitchell faced the only foreign competition; the redoubtable Macchi seaplanes from Italy.

The day before the race a dramatic snag arose. After all the workmen had left for the day, a Rolls Royce engineer discovered that as a result of a seized piston, the cylinder had been scored. A new block had to be fitted. The local police traced the men, recalled them to the workshops, and actually gave them lifts to get there. By working all through the night, the job was done and the S.6 prepared for flight by 10.30 a.m. – shortly before the race.

The British pilot in the race was Flight Lieutenant H.R.D. Waghorn. When he was approaching (as he thought) the last of his seven circuits of fifty kilometres each, his engine failed. It gave out near Cowes and so he alighted on the water off Old Castle Point, some miles from the finish. In fact he had miscounted the number of circuits – this last one was the eighth. He had already won the trophy at an average speed of 328.63 mph. The other S.6 had suffered a navigational mishap earlier on. A short while afterwards, Squadron Leader A.H. Orlebar also in an S.6 raised the world's speed record twice – to 336.3 mph and again to 357.7 mph.

So Britain had won the Schneider Trophy twice. A third victory and it would be hers permanently. But in the bleak economic climate of 1931 the British government refused further support. A private sponsor appeared in the person of Lady Houston, who offered £100,000 funding. Mitchell had no time to start on something entirely fresh, so he improved the S.6 into the S.6B.

This time the British had no competitors. The entries prepared by the Italians and French literally could not get off the water. The Americans had already opted out of the contest some years earlier. So the British were the only starters. They only needed to complete the course to gain the Schneider Trophy outright.

On 13 September 1931 thousands of people lined the coast and thronged the piers at Southsea, Gosport and elsewhere. I was one of them! Flight Lieutenant J.W. Boothman completed the course at an average speed of 340.08 mph. On the same day, Flight Lieutenant Stainforth set up a new world speed record of 379.05 mph. And then on 29 September he increased it to 407.05 mph.

No more Schneider Trophy contests were ever to take place – and the Royal Air Force disbanded the High Speed Flight which had been formed especially for the project. Fortunately the experience of the Schneider Trophy was not wasted. Mitchell and his staff felt that their work could be best channelled into the development of a high speed monoplane land fighter. As soon as the Air Ministry announced its specification for a day-and-night fighter monoplane with four guns, Mitchell urged his firm to tender.

Mitchell's offering, the Supermarine F7/30, did not meet with government approval. What it did was to act as an indispensable link in design between the S.6B and the Spitfire.

In any case, a new official specification was already out for an eight-gun monoplane fighter. The projected machine-gun power had been doubled, and at the same time the government decided that the gun most likely to meet the needs of the new fighter was the American Browning. Supermarine restyled their F7/30 to cope with this new specification.

On 5 March 1936, just four months almost to the day after the first flight of the Hurricane, the Spitfire prototype was flown from Eastleigh airfield by Captain J. 'Mutt' Summers, chief test pilot of the Vickers group. An onlooker described the machine as 'a highly polished silvery monoplane that looked almost ridiculously small, with a seemingly enormous wooden propeller'. The machine took off, the undercarriage went up and in a minute the Spitfire became a dot in the Hampshire sky. So far so good. Then Mitchell had to turn the prototype into the production model, complete with eight-gun armament.

In 1936 the British public had not heard of either of these two magic names, Spitfire and Hurricane. The Spitfire appeared for the first time in public on Saturday, 27 June 1936 at the famous pre-war RAF Hendon Air Display. The prototype Hurricane flew on the same day, skimming the crowd just before the Spitfire. It was the first time the two had flown in proximity. Not the last!

With his eye on the Air Ministry's production scheme promulgated in 1936, Squadron Leader Ralph Sorley, RAF officer responsible for the development of the Spitfire, wanted production to start early in that year. In the event, the order was placed only four months after the first flight of the prototype. The agreement was dated 3 July 1936. The contract was for 310 Spitfires. This would fulfil the plan for 500 Hurricanes and 300 Spitfires to be in service by March 1939.

Before the war, this sort of mass production represented a vast task to an aviation manufacturer. The stressed-skin construction called for tooling that was both expensive and time consuming. Tragically, R.J. Mitchell died on 11 June 1937 when only forty-two years old and before he could see the first Spitfire off the production line. The first Spitfire was in fact flight tested in May 1938. That autumn of 1938, Vickers (Aviation) and the Supermarine Aviation Works (Vickers) both became part of Vickers-Armstrong.

In 1938, at the time of Munich, Fighter Command of the Royal Air Force had twenty-nine fighter squadrons. Of these, only five had modern equipment – Hurricanes. Pilots of the other twenty-four squadrons were flying obsolete biplanes with fixed undercarriages, insignificant firepower and maximum level speeds of around 220 mph. This was just one year before the beginning of the Second World War.

The first Spitfire to enter service with the Royal Air Force reached 19 Squadron at Duxford on 4 August 1938. This had a two-bladed wooden propeller and no armour behind the seat for the pilot's protection. The rate of arrival after this first Spitfire was one a week. 19 and 66 Squadrons, both at Duxford, were the first two to be equipped with Spitfires during the next weeks. On 8 March 1939, it was officially announced that the Spitfire's maximum level speed was 362 mph at 18,500 feet and that its rate of climb was around 2,000 feet per minute. At last we had a fighter comparable to any in the world. The two squadrons at Duxford were followed by 41 Squadron at Catterick in Yorkshire, then 74 and 54 Squadrons both stationed at Hornchurch in Essex.

In July 1939, a two-pitch airscrew (coarse and fine) was fitted to the Spitfire which increased its top speed to 367 mph. In August – less than four weeks before the outbreak of the Second World War – these airscrews were being fitted to all production Spitfires.

The public first saw a Spitfire in RAF colours on Empire Air Day, 20 May 1939. The pilot belly-landed during the Duxford display and was fined five pounds by the Air Ministry! It was not unusual in those early days for pilots to forget to lower the undercarriage before landing. The small fine, soon discontinued, was a typical bureaucratic reprimand. The real answer was cockpit routine, or discipline, which newer pilots were taught from the start.

On 3 September 1939, there were some 400 Spitfires in service and over 2,000 on order; a very different state of affairs from a year earlier. But Britain was still short of fighters and, worse still, of pilots to fly them.

28

DOUGLAS BADER

The Legless Air Ace

Douglas Bader was one of the world's greatest fighter pilots – and as such he symbolized the spirit of Britain in the Second World War. But ever since the time when he lost his legs, Bader's life was bound to be a struggle. Luckily he found it funny, too. That helped him survive. He always referred to the rest of his life as 'the further adventures of the legless ass'.

What was Bader really like? He always saw issues as good or bad, black or white. He could be dogmatic, intransigent, even rude, but he was always also infinitely courageous, caring and loyal. He was positive, decisive, affirmative, and he believed in people, not places or things. He was called 'one of the greatest Christians alive' – even though he rarely went to church. He had an ambience of greatness. Perhaps he was destined for it. I first met Douglas during the decade when I was responsible for Royal Air Force publicity. We became close friends for the remaining thirteen years of his life. I am now the only living biographer of Bader.

The Bader story really goes back to 1931. Douglas was serving as a pilot officer in the RAF. He was twenty-one years old and a brilliant sportsman. He got his Cranwell colours at rugby, cricket, boxing and hockey. He was on the verge of being selected for a trial for the English rugby team. And he had already been chosen as a pilot for the RAF aeronautic display team at the annual Hendon Air Show.

On 14 December 1931, Douglas and two other pilots flew over to a nearby flying club, where they chatted to some of the chaps there. One or two of the civilian flyers had been trying to needle Douglas into showing them some aerobatics, but the RAF pilots were under

199

strict orders not to do so. Orders did not always apply to Douglas.

The RAF trio took off to fly back to their home base. Douglas brought up the rear. He was still smarting from that needling in the clubhouse and decided to show them what he could do. He turned, dived low over the airfield, and did a slow roll just a few feet off the ground. He made a slight error of judgment with his biplane, which crashed on to the grass in the middle of the field. Douglas finished up with the whole machine wrapped around him.

He was not dead. He was not even unconscious. But he had hurt himself very badly. His right leg had the rudder bar right through the knee and it was nearly severed from his body. His left leg was broken between the knee and ankle. They dragged Douglas out of the cockpit and got him into an ambulance. He was bleeding profusely from a severed artery. He just remembered reaching hospital. That was all he recalled for a day or two.

When the world filtered back to his brain, he saw a nursing sister standing in front of a window. He looked out of it at a blue sky with scraps of cloud fluffing across the sun. Then he saw a cradle contraption over his legs. The sister returned with the surgeon, who said to him:

'I'm afraid you've had a bit of an accident, old son, and we've had to take your right leg off.'

All Douglas replied was: 'I'm sorry I'm being such a nuisance.' Then his left leg began to hurt like hell. The doctor came back later to tell him: 'Look, we've got to reset that left leg. It's going to hurt a bit, so we're going to give you an anaesthetic.'

When he woke up again, his squadron leader came to see him. Douglas said: 'You know, this left leg hurts like hell. I can't think why they don't cut it off. Because the other one doesn't hurt at all.'

'Do you really want it to be cut off?' the squadron leader asked him.

'Yes – I just can't wait.'

'Well,' said the officer softly, 'as a matter of fact, they have cut it off.'

During this twilight period after he had lost his second leg, Douglas touched bottom. He felt weaker. The pain started to subside. In fact, he felt nothing. He was scarcely conscious. No pain, no effort, peace. Then he heard a slight sound outside the door. A murmur followed by someone saying: 'Sh! There's a boy *dying* in there.'

The voice reached his brain with clarity and intensity. He suddenly reacted. 'So that's why it's so cosy. So that's what they think. Well, they're bloody wrong. I'm going to do something about this.'

Douglas dragged himself to consciousness. Back came the pain and he knew he was fighting it. He started to get better slowly.

Douglas's recovery is an epic story on its own. Back in an RAF hospital at Uxbridge, he felt more at home among his fellow officers. Sometimes he went around in a wheelchair, or on a peg leg. His sense of humour returned.

It was during Douglas's stay at Uxbridge that he first met Thelma. One day he went out with two chums in a sports car with the idea of stopping somewhere for tea. The other pair had a broken leg and a broken arm. So with Douglas minus his legs, they made a rare sight. They found a roadhouse restaurant and drove in. People at tables in the garden stopped eating to watch this motley trio. The three RAF men found a table. And then the most beautiful girl Douglas had ever seen walked up to serve them. That was the meeting of Thelma and Douglas. On their later visits, Thelma always managed to serve them. Her father had been in the Royal Flying Corps.

Douglas had the natural optimism of youth. In due course, he became the first man in the world to walk on artificial legs. It was a real physical battle. He tried to walk. He fell down. Again and again. It hurt him – but he went on. At last, he could walk unaided. No parallel bars. No sticks. Just on his two tin legs. He drove down to Thelma's roadhouse and she was suitably impressed. That autumn they went out on their first real date. They visited London clubs and out-of-town roadhouses which were all the rage. He started to dance. They did a lot of dancing and canoodling. Thelma was very good at dancing and used to lead Douglas. In the canoodling, he led her – or so he always said!

Walking on his metal legs, Douglas insisted that he could still fly – only to be told that there was 'nothing in the King's regulations' to cover his case. He refused to accept the offer of a ground job and was invalided out of the service.

The 1930s passed. Douglas and Thelma married. He had several jobs which he hated before joining Shell. Then came 1939 and the war. Douglas argued his way to an RAF medical board and insisted that he was fit to fly. Passing his flying test, he was assigned for active service with a fighter squadron.

Early in 1940 he was taking off in a Spitfire when his engine failed and he crash-landed. Both his metal legs became badly bent, but an

RAF artificer straightened them and half an hour later he was up in the air again.

Douglas was promoted leader of the only Canadian fighter squadron in the RAF. Their pilots were demoralized from flying in France before its fall and they had suffered pretty badly. One of them voiced their sentiments: 'That's all we need – a leader with no legs.' Douglas sensed the situation and their resentment. He had to win their respect. The only way to do that was in the air. He walked out of their hut, climbed into his Hurricane, and took off. He piloted the fighter through loops, rolls, stalls, spins. The Canadians came out of their huts to watch. After that they were friends. Douglas moulded them into a front-line squadron in time for the Battle of Britain.

The first time that Douglas led his squadron in force was on 30 August. He and a dozen other Hurricanes were patrolling near London when they spotted fourteen blocks of six enemy bombers plus thirty Messerschmitts. Four Hurricanes had gone off to check up on some other reported aircraft, so that left nine to tackle the Germans. They fought and routed over 100 of the enemy at odds of 12 to 1. And in under an hour they returned to Duxford aerodrome without a bullet hole in any of their machines. Such was Douglas's leadership and skill. Here is how he described the flight at the time:

Thirteen of our squadron were on patrol near London looking for the Germans, who we knew were about in large formations. Soon we spotted one large formation, and it was rather an awe-inspiring sight – particularly to anyone who hadn't previously been in action. I counted fourteen blocks of six bombers – all bombers – with thirty Messerschmitt 110 fighters behind and above, so that altogether there were more than 100 enemy aircraft to deal with.

Four of the boys had gone off to check up on some unidentified aircraft which had appeared shortly before we sighted the big formation, and they weren't back in time to join in the fun. That left nine of us to tackle the big enemy formation.

I detailed the pilot from Calgary to take his section of three Hurricanes up to keep the thirty Messerschmitts busy. 'OK, OK,' he said, with obvious relish, and away he streaked to deal with that vastly superior number of enemy fighters.

The remaining six of us tackled the bombers. They were flying at 15,000 feet with the middle of the formation roughly over Enfield, heading east. When we first sighted them they looked just like a vast swarm of bees. With the sun at our backs and the advantage of greater height, conditions were ideal for a surprise attack, and as soon as we were all in position we went straight down on to them. We didn't adopt any set rules in attacking them – we just worked on the axiom that the shortest distance between two points is a straight line.

I therefore dived straight into the middle of the tightly-packed formation, closely followed by the rest of my flight. The enemy immediately broke up fanwise. I saw three Messerschmitt 110s do climbing turns left and three to the right. I saw one of our pilots go to the left and I attacked the right-hand three. Their tactics appeared to be climbing turns to a nearly stalled position to try to get on my tail. I tried a short burst of nearly three seconds into the first Messerschmitt 110 at nearly point-blank range as he was at the top of his zoom. The aeroplane seemed to burst into flames and disintegrate in the air.

I continued my zoom and found the second Messerschmitt below and to my right and just starting his dive after a stalled turn, so I turned in behind him and got a very early shot at about 100 to 150 yards' range. His evasive action, after my first burst, which lasted two to four seconds, consisted in pushing his stick violently backwards and forwards. The second time he did this, I got in a burst as he was at the top of his short zoom and I saw pieces fly off his starboard wing near the engine, and then the whole of his starboard wing went on fire and the aeroplane went away to the right in a steep, spiral dive, well on fire. I did not see anyone bale out of the fighter Messerschmitt 110s, although it is possible, but I was too busy to look round and worry about either of them once they caught fire.

I noticed in my mirror a Messerschmitt 110 coming up behind me and did a quick turn and saw five or six white streams coming out of his forward firing guns. It seemed as though he was using tracers in all his guns. As soon as I turned, he put his nose down and I temporarily lost him and eventually saw him travelling east, far below. Not once did a Messerschmitt 110 get sights on me. I saw nothing except Messerschmitt 110s, although I understand that there were Dorniers in the formation.

Now, there's one curious thing about this air fighting. One minute you see hundreds of aeroplanes in the sky and the next minute there's nothing. All you can do is to look through your sights at your particular target – and look in your mirror, too, if you are sensible, for any Messerschmitts which might be trying to get on to your tail.

Well, that particular battle lasted about five or ten minutes, and then, quite suddenly, the sky was clear of aircraft.

One pilot had sent a Hun bomber crashing into a green-house. Another bomber had gone headlong into a field filled with derelict motor-cars; it hit one of the cars, turned over, and caught fire. Another of our chaps had seen a twin-engined job of sorts go into a reservoir near Enfield. Yet another pilot saw his victim go down with his engine flat out; the plane dived into a field and dis-integrated into little pieces. Incidentally, that particular pilot brought down three Huns that day.

We hadn't shot them all down, of course. They hadn't waited for that, but made off home in all directions at high speed. But, apart from our bag of twelve (eight Messerschmitt 110 fighter-bombers, three Heinkel 111 bombers, and a fourth Heinkel bomber already partly damaged by another squadron), there were a number of others which were badly shot up and probably never got home, like one which went staggering out over Southend with one engine out of action.

As there was nothing left to shoot at we went home, picking up, as we went, the infuriated section which had been sent off to inves-tigate the unidentified aircraft and had missed our battle. They hadn't fired a single round between the four of them, and their language when they heard what they'd missed was unprintable. No-one in the squadron suffered any damage.

As a result of this success, the notion of a larger formation than a squadron was conceived and Douglas was given three squadrons.

The trouble was that they were north of the Thames and often called on too late to get into a favourable position for an attack.

On 7 September, the Germans switched from RAF targets to London. Over 300 bombers and hundreds of fighters took off to attack the capital. Bader was scrambled late. In adverse conditions, while still on the climb, they engaged quickly. An explosive bullet caused a big bang in Douglas's cockpit. It finished up against the petrol priming pump. A narrow escape. Douglas shot down two fighters. They claimed twenty destroyed for the loss of two precious pilots killed.

Ten days later, the Bader Wing was scrambled again – and late again. The Luftwaffe were in two groups, each of sixty aircraft. Douglas dived point-blank at the leader. He fired. His first victim emitted white smoke misting from both wings. Douglas was glad to see that at least one of the crew baled out. The results claimed by the Wing were twenty-one enemy destroyed as against two RAF pilots killed or missing. Douglas reported that two extra squadrons could have broken up the fleeing Germans still more severely. So on 14 September Douglas led five squadrons – three Hurricane and two Spitfire.

Then came the climax on 15 September. At about 11.30, Goering launched the first wave of the mass morning attack – over 100 aircraft followed by 150 more. They crossed the coast above Ramsgate, Folkestone and Dungeness. Some 100 bombers burst through our defences and reached the east and south suburbs of London. A number were intercepted just as Big Ben was striking noon. Twenty-one squadrons took off altogether to engage the enemy – five led by Bader.

For once the Wing had been called in time. They were heading towards the Luftwaffe at height – at the very time the enemy were over the English Channel. Douglas saw two enemy squadrons right under him. He managed to perfect the approach and opened fire in a steep dive on a Dornier. The shots hit its petrol pipe or tank. He went for another Dornier, but had to break away to avoid a Spitfire. Then he saw a Spitfire and Dornier collide – wrecking both instantly. By lunchtime they claimed twenty-six aircraft destroyed.

Hardly had they landed and refuelled when they were ordered up again. The Wing comprised forty-nine fighters instead of the fifty-six earlier. They saw masses of enemy bombers above them. Douglas pulled up and around quite violently. He partially blacked out and almost collided with his friend Denis Crowley-Milling. He spun off the latter's slipstream and straightened out at only 5,000 feet.

That day the Bader Wing had their many successes and some tragedies. A Polish pilot flying with Douglas was forced to bale out during a violent exchange of fire. For reasons unknown, he was unable to pull his ripcord. He was killed . . .

During the afternoon, the Wing claimed a further twenty-six aircraft. So, for an average of fifty-two fighters flying, the Wing claimed fifty-two aircraft destroyed. One enemy per aircraft. The Battle of Britain was won on that historic day. The Bader Wing had played a crucial part in the victory. They represented a quarter of all the RAF aircraft airborne.

But the war went on. In March 1941 Wing Commander Bader went over to the offensive, flying fighter sorties from Tangmere. He was the RAF's first wing leader. Douglas flew a further sixty or seventy sorties in just two or three months that summer. His personal score of enemy aircraft destroyed was about twenty.

When pulling up after an attack over France on 9 August, his Spitfire collided with a Messerschmitt. It slewed round and started to nose down. Dust cloaked the cockpit. Douglas was in a spiralling dive. He looked round to see that most of the machine was missing – sliced away by the collision. He had to get out – quickly. Helmet and mask came off. He got the canopy open. The air screeched in at him. His head reared over the windscreen and he was out. Or nearly. The foot of his artificial right leg caught in the cockpit. He could not get it free. But with the cockpit doing nearly 500 mph, the leather belt attached to the metal limb gave way under the pressure, and he floated out. He pulled the ring, the parachute opened, and he dropped through the clouds at 4,000 feet.

An enemy fighter flew towards him but did not open fire – or that would have been the end of the Bader story. Douglas survived the landing with two broken ribs, but lost consciousness. He revived to find three members of the Luftwaffe bending over him. Then he was taken to hospital. The Germans also retrieved and mended his missing leg trapped in the Spitfire – or what was left of it.

Thelma thought Douglas was alive, but back in England they all had a terrible time waiting to hear something. At last the boys from Tangmere told Thelma: 'You'll have to face it. He won't come back. One of us would have heard something.' Days dragged by. Eventually, Tangmere heard from the Red Cross that Douglas was in hospital at St Omer. Thelma went out with the boys and had a tremendous party. Then the boys returned to war and Douglas started to think how he could get back to Britain.

He escaped from the hospital, but was recaptured. Placed under close guard, any further effort to escape was impossible. But the RAF sent him a present. Sweeping across St Omer airfield, one aircraft dropped a yellow box, which floated down by parachute. The Germans gave him the contents: his spare right leg from Tangmere. So to hospital in Frankfurt; then several POW camps and finally to Colditz Castle, where he stayed for nearly three years.

Then on 15 April 1945, Douglas awoke to the sound of soldiers' feet in the castle courtyard below. He strapped on his two legs and followed the others downstairs. He saw the German guards surrendering their arms to American troops. He was free.

Douglas and Thelma resumed their lives. He rejoined Shell in 1946, going back to their aviation department. For the rest of his life, he spent much of his time actively aiding the disabled. And he flew his own aeroplane all over the world . . .

29

BUTCH O'HARE

Saving an Aircraft Carrier

The carrier *Lexington* was with a force of four heavy cruisers and ten destroyers, planning to attack Rabaul in New Britain, when they were spotted by enemy flying boats which wheeled off for some stronger support. Soon they were back and the first heavy bomber approached the *Lexington* and her escorts. Two of the six US fighters keeping constant watch overhead peeled off to attack it – and the plane quickly went down in flames. The second enemy plane went the same way. The next one copied the course of the original flying boats and went the same way. The next went home for reinforcements.

When they came, the stage was set for one of those fights to a finish when the lives of all the men witnessing it might hang on the outcome. Another half dozen American Navy fighters flew off the deck of the *Lexington* to join the first six.

Nine Japanese bombers in a V formation pointed straight at the carrier. The original fighter force was getting short of fuel before the battle began, but throttled forward to engage. In a spluttering few minutes, five of the enemy bombers left searing trails of flame in the sky as they plunged into the Pacific. This rattled the Japanese, who found the next phase too much for them. The US ships loosed all they had at these last four bombers, frightening the pilots so badly that their bombs sank harmlessly into the sea. The planes tried to turn and flee back to Rabaul, but the American fighters were still airborne and shot down all but one of them.

But something serious was taking shape as the fighters flew in pursuit of these last four planes. The *Lexington* had managed to get fifteen more fighters up to help in the chase, exchanging these for five

208

of the original ones which needed more fuel and ammunition. At the exact moment that all the airborne fighters except two were well away from the carrier dealing with the enemy planes, another nine bombers droned down toward the *Lexington*. And at the second the two US fighters took on this next wave, the machine guns of one of them jammed – so he could do nothing but fly clear to safety. This left one lone fighter flying between the enemy and the ship. Its pilot was Lieutenant Edward H. 'Butch' O'Hare.

O'Hare took on all nine.

He raced down on the V formation from the rear and their right. Down on the *Lexington* everyone who had a second to spare watched what happened next. O'Hare pressed his gun button just before his fighter crashed. Weaving underneath the rest, he then gave another bomber a burst. It limped out of the V, which was already a ragged arrow. Two more of the group lost bits of wings and fuselage as they struggled to save the formation. So five of the nine never reached the target to drop their bombs.

The quartet who got through did drop them, but hurriedly and inaccurately. They were anxious to get away from this daredevil. Then as the scattered group struggled to find some order, O'Hare went into them again. One, two, three. All went spiralling into the sea before his guns. In just four minutes, he shot down five of the nine bombers and hit three more.

But the brief battle was not yet through. For as these three sputtered homeward, each short of one or more engines, they ran right into the *Lexington*'s main force of fighters as it was flying jubilantly back from wiping out the first bombers. All three Japanese bombers received mortal machine-gun fire. The last plane ran for it as fast as a bomber could, pursued by Lieutenant Edward H. Allen in a Navy scout bomber. Both planes flew at about the same speed, but whenever the Yanks managed to come within range, the recoil from their guns restricted the scout bomber just long enough to allow the enemy to gain ground again. Although the enemy escaped, both Allen and Lieutenant Commander John S. Thack won the Navy Cross.

But to O'Hare went the coveted Medal of Honor. Admiral Brown said that the *Lexington* owed her life to him alone, so that is the answer to the question: Can one man save an aircraft carrier? Yes, O'Hare did it.

The sequel to the story must be told.

Off the Marshall Islands on 27 November of the following year,

O'Hare was flying from the carrier *Enterprise* at night. After a scrap with enemy planes, a lagging Japanese pilot became mixed up with three American Hellcats about to return to their carrier. O'Hare flew in one of these Hellcats, and in the firing that broke out when the Japanese was discovered, O'Hare's plane was hit. It lurched over. The flaming fighter took O'Hare with it into the sea. A tragic end.

30

GUY GIBSON

The Dam Busters' Raid

On 17 March 1943, No. 5 Bomber Group headquarters received a letter from Bomber Command telling them of a new mine weapon intended to be used against 'a large dam in Germany'. The attack had to be made during May, and a new squadron was formed to carry out the attack.

Four days later, this squadron started to take shape at Scampton, while the twenty Lancasters it would receive were being built. The whole project was both top secret and top priority. Everyone picked for it had to be top grade, too, air and ground crews alike. The personnel had to be chosen first of all, before the modified Lancasters were ready. The man chosen to command the new squadron was Guy Gibson. All he himself knew about the project at that stage was that it would involve low-level flying across country, and training started along these lines at once on standard Lancasters. All twenty crews reached Scampton before the end of the month, within ten days of the squadron being born.

All they had yet learned was that they would have to fly at 100 feet and at 240 miles an hour. A mine would have to be dropped from each bomber within forty yards of the precise point of release. They went into training over reservoirs and lakes in Wales and the Midlands, for only six weeks were left to perfect this demanding technique. This ability to fly at 100 to 150 feet over water in the dark, and to navigate and drop mines accurately as well, was the first key factor in the operation. There were many more, not the least of them being able to avoid enemy fighters and ack-ack in the actual target area.

But even Gibson did not yet know this target area, so he was literally flying in the dark. Then he met the inventor of the mines, Mr

B.N. Wallis – later famous as Barnes Wallis – who told him roughly how the mines would work. They would bounce along the water towards their target. The whole project became daily more fantastic.

Meanwhile, Gibson and his crew practised flying over Derwentwater reservoir in Yorkshire, which bore resemblances to the conditions expected over the ultimate targets. After some trial runs by day, Gibson discovered that he could estimate his altitude and direct a bomb at the specified speed with reasonable accuracy. But by night he only barely escaped actually striking the gloomy invisible water of the reservoir. And the attack was of course to be carried out at night. They would have to learn a lot in the coming few weeks. One of the many problems involved was solved when an accurate range-finder was devised which enabled the squadron to keep within a rough twenty-five yards of their target, and so within the forty yards' tolerance allowed by Barnes Wallis.

The following day, Gibson was finally let into the secret. They were to attack the great Ruhr dams of Germany: Möhne, Sorpe and Eder. The main target would be the Möhne Dam, 830 yards long, 150 feet high and 140 feet thick at its base – of sheer concrete and masonry. If Gibson and his squadron could smash one or more of these dams, the havoc caused to the enemy industries and communications would be tremendous.

Apart from the difficulty of flying to the rigid requirements vital for the success of the plan, there was one other problem: the mine had not yet had its full-scale trials! The first such trial came in mid-April when an inert mine was dropped from one of the modified Lancasters at the required height of 150 feet over water. The outer casing of the mine disintegrated as soon as it struck the sea off the Dorset coast. No time was lost in strengthening the casing, but this made no difference to the trials and the mine still shattered.

Gibson, too, had his worries, just as fundamental as the setbacks for Barnes Wallis. They found it impossible to fly at exactly 150 feet over the water and maintain that height accurately. Then one of the backroom 'boffins' found an answer: to train two spotlights down-wards from the nose and belly of the bomber so that their beams would meet at 150 feet below the Lancaster, making a spot where they intersected. In this way, with the help of a couple of Aldis lamps, the aircraft could be flown within a few feet of any required height simply by keeping the spotlight at water level.

The next panic came when the inventor found that they could only expect effectiveness from the modified mine if it were dropped from sixty feet instead of 150 feet. Without the spotlight device, this would have been quite out of the question. By the time they had put in some practice at sixty feet, the month of May had arrived.

Early in May, an inert mine was dropped from the new height of sixty feet and operated successfully; then an active mine went off exactly as expected. While this aspect went well, just one more problem presented itself at the operational end. A complicated signalling system had to be worked out to control about twenty bombers over several tricky targets. The answer was very high frequency radio-telephone sets, twenty in number. These arrived on 7 May, but a lot of routine testing and procedure had to be accomplished before the actual attack. This had been done by 9 May, except for minor adjustments.

The nearness of the operation had suddenly been brought home to them all by the dress rehearsals, the first of which was timed for the night of 6 May. A film company was actually called on to assist by building dummy structures in the Uppingham and Colchester reservoirs, so that the squadron had something tangible for a target as they roared in during their dress rehearsal raid.

Even this stage had not been reached without further hazards and headaches, for a few days earlier half of the dozen Lancasters in one trial had sustained bad damage – with rear turrets dented, elevators broken, and fins bent. The trouble occurred because the aircraft had been flying a few feet too low, and though the mines they dropped were only inert, they had caused gigantic splashes as they struck the water, which had affected the bombers flying at 232 miles an hour.

On 15 May, Gibson got word at last: 'Be prepared to take off tomorrow.' He sat up late that night committing the detailed operation to paper – just in case none of them got back. They had been so busy training that the danger of the mission might have escaped some of them, especially since it was only on the following morning that the aircrews knew the complete plan.

The first of nineteen Lancasters took off at 9.28 p.m. on 16 May. The main force of nine would go for the Möhne Dam and then, if it was destroyed before all their mines had gone, they would fly to the Eder. The second force of five was to head for the Sorpe Dam, while a third force of five was to form a reserve to fill in any gap, according to how the operation progressed.

They skimmed over the sea towards the Continent at a mere sixty feet or so, and went still lower after they crossed the Dutch coast. Moonlight helped them, but navigation at that altitude proved hard.

Gibson and the other two Lancasters in his immediate section of three hurtled overland, rolling right and left to confuse the defences. No guns opened fire. But in a couple of minutes they found themselves over the sea again! They had flown over one of the several islands they had tried to avoid, and instead of being inland were only now crossing the real Dutch coast. By good chance, none of the ack-ack guns on the island had opened fire on them. On their fresh course, Gibson's bomb-aimer had to shout to them regularly over the intercom to lift the aircraft to avoid trees or high-tension cables. All three aircraft in the section kept formation right up until the Rhine came into view. Then it was found to everyone's alarm that Gibson's Lancaster, leading the whole flight, was no less than six miles too far to the south and heading for Duisburg, one of the most heavily defended towns in the whole of the industrial Ruhr. Gibson made a sharp turn to remedy the potential danger of the situation and flew along the line of the Rhine, under heavy fire from barges on the river equipped with quick-firing weapons.

On to the Ruhr Valley, with half an hour to go before the Möhne Dam. Ceaseless anti-aircraft fire forced Gibson to take evasive action. The three were also being continually caught by searchlights, some of which Gibson managed to avoid or shake off by 'dodging behind trees' as he colourfully put it.

Then they flew over a new and heavily defended airfield near Dorsten, not marked on their maps, where all three were held by searchlights. Gibson's rear-gunner fired at the beams but stopped when some tall trees came between the lights and the aircraft. Suddenly the searchlights were extinguished by a long burst from the rear turret of one of the other two Lancasters.

It was about here that one of the aircraft of the first wave of nine was lost. Gibson sent a radio warning of this new airfield to the following aircraft. Lancasters B, N and Z formed the second section. Shortly before it was lost, aircraft B broke formation, presumably for the pilot to check his position. The pilot of Lancaster N, then flying at 100 feet, reported that soon afterwards he saw a bomber being shot at by anti-aircraft guns and returning their fire. Then he saw an explosion on the ground. The inference was that Lancaster B had crashed, its mine probably exploding at the same time. The other eight Lancasters flew on, past Dortmund and Hamm, avoiding more fire from the ground. Then hills rose ahead and open country apparently without defences. Gibson gained height to get over a hill and then saw the Möhne Dam lake ahead – and in a moment the dam itself. From all along the dam, which looked, Gibson said, rather like a battleship, guns were firing, as well as from a powerhouse below the dam but there were no searchlights. Gibson estimated that tracer was coming from five positions, and probably a dozen guns in all. The Lancasters all circled around getting their bearings, and each time one of them came within range of the guns on the dam, they received accurate fire. One of the eight aircraft was hit, though not fatally.

The attack on the Sorpe Dam had been planned for this precise time, as an effective diversion from the efforts of the main force of Lancasters against the Möhne. But only one of the five aircraft aiming for the Sorpe Dam had in fact reached it. They had met heavy opposition early on. Lancasters K and E had both been shot down near the Dutch coast; H had hit the sea and lost its mine in the process, so had returned to Scampton; W had been hit by flak which disrupted the intercom, so that the pilot had had to return home. Only Lancaster T attacked the Sorpe Dam, a minute or two before 3 a.m. on 17 May.

Back at the Möhne Dam, the Lancasters had scattered, ready for the attack. Gibson was due in first. He made a wide circle, and then came down over the hills at the eastern end of the Möhne lake. He dived towards the water and flew at exactly sixty feet, with the spotlights meeting on the water below. With these lights on, the bomber made a still simpler target for the gunners on the dam, who could see it coming from more than two miles away. Tracer shells converged towards it as Gibson flew straight and level towards the dam. The bomber's gunners replied. Gibson said afterwards that he expected to die at any moment. But the Lancaster was not hit anywhere. The mine was released and Gibson flew in a circle.

Looking back at the lake, the crew saw fountains of water, white in the moonlight and 1,000 feet high. The surface of the lake had been broken and sheets of water were pouring over the dam. At first, Gibson thought it had burst at the initial attempt, but he soon realized that it was only water churned up by the explosion. The mine had gone off five yards from the dam, but Gibson had to signal home that there was no apparent breach. Back in England, 'Bomber' Harris, Barnes Wallis and the rest received the news breathlessly and waited for the next report. They had to hang on for fully thirteen minutes.

Gibson waited for the water to subside and then signalled to Lancaster M to make its attack. The same thing happened all over again. The enemy guns focused on the lone bomber, looking very vulnerable. Some 100 yards from the dam, a jet of flame sprang from the aircraft. Gibson inferred that the bomb-aimer had been wounded because the mine fell late and onto the powerhouse below.

The pilot was striving desperately to gain height for his crew to bale out of the blazing bomber. He got up to 500 feet, and then there was a flash in the sky, and one wing fell off. The whole aircraft came apart in the air, and fell to the ground in fragments. Almost immediately afterwards the mine that had fallen on the powerhouse exploded. This caused so much smoke that Gibson had to wait some minutes for it to clear before he could direct the next aircraft to attack.

For this third attempt, Guy Gibson had a plan. As Lancaster P flew towards the dam, Gibson went alongside, a little ahead of it, and then turned. His rear-gunner fired at the flak position on the dam and at the same time helped to draw off their fire from the bomber about to attack.

Lancaster P was hit several times despite Gibson's help, and all the petrol drained from one of the wing tanks – but the mine was accurately released and exploded fifty yards from the dam. Again circling near the scene, Gibson thought he saw some movement of the wall itself, but although the same huge fountain of water was thrust up, it was disappointingly clear that the dam had not yet been breached.

Now it came to Lancaster A's turn. Gibson developed his diversionary tactics still further this time, and as the bomber began its run in towards the dam, Gibson flew up and down on the farther side of the dam and told his gunners to fire on the enemy's positions. To make sure that they would concentrate on him rather than Lancaster A, Gibson had his identification lights switched on. The plan was successful, and the enemy did in fact keep their guns trained on his Lancaster while the attacking one flew straight towards the dam. As the mine exploded a huge wave went over the dam, but although it had gone off in contact with the wall they were still unable to report any apparent breach. Back at headquarters the tension was becoming increasingly unbearable, as each attack failed to bring about the desired effect.

Gibson ordered Lancaster J to attack. The fifth mine went up almost exactly in the correct spot. Just before the moment of release, however, the pilot reported seeing a breach in the centre. The bomber's own mine flung up the by now usual fantastic fountain, and then the aircraft became badly harried by enemy gunfire. Gibson himself could not see the dam at that moment, so was in no position to confirm a breach. He knew that time was running out, however, so decided to send the next bomber into the attack at once. Just as he had ordered Lancaster L to start, he turned and came close to the wall of the dam.

But it had rolled over.

Quickly he told Lancaster L to turn away. Gibson flew close and looked again. Then he saw plainly that there was a breach in the dam 150 yards wide. A huge cataract of water was churning through the breach. At 00.56 a.m. Gibson signalled to group headquarters the prearranged code-word 'Nigger', meaning that the Möhne Dam had been breached. Nigger, his dog, had been run over and killed the evening of the day before the attack.

The valley below the dam was filling with fog, evaporating from the water that was pouring down it. It was moving in an unbelievable wave, and in front of this Gibson could see the headlights of cars racing to safety. These headlights changed colour, first to green, and then eventually to dark purple, as the water overtook some of them. The water surged on towards the eastern end of the Ruhr Valley. The powerhouse beside the dam was by now completely submerged.

Gibson circled for three minutes and then called up the rest of his force. He told aircraft J and P and make for home. Lancaster M had been shot down. The rest of the force Gibson ordered to set course for the Eder Dam. Gibson's own Lancaster G and Lancaster A no longer had their mines, but they went as well; L, Z and N still carried their mines intact.

It was getting late in the night by the time they all reached the Eder Dam, which lay in a deep valley among wooded hills, and at the far end of the lake was a hill about 1,000 feet high with a castle on top of it. They had to approach the dam by flying over this hill, and then diving steeply from above the castle, down to sixty feet over the water. Lancaster L made three runs before the bomb-aimer released his mine. A great spurt of water was followed by a small gap towards the east side of the dam. Next followed Z, after two tries. Gibson saw a vivid explosion on the parapet of the dam itself, which lit up the whole valley. Then no more was seen of the Lancaster, which must have been blown up by its own mine on the parapet . . .

Lancaster N attacked, successfully this time at 1.52 a.m. A cone of water rose up, then a thirty-foot breach appeared below the top of the dam, leaving the top intact for a moment. A torrent of water cascaded downwards and rushed in a tidal wave to the valley below. Gibson's wireless operator signalled the code-word 'Dinghy'. The Eder Dam had been breached, too.

So the five aircraft set course for home, with the enemy's fighter force now fully aroused. Lancaster A failed to return. Some time on the way back, Gibson's rear-gunner warned him that there was an enemy aircraft behind. Gibson lost height, though he was already flying very low, and made towards the west, where the sky was darkest; by this manoeuvre he evaded the enemy.

One of the reserve Lancasters managed to get through to attack the Sorpe Dam at 3.14 a.m.

Eight of the Lancasters making this historic raid were lost; eight bombers, and more distressing, eight crews. But without Gibson's heroism, both at the Möhne and the Eder, in drawing enemy fire on his own plane, the losses would have been even heavier.

There is no need to repeat the catastrophe and chaos caused by the result of the raid. The headlines have told the story before:

'Growing devastation in the Ruhr.'

'Flood waters sweep into Kassel.'

'Damage to German war industries.'

'Dam floods stretch for sixty miles.'

Later it came to light that the dams had not been as badly hit as believed – but it was still a heroic operation. Later on, Churchill asked Guy Gibson, who was awarded the Victoria Cross for his part in the operation, to tour the United States on behalf of Britain, and he was of course fêted wherever he went. Gibson returned to flying duties and there is a school of thought that suggests he became over-confident and was not sufficiently experienced with the Mosquito he was flying on 19 September 1944. He led one last raid on Rheydt, in the Rhineland, a strongly defended rail centre and traffic terminus for the Ruhr.

He was flying below the main force, guiding the bombing, talking to his fellow pilots, telling them where and when to strike. Over the target, his bombers, coming in to bomb high above him, heard his voice on the radio, calm, unhurried. His instructions came clearly, and they followed his orders. The bombs hit an ammunition train and started a series of fires and explosions. The crews heard his final orders. His plane crashed in Steenbergen, near Bergen-op-Zoom, on the East Scheldt estuary, where his body was found and buried.

31

DENTON SCOTT

Gunner over Lorient

What was a bombing raid *really* like? Come over Europe to Lorient in a B-17 with Sergeant Scott. This is how he felt:

The moment you climb past the bomb bay, you forget, forget altogether once you shudder involuntarily at the monstrous, sinister cases, fused ready to explode. You shudder, but you force yourself not to think about that, and you know that you are a prisoner of this ship, this gaunt fuselage, a ward of those four motors – for many long and tedious hours to come. That imprisonment can be broken only by three factors and they are, in order, disaster by explosion and parachuting to another prison, death or a safe return.

The nose of a B-17 is cramped and small, and once there you know you are no longer a part of anything except this ship.

You look out at the black tarmac, at the camouflaged hangars, and they are remote and distant. They are a part of a world which does not concern you in the slightest. They are a part of a world, seen in a dream, securely moored to the safety of the earth itself – a world you are leaving for eight hours, perhaps forever.

This is your world now; the tarmac flashing by on take-off, the emptiness of the sky, the vertigo caused by looking straight down at the earth below with only glass supporting you. It is a sparsely populated world; the only men in it are the men imprisoned with you. This is your world; the strong faces around you, the acrid smell of sweating flesh, the gun you man. This is a world in which four motors are a human, tangible part of your crew, because motors can be temperamental and therefore assume a personality – a personality at which you can curse if they fail, which you can beseech if they falter, which you can almost subconsciously praise if they beat forever strong. This is your world.

We wove out to sea in perfect formation. Men speak among themselves in this world not as men speak in the world we know. Speech is an automatic reflex, born of fear and excitement. Speech in our world is the speech of Dutch Schultz when the gangster delivered his death-bed soliloquy. The tongue speaks before the mind thinks. It is almost a world of subconscious reactions. A man cannot, and will not, stop to rationalize his way into the arms of death, or of Jerry.

This is why Santoro, the bombardier, turns to me and says: 'For Christ's sake, don't get rattled. Just do what I do.'

Now Santoro is a mild fellow, ordinarily, patient and untiring. On the ground he would have said: 'Now, Scotty, the main thing is to take it easy and relax. It is just like any other game where you need quick reflexes. Tensing only slows you up.' But now, we are over the Channel, and it's 'For Christ's sake . . .'

All questions and answers are clipped and grievously accentuated by the circumstances, as another voice through the interphone: 'Scotty, don't pay any attention to that son of a bitch. All bombardiers are nuts.'

We are told to test our guns. There again, spontaneous reactions. I had pressed the trigger of the .30 caliber and had watched the tracers stream down toward the sea, had accomplished this order as an automatic reflex, without hesitation, without thinking. The last bullet had sliced its red-hot path into the cold waters below before I realized specifically and rationally that I had been given an order and had complied with that order.

We are nearing the coast, nearing the flak and the fighters, the targets, into a clear and sunlit battlefield, a land of quiet, swift violence, on which the traces of violence leave no mark save for a vanishing cloud of smoke, or the white, pathetic shroud of a parachute blooming against the blue skies and slowly leaving this battleground that refuses to be despoiled by war.

We are nearing the coast, flying low now at just 1,500 feet. And now we begin the long haul up to the front, up through the mist, into a land of broken patches of light and darkness and then entirely above the clouds into the clear. The sun is bright in the nose, and warm. There is a natural feeling of security in sunlight, but when that sense of warmth and security is tempered first by the knowledge that the air outside is cold and sterile and then by the knowledge that the sunlight is your enemy, it produces an effect far more eerie than fear in the night, since the primary association of fear is with darkness.

If men sing in the sky, going into battle, as they say men sing, it is the singing of a small boy who finds in passing a graveyard by night that the action of his lungs reduces the tingling in his spine and the awkward involuntary tendency of his legs to break into a fast run and get out as fast as he can.

We did not sing.

'Fighters at nine o'clock! Fighters at nine o'clock! Oh, you little . . .'

They are FW109s (*sic*), and they are rubbed down and polished so they glitter in the sky, and they are hard to see. They come right at us. Hausman opens up. I look straight into their props; they come straight towards us. They then veer away, leave by lowering a wing and just sliding off and away from us, turning slowly up and over, exposing their slick Nazi bellies to the sky above, and then just floating off. There is no sensation of speed, strangely; I always thought there would be a sensation of speed; but they just float away like feathers in a breeze.

We are coming over Lorient now; Lorient with its docks and quaysides and its sinister submarine pens. We come steadily, thundering relentlessly towards the target. The charge of the light brigade is no more impressive than the firm, sure run through blast troubled skies of a bombing run. The city spreads out far below us through the nose. Santoro, the bombardier, squints through his sights. The windows are glazed with ice, and Santoro curses. He presses the button and the bombs go tumbling from the opened bomb bay doors, down through the clear blue skies, down through five solid miles of space, gathering velocity, becoming steadily smaller and smaller and finally falling out of sight. Then the brief eruption down below.

I look ahead. One B-17 slips out of the group, faltering and crippled, helpless. Its right wing, riveted with science and the delicate touch of experts, begins shredding off. Chunks of metal flutter through the sky, caught up sometimes in the prop-wash of oncoming planes. She loses speed, and then gains it. The right wing

222

is breaking into bits. Then the parachutes, one by one, billowing out against the blue sky.

The flak is becoming hot and heavy, black deadly puffs of the stuff erupting all around the ship. Santoro rages back and forth in the restricted confines of the nose, cursing the men for not cleaning the windows. He curses the Germans. He hurls vile imprecations at the men. He curses the major in the leading plane for flying too high, for giving the wrong kind of evasive action. The Jerry fighters come in through the ripening fields of flak, and he curses them too. The red tracers stream past the ship. Two red balls of flame rise in front of the nose and disappear. Me. cannon blasts, somebody yells, and we look through the frosted windows. The two Me109's are coming in at 300 miles an hour. I grab my gun and let go. The sweat is pouring from my face. Once, the oxygen mask loosens and I stop to fix it on my face. Somebody is yelling through the intercom that the supercharger on the number three engine has blown. We have driven the Me's back, and now our problem is to stay in the protecting line of our formation or risk getting picked off by fighters.

We streak out across the Channel. The fighters don't follow. The sweat dries on our faces. It is cool and quiet now, and the sky is peaceful. We come down again, slowly, surely from our great height to 1,500 feet once more. At times, we can see water. It seemed very blue. The tension had been broken but we did not sing. Until we landed we still would not have established contact with that world we had left on take-off. Even when we made land-fall once more, the sight of men's houses, and the farmlands, and the green Cornish hills below were nothing more than impersonal landscape, a painting that held nothing but objectivity.

What I did feel was a sudden physical release from strain, but more acutely a deep affinity to every man on this ship, my fellow prisoners. The swearing and the violence in the sky had only brought ten men closer together in eight hours than eight years might have in that other, more normal world, such being the inevitable bonds between men who have suffered fear together and fought against it. This is perhaps the strongest of all ties among men; but that affinity now was only of the confines of our ship; for the moment, it did not extend to those outside the circle of those experiences we had just lived through.

We had been to a battlefield, not of this earth and not of the men in it. There is a chasm greater than 25,000 feet of bright blue altitude between these two worlds.

It is a hard and terrible transition to come back. I hope we all make it . . . after so much sweating and swearing and swallowing our hearts.

32

LEONARD CHESHIRE
Pathfinder Supreme

In October 1943 Leonard Cheshire took command of 617 Squadron and opened his fourth operational tour as a wing commander. He had relinquished the rank of group captain at his own request to take up flying duties again. He was already one of the most decorated men in the Royal Air Force.

He soon began to devise a fresh way of ensuring accuracy against comparatively small targets. It developed as the new marking system by an aircraft flying lower than the rest of the force. Cheshire pioneered this 'master bomber' technique with 617 Squadron, confirming its effect in practice by attacks on the flying bomb sites in the Pas de Calais. The method was later adopted for a series of small specialized raids on targets in France vitally associated with German aircraft production. By the end of March 1944 eleven of these twelve targets had been destroyed or damaged, using the new marker system of attack and a 12,000-pound blast-bomb.

The very first raid with this remarkable bomb was on an aero engine factory at Limoges on 8 February. Cheshire led twelve Lancasters through cloud to reach the target in moonlight. He then dipped his marker Lancaster down to a mere 200 feet over the factory and dropped a load of incendiaries right in the middle of it. These burst at once, throwing up volumes of smoke. The deputy leader then dropped two red-spot fires from 7,000 feet into the incendiaries, so the rest of the bombers had a perfect aiming point. Four of the five 12,000-pound monsters fell right on the factory, each obtaining direct hits on separate buildings. The damage was therefore quite devastating.

Cheshire soon realized that something more manoeuvrable than a

Lancaster was needed for the marker, and so got two Mosquitoes for this low-level task.

The 'master bomber' technique quickly established itself as adaptable to all conditions, where more normal methods would have failed. On 10 March the squadron target was a needle bearing factory comprising an area only 170 by 90 yards. Despite the weather forecast of a full moon and clear visibility, a screen of cloud obscured practically all the moonlight. Cheshire and his deputy tried repeatedly to pick out and mark the target, but decided it was no good using the red-spot fires or green indicators as intended. Improvising immediately, Cheshire dropped incendiaries on the eastern and western edges of the target, and then told the force to bomb between these twin glows. Although their success seemed doubtful, later daylight reconnaissance proved that they had succeeded beyond all their expectations, and almost entirely destroyed the vital small factory.

Still operating over France, one of Cheshire's next targets called for bombing on an altogether larger scale: the railway marshalling yards at La Chappelle, just north of Paris. The night of 20–21 April was chosen for the attack, as part of the general pre-invasion softening up and dislocation of communications in the entire northern France region. 617 Squadron was only one of many participating and the plan called for separate attacks on two aiming points within the overall target of the marshalling yards. More than 250 aircraft were due to be employed.

Bombing by now had developed into a highly skilful and scientific operation. First of all, at 00.03 a.m. six Mosquitoes reached the target area two minutes ahead of the time for the start of the attack. These aircraft dropped 'window' – strips of metal-covered paper – to confuse the enemy's radar-directed air and ground defences.

Aircraft from a group other than Cheshire's were due to drop green target indicators first of all, but although these devices were released they failed to cascade at once. So Cheshire had little time left to find and mark the exact bombing point. He operated rapidly, however, and located the aiming point – marking it with red-spot fires and telling his deputy to add more fires for a clearer indication. He gave orders for the controller of the force to instruct bombing to begin, but a further delay occurred due to a failure in the VHF radio-telephone between Cheshire and the controller. The latter did not receive the instructions till after the main force of bombers was actually in the La Chappelle area. Despite the delay and congestion, the

226

attack proceeded smoothly from then on, and subsequent reconnaissance revealed that the entire zone around the aiming point lay utterly irreparable. This yielded further proof of the efficacy of the marker technique, which had even survived setbacks such as the delay of the first indicators to cascade and the interruption of communication between Cheshire and the attack controller.

Much of the Allied bombing potential was naturally being directed against the invasion areas and the links with it, but Cheshire and his squadron fulfilled a wish to try out the marker technique where it would be most severely tested: against targets in Germany itself. Two raids during April especially proved its worth, the first on Brunswick, the second on Munich.

Cheshire's group, No. 5, received orders to bomb Brunswick on 22 April with a strong force, which turned out to be 265 aircraft. Two Mosquitoes flew ahead to report on the weather to the twenty Lancasters due to mark the target – the industrial region of Brunswick. But trouble developed with their VHF radio-telephones, so no such reports were returned. The next confusion came when the enemy – wise to the new flare system – began laying their own dummy target indicators. They looked like the genuine article, but unluckily for the Germans, they were the wrong colour. The lack of contact with the two Mosquitoes, however, was one of the things which caused the first of the flare force to drop its flares in the wrong area by about five miles.

The error did not prove too serious, though, for the ever-alert Cheshire made a low-level reconnaissance by the light they had created, and realized the mistake. He did not release his vital markers yet, waiting for another batch of flares to go down. This shot was much more on the mark, and by their light the aiming point could be assessed as accurately as necessary.

With the right region marked by the familiar red-spot fires, Cheshire authorized the attack to begin. But all did not go smoothly, because of the difficulty in the VHF communications. The interference on the radio-telephone resulted in orders being partly misinterpreted, so that some of the crews bombed the dummy green target indicators instead of the accurately placed red-spot fires. Cheshire had to report that only half the bombs of the main force fell in the target area, the rest exploding in the wrong area that had been illuminated by the green indicators. Nevertheless, a railway equipment works, an artillery tractor plant and other industrial objectives were struck by at least fifty per cent of the 741 tons dropped during the operation. Only three of the 265 aircraft were lost – a remarkably low proportion for a raid so deep into the German heartland.

Directly after Brunswick followed the famous Munich raid. Munich was selected for this attack so that the method of marking at low level could be tested against a heavily defended target, again in the heart of the Reich. Munich had particularly fierce anti-aircraft and searchlight defences. The number of guns in the immediate area of the city was thought to be about 200: nearly one for each aircraft.

It was only two nights after the Brunswick bombing, on 24 April, that exactly the same number of aircraft aimed for the city so dear to Hitler and the Nazi movement. All aircraft except ten actually attacked. The scientific approach reached one sophisticated stage further with the inclusion of a feint raid on Milan by half a dozen Lancasters of 617 Squadron to lure enemy fighters from Munich itself.

The main force flew via south-west France to avoid some defences. But four Mosquitoes carrying out the marking flew direct. From Augsburg to Munich they endured continuous and nerve-jangling ack-ack fire, yet they reached Munich precisely on scheduled time. Cheshire's aircraft was caught in a cone of searchlights and every gun within range opened fire on it. He dived to 700 feet, identified the aiming point, and dropped his red-spot fires at 1.41 a.m. The other three marker Mosquitoes did likewise.

The main force then flew into the attack. Cheshire continued to fly over the city at a mere 1,000 feet as the bombs were falling. Shell fragments hit his aircraft, but he went on with his control of the operation. Searchlights so blinded him at one stage that he nearly lost control. Still at only the height of the Empire State Building, he stayed till he was sure he could do no more. But extricating himself to head for home proved worse than flying in. He had to suffer withering fire for twelve minutes before he finally got clear. But he did. Out of the 265 aircraft taking off, nine were lost – a proportion of three and a half per cent or one in thirty. Typical odds of survival.

The damage done was out of all scale to the size of the force, and much of Munich seemed affected, including Nazi buildings.

To Leonard Cheshire the final weeks before the invasion meant more operations with his marker method. During his fourth tour of duty, he led 617 Squadron on every occasion. One such operation early in May 1944 was against the large military depot and tank park at Mailly-le-Camp, where thousands of enemy troops were believed to be located. Cheshire's Mosquito hummed over the area in clear moonlight, but despite the fact that this was the only operation of the night, he managed to mark the target correctly. All enemy fighters could be made available against the raid but it made no difference. The attack went ahead as planned, but because of the bright moonlight and quantity of fighters against them, forty-two bombers were lost out of the 338 that set out from England.

As his contribution to D-Day, Cheshire led Operation Taxable. This was designed to mislead the enemy radar defences between Dover and Cap d'Antifer into thinking that an armada was approaching that part of the coast. Sixteen Lancasters and eighteen small ships were chosen to create this illusion. Some of the ships towed balloons with reflectors attached, to simulate the sort of radar echoes emitted by large ships. The Lancasters had the more unusual job, though. They had to stooge around at precise points in flattened ellipses and release 'window'.

Cheshire said:

The tactics were to use two formations of aircraft with the rear formation seven miles behind the leaders, each aircraft being separated laterally by two miles. Individual aircraft flew a straight course of seven miles, turned round, and flew on the reciprocal course one mile away. On completion of the second leg, it returned to its former course and repeated the procedure over again, advancing far enough to keep in line with the convoy's speed of seven knots.

An average of two bundles of 'window' were jettisoned on each circuit. The operation started soon after dusk on D-1 and went on steadily until the D-Day landings along the Normandy coast. It played a valuable part in helping to achieve surprise for the greatest invasion in history.

So D-Day came and went. And with it came a new weapon for 617 Squadron, even bigger than the blast-bomb. This was the terrifying Tallboy, a 14,000-pounder which reached the ground at a speed faster than that of sound – so no warning preceded its arrival. It was developed for targets where the deepest penetration was needed, and extreme accuracy would be essential.

Tallboy made its debut on 8 June, when 617 Squadron attacked the Saumur railway tunnel, which ran north-east to the Normandy front. Four Lancasters of another squadron were detailed to drop flares, so that Cheshire could lead the assault by marking the target. This small flare force encountered difficulty, yet although many flares dropped wide, Cheshire could make out his whereabouts just sufficiently to release his familiar red-spot fires into the cutting leading to the tunnel, only forty yards from the actual mouth. Nineteen Lancasters made the attack with Tallboys after several dummy runs, to be sure they were in the precise position. Here they had to be exact, but it could hardly be expected that many of their giant bombs would drop in so small an area. In fact, one fell on the roof of the tunnel, the crater caused by this being 100 feet wide, and three exploded in the deep cutting approaching the tunnel, blocking the whole line with craters still wider than the one on the roof. And the main line stayed blocked until the Allied armies occupied the area. So the operation succeeded in its purpose, even if the actual entrance to the Saumur was not definitely blocked. The railway was the object, after all.

Jubilant at the dramatically devastating impact of these bombs, 617 Squadron looked forward to the chance of using them again. This came within a week. On 14 June Cheshire led a small section of Lancasters from 617 to attack the E-boat pens at Le Havre. The aim was to try and stop the activities of these small vessels against the supply line of the Normandy beachhead. They carried Tallboy bombs to penetrate the thick concrete roofs designed to protect the pens from the air. Needless to say, the marker for the mission was once more Cheshire.

He was as determined as ever to leave an accurate mark for the following bombers, so he dived well below the altitude range of the anti-aircraft guns, which peppered the aircraft. Their barrage geared up to a great crescendo as he descended. They actually hit his aeroplane repeatedly, but he still dived lower and lower, in daylight and with no cloud cover. He only released his markers when he felt sure the devices would do their job. The aircraft was blazing by now, but somehow Cheshire got out of that holocaust of Le Havre – and made England again. The force following scored several direct hits on the E-boat pens, and one of the Tallboy bombs pierced the roof, destroying part of the wall. Leonard Cheshire survived the war to become even more celebrated in peace. But that is another story . . .

33

GEORGE BUSH

The Flying Casket

Autumn 1943: US Navy pilot Ensign George Bush was training for future action in torpedo-bombers. After finishing his flight training, Bush was posted (or 'assigned') to the USS *San Jacinto*, a light aircraft carrier. It was Spring 1944 as the *San Jacinto* sped west over the watery vastnesses of the Pacific. Bush would be piloting a TBM Avenger, designed to carry and drop a 2,000-pound torpedo or similar bomb load. It was called 'low and slow' by some of the pilots, and flying caskets by other people. But Bush rather fancied the idea of diving almost to water-level and then gliding along to release his torpedo.

Bush's first sight of fatalities came one day after he himself had landed safely on the carrier. Another pilot crashed into one of the ship's gun positions. George saw all four of the gun crew killed before him. Some of the Avenger's early assignments were shielding land forces as they fought from island to island, or the Avengers glide-bombed specific enemy strongpoints on land. On still other occasions, they searched for submarines and in this role they carried depth-charges ready to be dropped.

Bush was one of the pilots providing low-altitude screening for the Americans when they hit Guam and Saipan, often flying through frightening ack-ack counter-attack. He said later: 'We could see the troops going ashore and the big guns from the battleships firing over them. All I could do was count my blessings that I was up there instead of down below.'

In Europe, D-Day came and went. Mid-June now in the Pacific, as the enemy instigated air attacks on the US ships grouped off Guam, Saipan, and other Mariana islands. The *San Jacinto* inevitably formed one of the prime aims for the 300-strong air armada. The carrier's fighters took off first to counter the threat, but the order went out for the Avengers to fly off, too, to avoid any danger of their being bombed while on their own flight deck.

Actually as George Bush was about to be catapulted into the air, he suddenly saw that the Avenger had oil pressure trouble in its engine. The launch went ahead, but the engine faltered in only a minute or two. George was carrying his normal crew complement of two others – and a weapon load weighing 2,000 pounds. Bush guided, coaxed, the Avenger over the wave-tops, hauled the nose upwards and then the tail just grazed the sea. The nose went forward almost gracefully and the crew of three moved rapidly from wing to raft. They began quite a frantic paddle motion, thinking of the depth-charges still aboard the sinking Avenger. At a predetermined depth, the weapons went off – without harming any of the trio. They were saved by a US destroyer and duly returned to their carrier. Just a microcosm in the whole sea war.

Through the midsummer months, the same pattern of operations followed: either attacking enemy land-targets on the islands, or seeking Japanese submarines. June, July, August. On 1 September 1944, Bush and the rest of his Avenger squadron had as their target an enemy radio communication post on one of the Bonin Islands. They were getting nearer to Japan itself now – only five or six hundred miles away. Ack-ack opposition interfered with the attack, which was only partially successful. The Avenger pilots learned that the enemy radios still transmitted, so it proved no surprise when they received word that they would be resuming their attack on the following day.

George Bush had Jack Delaney as his radioman/gunner. And a pal of Bush's, gunnery officer Ted White, asked if he could accompany them on the raid. White received permission from their commanding officer and the three of them catapulted off promptly on time. The Avenger was one of four from the carrier, escorted by a squadron-force of protective fighters. The Avengers had their full complement of bombs for the attack – four Avengers each with four bombs adding up to 2,000 pounds per plane; a dangerous load to be carrying as they flew slowly into really shaking shellfire from the ground.

The opening pair of Avengers included the one flown by the squadron commander. They dropped their loads through the ground firing, and observed strikes on a transmitting tower as well as hitting other adjacent targets. Then George Bush and the fourth Avenger

232

prepared to go in. Bush commenced the dive preparatory to dropping, but almost at once his aircraft received an alarming physical impact. An ack-ack shell tore at the Avenger's engine. Fire threatened the wings of the bomber and the usual acrid smoke thickened around the cockpit. Bush continued the course of the dive; the four bombs were released and scored hits on the radio station and then they pulled away – fast.

Bush swung around in the direction of open waters, as he knew the Avenger was doomed. Over the bomber's intercom, he told Ted White and Jack Delaney:

'Bail out. Bail out.'

Bush did not get an answer, so he put the bomber on as level a heading as he could, and bailed out himself. But in so doing, he pulled the cord of his parachute before he was fully free of the plane. The parachute became enmeshed in the tail of the Avenger and Bush hit his head on the tail. By some stroke of fortune, the parachute wrenched itself free under the wind pressure and took Bush with it. The descent was too quick but did not injure him. Bush shook the harness of the parachute off him and managed to strike out towards the life raft. Once aboard the raft, he looked all round the 360 degrees of seascape engulfing the small craft – but he could not see either of the other two aircrew. He paddled strongly to try to keep the raft away from the island they had been attacking. He did not want to end up as a prisoner of war in Japanese hands.

Bush had hit his head badly on the plane's tail and it was still bleeding after an hour or more. He went on paddling by instinct and after a couple of hours he felt really ill; head hurting, arms aching, sick after swallowing seawater. 'It seemed just the end of the world', he said later. At that stage, he did not know if there was going to be any 'later'.

George Bush needed a minor miracle. It appeared in the form of a moving dot that increased in size by the second. The other Avenger crews in the attack had in fact spotted his raft and radioed his position back to base. The message reached the US Submarine *Finback*. The dot that Bush was watching turned out to be the periscope of the *Finback*. Like some revelation, he watched while the conning tower of the submarine heaved onto the surface, and soon the whole mammal-like bulk dripped itself glossily dry. It only took a few minutes for the *Finback* crew to get Bush on board, before the craft vanished once more below the surface.

Only one of the crew of two were spotted bailing out of Bush's Avenger, but the man's parachute failed to deploy properly. The second man must have gone down with the plane. He may have been killed or injured but in either case he was never seen again. The loss of his two aircrew has always been a shadow over George Bush's survival.

That was not quite the end of the story. The *Finback* had picked up three other US Navy aircrew from the sea and the four fliers had to remain submerged in the *Finback* for about a month. They even experienced being depth-charged by an enemy bomber. Bush said later: 'That depth-charging got to me. It just shook the boat, and those guys would say, "Oh, that wasn't close".'

It was actually almost two months before Bush got back to the *San Jacinto*. The date: the end of October. US assault troops were landing on Leyte. George Bush now had a new Avenger aircraft, which he flew on further air strikes aimed at shore installations in the Philippines, as well as enemy shipping off the coast. He went on flying until nearly Christmas, when he was sent home. His flying log read as follows: 1,228 hours airborne; 126 carrier landings; 58 combat missions.

Less than a fortnight after Christmas, George Bush married Barbara Pierce on 6 January 1945. Neither of them knew that one day they would be living in The White House, Washington . . .

34

THE ATOMIC BOMBS

While the US Third Fleet and British Task Force 37 were striking at the very heart of Japan – Tokyo's airfields – the cruiser *Indianapolis* set sail from San Francisco on a crucial and top secret mission.

By 24 July 1945, the Allied fleets were in virtual command of all the waters washing the quickly diminishing Japanese Empire. The fliers of the Third Fleet found some of the remnants of the enemy navy at anchor in Kure harbour. Around the clock, US navy planes pulverized them with bombs, bullets and rockets. Hit after hit wrecked the Japanese warships, trapped in the harbour below. Then night fighters and torpedo planes intensified the attack.

In two days the Third Fleet sank or damaged a quarter of a million tons of enemy warships and got 130 planes while losing only thirty-two of their own. Some of these pilots were saved, however. Ensign Herb Law, flying from the ship *Belleau Wood*, was one.

He was badly hit in the left leg while attacking an airfield, and his plane started smoking. He was too low to bail out, and somehow landed and escaped from the agonized aircraft. As he tried to bandage his bleeding leg, a woman ran out of the bushes and fired at him from ten yards, but missed. She ran off for help, and the enemy soon found him.

They took off his clothes, bound him, and gave him no food or water for three days. He was beaten with clubs, fists, leather straps and, in general, used as a judo guinea pig. But he survived to tell his story.

On 28 July, the navy fliers returned to the scene of the shambles at Kure and finished off all the ships they could see there. An air of expectant inevitability surrounded the events of those last few days

235

of July. Throughout 28 July, too, navy planes focused their fire on the battleship *Haruna*, which stayed afloat for a few hours, but at last gave up and sank in shallow water. The crowning disgrace to the enemy was to see her turrets still sticking above the level of the water as it lapped around them. By nightfall the Japanese Navy no longer existed as a serious fighting force. Only a few stray submarines and other small craft still survived in the open seas.

That night, more planes pitched into the important port of Hamamatsu. Another scene was designed for the climax to the whole war. To tell it, we return to the *Indianapolis*, which had left San Francisco the day the Third Fleet planes were raiding Tokyo. The ship sailed under the Golden Gate at 08.36 a.m. – with a big box on board.

This wooden box contained the main nuclear parts of the first atomic bomb. Tests of the bomb had just been completed at the time of the Potsdam peace conference, then in progress in Europe, and President Truman got news of its success while he was actually there. The Allies agreed to use it only if the Japanese refused to give in.

The wake of the *Indianapolis* spread quickly westward from San Francisco to Pearl Harbor. After refuelling, she surged on again, this time to Tinian, anchoring in the harbour there about 11.00 a.m. on 26 July. The vital section of the bomb was unloaded, and two days later the rest of the nuclear parts for both the Hiroshima and Nagasaki bombs arrived by air.

On 29 July, with her part played, the *Indianapolis* sailed unescorted out of Tinian on her way from Leyte to Guam. The famous cruiser made the usual zigzag course during the day until darkness fell. Then she straightened up for a normal night. But by one of those million to one chances, a solitary submarine of the shattered Japanese fleet happened to be lying on the surface actually at right angles to the course which the *Indianapolis* was plying – and at exactly the right range for firing torpedoes. The captain of the submarine waited in the gloom of those first few minutes of 30 July, until the cruiser sailed unaware into the trap.

The Japanese captain aimed forward and hit the bow area twice. The great cruiser began to settle by the bow. With all her complex communication gear struck, it was hard to give orders. Soon afterwards, Captain Charles B. McVay III, was forced to give the order, 'Abandon ship'.

In the nightmare of that night, no SOS signal went out from her radio. And it was four days later when the pilot of a Ventura reconnaissance plane chanced to see the oil slick from the sunken ship – and the dots of many men's heads kept afloat by their life jackets. Eventually, 316 men were rescued from the *Indianapolis* . . .

At 2.45 a.m. on 6 August 1945 the crews of the three B-29s scheduled to drop the first atomic bomb went aboard their aircraft after a tropical rainstorm. The bomb-carrying plane, commanded by Colonel Paul Tibbetts, took off first and went up to 4,000 feet.

The bomb commander assembled the nuclear weapon slowly, with infinite care. Then they all ate breakfast, while the B-29 throbbed on towards Iwo. At dawn they met the other two aircraft and together the trio climbed to 10,000 feet, where the weather was better.

They had been in the clouds most of the time till then, and the rain had spattered the screens. But otherwise it still seemed to them all a quiet flight. Except that they carried the means of ending the war in a single flash of fission. They did not talk too much now.

Before climbing they had armed the bomb. Now the bombers gained altitude. Navigation was right – to the minute and the mile.

They saw Hiroshima huddled below, far below. The weather had become clear, yet with a slight haze. One of the two escorting B-29s circled to come in some miles behind the bomb-dropper to take pictures. The other one stayed on their beam.

Only about four minutes more. Then three. Then two. The bombardier gazed through his periscope, motionless – if not emotionless. One and a half minutes. After that he did not touch the bombsight once.

They were coming in high and fast now. The second hands of their watches crept around to zero and a hush radiated through the plane. The sky seemed still, horizons muted. Then the bomb fell, within fifteen seconds of the exact moment that had been planned six months earlier.

The B-29 turned sharply to try to get as clear as possible of the stupendous shock which would soon be arising. They lived through a strange ninety seconds more, while the bomb dropped.

A flash in the firmament. The bomb burst vividly, vehemently. A ball of fire from the flashpoint, growing each semisecond. The historic mushroom-shaped cloud pumped up bigger and bigger. The plane was banking at about that moment and snapped like a tin roof. The crew looked at one another. Then they heard the noise. A sharp crack and crash followed by a long roll like thunder.

They circled around only a mile or so above the holocaust, taking pictures of the cloud that was boiling before their eyes. Black smoke, and orange, blue, grey. That was all they saw, for the dust hid the whole city. They could not speak, only watch hypnotized.

Suddenly it was over for them, as the breeze caught the ball, breaking it into a raging, ragged, billowing cloud. They headed for home. The flight meant a long seven-hour haul and most of them slept some of the time, for they had been awake for a day and a half.

By mid-afternoon the three B-29s buzzed down at 300 mph, lost height and landed. The Japanese had refused to surrender. Now 70,000 of them were killed by the bomb and as many injured.

Everything up to a mile from the flashpoint was destroyed, except for a small number of reinforced concrete buildings designed to withstand earthquake shock. Even multi-storey brick buildings had been demolished. Beyond that range, roof tiles had been bubbled or melted by the flash heat. And there were many other eccentricities. People scorched to walls in grotesque silhouette. Some 60,000 of the 90,000 buildings in the city were either destroyed or severely damaged; two in every three structures. The atomic age had been born.

Three days later, it all began again. The nightmare of Nagasaki started at 11.02 a.m. on the morning of 9 August. And it was only because of bad weather that Nagasaki was the target at all for the second atomic bomb.

The town lay at the head of a long bay, forming the best natural harbour on the southern Japanese home island of Kyushu. The main commercial and residential area of the city was on a small plain near the end of the bay. Two rivers split by a mountain spur formed the two valleys in which the city lay. This spur and the irregular layout of the land reduced the area of destruction after the bomb, so that at first glance Nagasaki appeared to have been less devastated than Hiroshima. The heavily built-up area was confined to less than four square miles out of a total of some thirty-five square miles of the whole city.

Nagasaki had been one of the largest seaports in southern Japan and was very important for its varied industries, such as ordnance, ships, military equipment and other war materials. In contrast to many modern aspects of Nagasaki, the dwellings were without exception flimsy wood or wood-frame buildings, with wooden walls, perhaps plaster, and tile roofs. Many of the smaller industries and businesses were also in this kind of wooden building or flimsily-mounted masonry structures.

Nagasaki had never been subjected to large-scale bombing before the atomic bomb. But on 1 August 1945, some high explosives were actually dropped on the city. A few of these bombs hit the shipyards and dock areas in the south-west part. Several of the bombs struck the Mitsubishi Steel and Arms Works, and half a dozen landed at the Nagasaki Medical School and Hospital, with three direct hits on buildings there.

While the damage from these bombs was relatively small, it created considerable concern, and quite a number of people – principally schoolchildren – were evacuated to rural areas for safety, so reducing the population actually in the city at the time of the atomic attack.

On the morning of 9 August an air raid alarm echoed through Nagasaki at about 7.50 a.m. local time, but the all-clear followed forty minutes later. When only two B-29 Super-Fortresses were sighted at 10.53 a.m., the Japanese apparently assumed that they were only on reconnaissance. No further air raid alarm was deemed necessary.

Dead on 11.00 a.m., the observation B-29 dropped instruments attached to three parachutes, and at 11.02 a.m. the other aircraft released the atomic bomb. Commander F.L. Ashworth, United States Navy, was in technical command of the bomb, charged with the task of assuring that it was successfully dropped at the proper place and time. This second atomic mission was much more eventful for the crews than the first had been. Again, the men had been specially selected and trained. But then bad weather introduced some momentous complications.

Commander Ashworth described the whole operation like this:

The night of our take-off was one of tropical rain squalls, and flashes of lightning stabbed into the darkness with disconcerting regularity. The weather forecast told us of storms all the way from the Marianas to the 'Empire'.

Our rendezvous was to be off the south-east coast of Kyushu, and 1,500 miles away. There we were to join with our two companion observation B-29s that took off a few minutes behind us. Skilful piloting and expert navigation brought us to the rendezvous without incident.

About five minutes after our arrival, we were joined by the first of our B-29s. The second, however, failed to arrive, having apparently been thrown off its course by storms during the night. We waited thirty minutes and then proceeded without the second plane toward the target area.

During the approach to the target, the special instruments installed in the plane told us that the bomb was ready to function. We were prepared to drop the second atomic bomb on Japan.

But fate was against us, for the target was completely obscured by smoke and haze. Three times we attempted bombing runs, but without success. Then with anti-aircraft fire bursting around us and with a number of enemy fighters coming up after us, we headed for our secondary target – Nagasaki.

The bomb burst with a blinding flash, and a huge column of black smoke swirled up toward us.

Out of this column of smoke there boiled a great swirling mushroom of grey smoke – luminous with red, flashing flame – that reached to 40,000 feet in less than eight minutes. Below through the clouds we could see the pall of black smoke ringed with fire that covered what had been the industrial area of Nagasaki.

By this time our fuel supply was dangerously low, so after one quick circle of Nagasaki, we headed direct for Okinawa for an emergency landing and refuelling.

The bomb actually exploded high over the industrial valley of Nagasaki, almost midway between the Mitsubishi Works in the south and the Mitsubishi-Urakami Ordnance Works (for torpedoes) in the north, the two main targets of the city.

Nearly everything within half a mile of the flashpoint vanished – including heavy structures. And including people. All Japanese homes were destroyed up to three times this distance – one-and-a-half miles. Within a radius of as much as three-quarters of a mile, both people and animals died almost instantaneously.

So to the summary of damage at Nagasaki: 14,000 dwellings were destroyed and 5,400 half-destroyed. This destruction was limited by the layout of the city. And the casualties: the source which recorded the Hiroshima figure as 66,000 dead and 69,000 injured, gives the equivalent Nagasaki totals as 39,000 dead and 25,000 injured.

The war was over within a week.

35

THE JET AGE

The British engineer Frank Whittle patented the basic design for the turbo-jet engine as long ago as 1930 – and he worked on jet propulsion in the Royal Air Force from 1937 to 1946. The Whittle jet engine was incorporated in the experimental Gloster E 28/39 aircraft, which flew first in May 1941. German and American jet aircraft were actually built using his basic principles.

At the end of the war, Britain and America were the only nations actually engaged in jet fighter construction. The De Havilland Vampire jet exceeded the 500 mph mark. The Venom was the next version of the Vampire and then the Gloster Meteor proceeded to outdo both of them. Around the same time, the first US jet fighter after the war was the famous Shooting Star. This could claim a top speed just over 650 mph, while the Thunderjet from Republic flew a fraction faster. But the sound barrier had not yet been broken. Evolving from the Mustang, the North American Sabre dated also from around 1947 and nudged the speed record a few mph higher to 671. Soon the Russians had jet fighters flying in the form of the MiG15.

Britain then re-entered the speed stakes fleetingly. The Hawker Hunter was powered by a Rolls Royce Avon engine and for a short while in the Coronation Year of 1953 held the world speed record of 728 mph. The latest advance in jet propulsion was of course reheat. The Hunter proved highly popular and was exported to many countries, while the Black Arrows RAF display team flew Hunters, too.

The reality of breaking the sound barrier was flying supersonic in level flight – not in a dive. The American Skyray from Douglas cranked the speed record above 750 mph and virtually touched

Mach 1 while level. The swept-wing Sabre was really the first fighter to attain supersonic level flight. This also occurred in 1953. And so it went on; the Starfighter from Lockheed and more Russian MiGs. The very last time that Britain went down as holding the world speed record was in 1956, when the research aircraft, Fairey Delta, leap-frogged over the recent records to register 1,132 mph. But the design was never developed further into production.

It would be tedious to list at length all the advances after this. The Gloster Javelin was another delta-wing shape, designed as a two-man night fighter. The Gnat turned out to be too small as a fighter but ideal as a jet trainer for the Royal Air Force – and for the famous Red Arrows aerobatic team. The French Mirage appeared in dashing Gallic style. Then the RAF Mach 2 interceptor fighter was the two-jet-Avon powered Lightning, with the engines mounted one above the other. Both the Lightning and Gnat reappear in the next two chapters. Following the famous Lightning, the Royal Air Force remained in technological prominence with the Phantom, Harrier jump jet, Jaguar and the Tornado. The last must be the noisiest one of all!

Meanwhile, several of these jets were excelling themselves in famous air races sponsored by the London *Daily Mail*. These contests were conceived to commemorate the newspaper's sponsorship of the original air races – as far back as Blériot. The first of these new races was flown between Paris and London – from the Arc de Triomphe to Marble Arch. This at once became known as the Arch-to-Arc or vice-versa. The outright winner was 65 Squadron, RAF (Squadron Leader Maughan) whose team completed the course in a mere forty and three-quarters minutes. To accomplish this feat, their Hunter was backed up by a pair of helicopters plus two motor-bikes!

Both races were split into several categories so that entrants with different flying machines had an opportunity to compete in their particular type. In 1969 the second of the pair of races was on a more global scale – from the top of the Post Office Tower in London to the equivalent level of the Empire State Building in New York. Competitors displayed imaginative ingenuity. Civilians, celebrities and Service teams competed and the Services as usual came out winners in both transatlantic directions.

The record time recorded from London to New York logged in at six hours eleven minutes fifty-seven seconds. A still-novel RAF Harrier jump jet was the aircraft behind the feat. The vertical take-off and landing plane caused a sensational splash of publicity when it hovered down to land actually in the hubbub of downtown New York.

For the New York to London direction, the Harrier also helped achieve a fast time by landing at St Pancras railway station – only a short way from the Post Office Tower. But the Royal Navy won the laurels in this direction. A Phantom jet helped register the truly staggering time of five hours eleven minutes twenty-two seconds. Presumably with a strong westerly tailwind!

36

THE FIREBIRDS AND
THE RED ARROWS

I must dedicate the next two chapters to all the RAF aircrew who flew me with such skill for many years. And although it is told through my eyes, the story is essentially theirs.

Before I joined Royal Air Force publicity, I had only ever made one flight. And that was a very brief affair by helicopter from Gosport to Lee-on-Solent and back. I suppose I should have realized that RAF publicity would entail flying – and it did. I was plunged in at once with a return trip to Singapore in the days when the Comet was still new. Then on a subsequent flight over the same route, two engines failed in the middle of the night near the Persian Gulf and the Comet had to make an emergency landing at Teheran on the remaining pair.

The fault was found and we were back in the air again. A brilliant yellow-peach sunrise at 3.08 a.m. cheered me up and then three hours later came the descent to Gan. As the jet crossed the Equator, we suddenly sighted Gan, one and three-quarter miles by three-quarters of a mile, most southerly of the Maldive Islands and some 600 miles south of Colombo. A palm-fanned, emerald and coral isle set in a sapphire sea, Gan marked the most westerly outpost of the Far East Air Force.

There are few seasonal changes on Gan and few unpleasant creatures. Bird life is limited, mosquitoes are rare, cats were then the only common animal and the sea sported prolific multi-coloured fish. As the Comet came closer, the colours cleared to turquoise reefs and an oil-blue sea. The 3,000-yard runway was literally the length of the island, and the Comet came in over a lagoon only inches above the shallows.

My next take-off and landing was less idyllic, though much nearer home. I arrived at RAF Wattisham in Suffolk blissfully unaware of what the following few hours would mean for me. The flight was to be in a Lightning at twice the speed of sound. Remember that this was back in the early 1960s. It all sounded rather glamorous, flying with the Firebirds aerobatic squadron at about 1,400 miles an hour. The reality felt a little less so.

I was driven along the RAF station's roads to the buff-brick building of the sick quarters. Here the senior medical officer explained the precautions that have to be taken when flying at high speeds and altitude. The flow of air in and out of the ears must not be impeded, and variations of pressure can damage a weak eardrum. Similarly a cheek sinus must not be blocked, and no-one with a sore throat, cold or cough can fly under these conditions.

After examining me, he issued a medical inspection report that I was fit to fly up to an altitude of 40,000 feet. This was the limit unless someone passed a special decompression test. From there I passed on to the central clothing section to be kitted up. This included flying overalls, gloves, a G-type helmet, oxygen mask, safety helmet and a Mae West, complete with its own radio homing beacon for use in case of ejection into the sea. Metal leg restrainers would keep the knees firmly together on ejection. For higher altitudes up to 60,000 feet, pilots had special pressure kits to help counteract the substantial stresses imposed at that height in an aircraft travelling at over Mach 2 – or a mile in under three seconds.

Then I was ready to meet the Lightning, at the time our No. 1 day and night all-weather weapon against enemy attack. The first truly supersonic aircraft of the RAF, the Lightning was powered by two Rolls Royce Avon turbojet engines with reheat. Its ascent straight from take-off could be as steep as eighty degrees. I hoped the climb would not be quite as rocket-like as that.

It could be scrambled to take-off in under a minute. In well under three minutes it could climb to heights greater than any attained in the Battle of Britain. Lock-on gear enabled its radar to track a target's movements and prevent contact being lost. Even as long ago as this, the radar information was being processed through computers and with the guidance provided to the pilot and his attack sight, he could close to missile-firing range. At this point, the homing-heads locked-on to fire electronically. He never needed to see his target. All of this is quite commonplace today, of course, though new in those days.

The pilot flying me was Malcolm Moore, a thirty-year-old flight lieutenant. We walked over to the two-seater trainer Lightning. Like all the other aircraft in the Firebirds, this had the squadron's red-and-white chequers on each side of the nose, red spines and tail units and red leading edges to wings and tailplanes. The aircraft's dramatic sixty-degree sweptback wings were chopped off with sudden sheerness, giving the whole design a look of a missile as much as a manned craft. The sleek silver body threw back the sun.

Malcolm and I climbed our respective ladders, sat down, and strapped ourselves firmly into the seats. Each seat ejected as a unit; a succession of small charges would shoot the occupant clear of the tailplanes and he would fall free to 10,000 feet, when the parachute system operated. The only thing left to be done was to withdraw the safety pins from the ejector seat release to make it operational.

At last we were all ready. Malcolm was carrying out his series of standard cockpit checks, and then he pressed the 'engine start master'. Another knob closed the canopy smoothly. Taxiing from its position in front of the huge hangar, the Lightning jolted gently round to the take-off runway. Our course was to be on a bearing of 040, roughly north-east, till we got to the North Sea.

'Clear to line up', came over the air.

As yet the Lightning was leashed, not hinting at its hidden power. But its nose was pressed eagerly upwards, as if impatiently scenting the air. We were swinging on to the take-off runway, where a crazy Clapham Junction of tyre tracks reminded me of the thousands of past sorties made from this historic field. Everything was still pretty peaceful, though the engine did vibrate a bit. We lined up on the dotted white centre line. Seventy-five per cent engines, then eight-five; they didn't talk of revs.

'Affirmative take-off.'

Malcolm released brakes and we suddenly surged forward. He read the knots and the gain was as fast as it took him to speak the words. Or faster.

'100, 120, 130, 150 . . .'

At 150 knots the nose-wheel lifted off the ground. '165, 176 . . .' At 175 knots the aircraft was airborne with a rush. The speed over the stained runway seemed staggering.

'Brakes and undercarriage up', Malcolm told me over the intercom, which was controlled by a switch on the oxygen mask. I was still finding breathing hard, because I was not used to wearing the mask. A shallow climb for a few seconds, before Wattisham fell away and each moment put more and more air space between us and the watercolours of the Suffolk landscape. Malcolm nosed us into a twenty-two-degree climb, and the speed had doubled since take-off; 350 knots, then 420. Pressure pounded on my ears as we quivered through the clouds.

On the upper side of the cloud-base, I looked down through the gaps at the patchwork of pale green and rust fields, their colours draining with every extra thousand feet we thrust upwards.

'Eighteen thousand feet and doing Mach point nine', Malcolm announced.

The Lightning could have exceeded the speed of sound in a climb, without reheat, too. We were leaving the heavy lather of clouds and coming up to the Norfolk coast. The light line, thin as thread, was the beach. The sheen on the water made it seem solid, not liquid. More like beaten silver. A blob of a boat was the only evidence that it really was sea.

Cold factual talk continued between the base and Malcolm. We were coming up to what was once called the sound barrier. And not that long ago. '33,000 . . . 36,000.' We were also up to our cruising altitude.

'I am now going high speed', Malcolm reported over the radio. We were already verging on Mach 1. Before we increased, though, we heard: 'Contact two o'clock.'

At once I peered out to try and spot another aircraft. I thought of collision courses and I did not really want to eject at this height. Or any other. The thought of free-falling 26,000 feet did not seem too funny. I continued to scan the sky, realizing anew the intensity of its colour at these heights. Overhead, the deepest azure through the canopy in the mid-distance lightening to Air Force blue and then paling off to a turquoise horizon. The sun was beating strongly on us.

The Mach meter was hovering around 1.0 when Malcolm applied reheat. With a frightening jerk, we got a great rocket of a thrust, as if a giant had punched us hard. I felt forced through the back of the seat, as one would if a car could suddenly start from scratch to 100 mph in a second or so. It was as quick as that. And as severe as that. Mach 1.25.

Then it went up to Mach 1.45 . . . 1.5 . . . 1.55.

So this was it. The filmy blue net of the sea strewn seven miles below, and if we could have seen it, scarlet flame flashing from the reheat. Inside the cockpit, Malcolm and I isolated from the world, hurtling for Holland at well over a thousand miles an hour. There ahead were strung the necklet of Dutch islands.

Hypnotized by the strange sensation around me, I suddenly saw a small fly flitting on the windscreen inside the cockpit. Unworried by lack of oxygen. Free from pressure problems. It had come all this way with us and would return to Wattisham.

I was just beginning to feel a bit blasé, that there was nothing so very special about supersonic flight in a fighter – when it happened. Malcolm decided to decrease speed, by several hundred knots in several seconds. I had a feeling that I was going straight through the windscreen. Like stopping dead in a car at 100 mph. The reverse of the reheat thrust. But I could not fall forward. I was strapped in tight. The stress was severe, to someone not used to it. And I was not.

Then he made a sharp turn. The Lightning was amazingly manoeuvrable. An inch on the control column and we took a drastic turn. Gravity dragged at me. I was twice, three times, nearly four times, as heavy as normal. Making any move was out of the question. I could not lift my hand. My head felt like lead. The strain on the aircraft must have been immense, but not as bad as it was on me. I was not made of the latest light alloys.

Back on the homeward course, we were closing with the coast at a mere ten miles a minute. I breathed more comfortably, not noticing the mask. Then through the sharply raked windscreen, I saw a large section of the East Anglian coastline bulging below. Malcolm fixed the distance at nearly fifty miles. Five minutes later we were up to the coast, as the radar screen picked up a large blip. It turned out to be a V-bomber far above us, and we were still at 36,000 feet. If it had been an enemy bomber, we could have intercepted up to twelve miles high. Luckily it wasn't.

As we crossed the coast, Great Yarmouth formed one square inch of screen. Malcolm banked steeply. Sharp descent then, with pressure and pain in my ears. From 36,000 to 18,000 to 2,000. All in a minute or two. Diving directly through the cloud cover, we saw the Suffolk scene. We straightened out, easing the pressure. Then we approached for our landing run. Orange flares lit the end of the runway. Lower, but still fast; 200 knots. Undercarriage down. The runway loomed.

At 165 knots we touched down, roared along the tarmac, and let out the dragnet parachute to save wear on brakes. In a moment we halved our speed and slowed to a stop. That was my initiation into high-speed flight; safely piloted by Malcolm Moore.

Soon after this, the Firebirds aerobatic squadron was disbanded. Then the Red Arrows team was formed and someone had the idea that I might be allowed to accompany them on one of their regular displays. I suppose it was a privilege to be about the first person ever to do so, but I felt a little apprehensive all the same . . .

What was it like flying with the leader of our aerobatic team? I found out, with a vengeance. I had to report to RAF Fairford in Gloucestershire. I did not know quite what to expect, though I had that Lightning flight as a reminder. At least Malcolm Moore had flown us in a normal manner. These pilots would be going berserk all over the sky! All right if you were watching from the ground. And worse than that, they would be trying to fly as close together as possible; literally a few feet between wingtips. Another fine mess I'd got myself into.

The seven crimson Gnat advanced jet trainers were lined up ready to taxi to the runway. Again wearing flying overalls, 'bone dome' and metal leg restrainers, I was strapped securely into the rear seat of the transonic trainer. I adjusted my oxygen mask as the canopy snapped shut. At 3.41 p.m. the ground crew ran clear of the aircraft. We were in the first Gnat to move off. The leader of the Red Arrows, and my personal pilot, was Flight Lieutenant Lee Jones. He controlled his team through radio.

'Red 10, flap 90 – go.'

'Up to sixty per cent – go.'

'Taxiing forward – now.'

Then we stopped for a second.

'Brakes on – go.'

'Red Arrows line up seven.'

We were taxiing on to the runway. The die was cast.

'Up to ninety – go.'

The Bristol Siddeley Orpheus jet rose to a distant roar. At 3.48 p.m. we took off smoothly with the other Gnats in close formation.

'Gear up – go.'

'Wing over port – now.'

So into a series of amazing manoeuvres in various formations – arrow, rhombus, half-swan, wineglass, big tee, vixen and vampire.

249

The pre-flight briefing began to make sense. '. . . in arrow formation smoking, changing to rhombus, rolling port in rhombus, cut smoke, from arrow slide to half-swan, dive on half-swan, pull up for loop . . .'

We went into a steep climb, with the other Gnats on our tail. I felt the force of G. As I did, my G-suit inflated hard, hurting my legs and stomach. Suddenly I was four times as heavy as usual. Not twelve and a half stones but fifty stones! Before I got used to breathing in my mask while weighing so much, I found myself muttering B.R.E.A.T.H.E. for the first seven times that I inhaled. I could hear my lungs amplified over the intercom. The pressure went on. It was all I could do to keep a clear mind – to keep conscious at all. My neck muscles ached with the effort of supporting a head that seemed to be bulging and felt like a heavy metal sculpture.

The Gnats corkscrewed through the sky as we flew into our first roll. Fleetingly the ground shifted across the windscreen from one side, to overhead, to the other side. Then we dived – 4G again at a speed of 400 knots. The ground loomed up alarmingly. I hoped Lee Jones felt more alert than I did. We pulled out of our dive and slid into the next formation, like a seamless aerobatic legato.

Then we rocketed into another steep climb for our first formation loop. The sun scorched. That same sense of endless sky beyond the transparency of the canopy. We pulled into the vertical and G was still severe, though the team was of course used to it. I was not, at my advanced age of forty.

Suddenly we were over the top with no real sense of being upside down. But seeing is believing. I looked up through the windscreen and there spread overhead lay the soft green English landscape, like photographic paper on a ceiling. I could see the airfield, the runways, the control tower and the crowd. Even a midget man standing the wrong way up on the tower.

As the moment at the top of the loop passed, we somersaulted down towards the vertical, with all aircraft still in perfect formation – flown with superlative skill. Time after time we flew over Fairford, in ever-changing patterns, repeating the rolls and the loops. Over the radio came the steady voice of Lee:

'Arrows going down for a vampire loop.'

'Smoke on – go.'

'Pulling up – now.'

We changed to arrow formation as we went over the top again.

'Arrow – go.'

'Smoke off – go.'

Then we were flying very fast and low along the crowd line. My head crashed against the right-hand side of the canopy and each aircraft was rolling very, very fast. We were in a 'twinkle' roll, turning about our axis at a rate greater than one revolution per second. The horizon spun, I glimpsed a blur of green, and we were level and once more pulling up into a hard wingover.

Towards the end of the show, two of the Red Arrows broke off to do low-level 'rocketry', flying from opposite sides of the airfield and crossing over close to each other. This was accompanied by smoke streaming from them to heighten the dramatic effect.

The finale. We were approaching the crowd in very open formation to pull up in a 'join-up' loop – with all the aircraft converging again on the leader; us. The formation was as one just before the top of the loop. We completed the loop and turned towards the crowd, again very low, before pulling up for a set-piece 'bomb-burst' all over the sky in the shape of a seven-strong fan formed from smoke trails at various angles.

The outside Gnats went out at the lowest angle and our lead aircraft climbed straight up at 7G as the focus of the fan. Then we made a loop break and ran in for the landing. I had to take their word about the 7G, because I could not honestly swear to remaining conscious! The display had lasted just sixteen minutes. My first and last venture with the Red Arrows. But thank you, Lee Jones.

The changing personnel of the team have maintained their status as the finest aerobatic team in the world. A reputation preserved not without loss of life . . .

37

TEST-FLYING THE VC10

I flew in virtually all types of RAF aircraft over the following years. Certainly my most remarkable experiences were associated with that splendid long-distance transport, the VC10. The RAF's own version of the VC10 was due to enter service in the mid-1960s. And the commercial versions were being test-flown by picked RAF aircrew and pilots of the British Aircraft Corporation. I went along, too, on a series of test-flights, first with the VC10 and then the Super VC10, before the RAF version took to the air.

That is how one day in 1965 I found myself high over the West Country in an early prototype VC10. I was sitting right behind the test pilot. We were about to start stall trials. Stall means loss of control caused through insufficient speed. The VC10 had all possible safeguards to stop a stall occurring. We were testing those devices. If they worked, a stall should never happen in production models of the airliner.

There were several stages of warning for a pilot approaching a stall – stick-shaker, stick-knocker, stick-pusher. So to the first of the seventeen stall trials. The air brakes reduced our speed. The undercarriage was up, and engines were at idling thrust. The air speed indicator fell towards 100 knots. The nose was well up. It was a tense time – the start of the first stall test.

Suddenly all my senses were assailed. The shaker and knocker machine-gunned out virtually together. The klaxon and stick-pushers followed straight after. The cabin was swamped with sound. Red lights blinked brilliantly. The stick-pusher was the automatic device to shove the control column – or stick – fully forward to bring the nose down. The whole flight deck quivered, quaked. The elevators outside were fluttering. So was my pulse. The nose dipped dramatically. I felt as if I were plunging down on a switchback railway, but the pilots concentrated calmly on their exacting job.

The altimeter reading revolved like a fruit machine: 20,000 feet; 19,500; 19,000; 18,500; 18,000; 17,500; 17,000. The ninety-eight-ton giant jet had dived 3,000 feet. Despite the violent vibration, all the protections had operated perfectly and the VC10 maintained its lateral stability and did not dip a wing. A thousand yards lower in the sky, the pilot applied power, pulled out of the dive and we were swiftly levelling off again. Once more it was like a switchback, but at the bottom this time. Stall test number one was over. Numbers 2, 3, 4 and 5 followed.

The undercarriage came down for stall No. 6 and the speed was cut to a mere ninety knots. The chewing gum stuck to my teeth. We had been airborne for an hour. So it went on. Climbing, stall situation, diving, straightening out. And each time the same shaking, quaking, rattling and screeching. No pilot could ignore these warnings.

Numbers 7–14. Undercart up or down; flaps up or down; slats in or out. Then the pilot was trying it with ninety per cent power, cutting one engine. Both he and the co-pilot were studies in relaxed concentration.

'It'll really sit up and beg this time', said one of the aircrew.

I rather wished I were at home with our black poodle.

The same stall signs. The same shuddering, juddering. I was taken right out of my seat; lifted clear off it as we went over the top into the dive. Then we roared down with a rush. The last two tests were dynamic stalls, while turning right and then left. These were the most severe and serious stalls in an aircraft. All four engines were lit and the 235,000 pounds of aircraft started its turn. It had eighty-four per cent power and the undercarriage was down. Once again the clangour in the cabin, with everything going off at the same time. The same sensation as the stick was shoved forward. The airliner dipped into a steep bank and the start of a spin. I felt all screwed round as it fell. A few seconds later the pilot pulled it out. Just the left-hand turn to do, then it was all over. A routine day in the life of a test pilot.

Those were stall trials of the VC10. So from the Standard VC10 to the Super VC10. We were roaring down the runway in a Super VC10. 'Now', clipped the test pilot, and the port outer engine instantly died.

That was the start of one typical test flight in the gigantic jet at

253

Torrejon airfield, near Madrid. The day had begun as I walked over to the massive aircraft with its ninety-odd portholes dotted along a fuselage thirteen feet longer than the Standard VC10. Two clusters of four wheels supported the 120 tons, together with the two smaller nosewheels. G-ASGB was scarcely a month old. The letters identified this second prototype Super VC10 on its high forty-feet tail, which dominated, dwarfed, the little Spanish fighter aircraft scattered nearby. The interior of the aircraft was crammed with hundreds of instruments for reading its performance. Testing an aeroplane was and still is a highly scientific business. The VC10 project pilot, BAC's Bill Cairns, wore dark green glasses and his normal brown lounge suit. He sat in the left-hand seat. The co-pilot, Flight Lieutenant Alf Musgrove, and the flight engineer were already both busy at their banks of instruments. Musgrove was later promoted to squadron leader.

'We'll be starting engines in five minutes', Musgrove reported.

'Let me know when you're ready for the check list.'

'Your radio altimeter was ticking.'

'We'll be about 40 minutes on circuit.'

Then the long check list started:

'Brakes on . . .'

The engines erupted and we were soon taxiing round the peritrack towards the main runway. Clear skies. Clouds skimmed the distant hills. The four Conway engines revved as the Super VC10 shivered like a leashed animal waiting to spring forward. We surged ahead, commencing the roll down the 13,000-feet runway. We were roaring down it now. Power pulsed through the aircraft. I was thrust back into my seat. We were nearing V1. That was the critical final refusal speed. The point of decision. If the speed were above the necessary for lift-off, we could go ahead. Otherwise we could not.

Faster to ninety knots, ninety-one, ninety-two, ninety-three. 'Now', called Cairns. Musgrove pulled back the throttle and shut down No. 1 engine. Sometimes he closed the fuel cock instead. The Super VC10 lost 25,000 lb of take-off thrust in a flash, yet we heard only a slight sigh at this loss of power. There was hardly any perceptible effect, just a slight shudder as the jet shrugged and continued to take-off in mere seconds. Cairns did not even have to adjust rudder. He just exerted extra pressure with his feet and applied elevator. Take-off was being achieved at minimum possible speed, well below the normal stipulated, to cover a pilot's possible error in operation.

Onlookers heard the gathering roar as the nose suddenly tilted. This was VR: rotation or unstick speed. Another moment and it was V2, the speed at thirty-five feet. The crack and boom and blast of the jets, though inside all was quiet. The aircraft assumed a sharp body angle, with its rear right down and almost scraping the ground. At such angles of ascent, the airflow could be distorted and the engines left gasping for air.

We were high in the air. The Super VC10 swept in a majestic climb straight off the runway, continued to ascend, and circled at 180 knots – still on only three engines. A thousand feet below, the shadow of the airliner rippled over the brown earth and across a row of trees lining a river. We went on circling until we came in for a three-engine landing.

On the roof of a nearby building, alongside radar scanners and aerials, stood advanced camera-recording apparatus which could be triggered off electronically from the aircraft itself. The pilot was also linked to the camera crew by radio. As the airliner lost height and approached the runway for the recorded landing, the countdown started – 'five, four, three, two, one.' At zero a button was pressed in the aircraft to energize the camera automatically. This was at thirty-feet altitude. At the same second, Cairns cut off engines. The camera took a series of shots during the six seconds to touchdown and then went on recording. It was all still smooth as the plane joined its shadow on the runway.

In addition to the camera record, there was a camera aboard the aircraft taking the readings of instruments, such as altimeters, air speed indicators, heading, yaw, pitch and roll, a vertical camera, a camera on the end of the runway and records of parameter readings, giving stress and other figures during the relevant periods. These records were fed into a computer to interpret the results of trials after each day's flights. Take-offs were similarly recorded from 'brakes off' to 100-feet height.

We repeated the whole operation and next tried a full four-engine take-off. The runway really rushed past. To get a fresh impression, I viewed this take-off through the periscope right at the rear of the cabin. I gripped the periscope handles as the plane accelerated. Through the circle of the viewer, I watched a strange scene unfold. Beyond a mist of jetstream, the ground seemed to be shooting away. I was forced towards the tail as we lifted off. I had to stand sideways to keep upright at all. In a split second the runway dropped steeply, like an astronaut's view of the receding earth. It looked almost like vertical take-off.

Then we were off on another target. For this series, we were flying on three engines only towards a long lake. At low altitude over the slight hills, neat vineyards, and wilder country, the airliner was dead quiet, dead steady. There ahead curled the lake, glistening green-silver in the sun. We banked, descended, and then climbed at 136 knots for five minutes – minimum speed and maximum permitted time for running engines at full power. This was a 'ferry baulked landing climb', meaning a ferry flight with one engine out of action throughout. It simulated an overshoot on coming in to land and proved an ability to clear hills around an airfield. The five-minute climb was eventually up, and we were banking, Spain seen on its side.

'Gear up, please.' The undercarriage had been down during that run.

'Shut down No. 2 engine', Cairns to Musgrove.

'Twenty degree flap.'

The next test was a 'ferry second segment climb'. This meant with Nos. 1 and 2 engines off. Both the port engines were completely out of action. Only the other two continued to run. Yet these two had to lift the quarter-of-a-million-pound load. That was the theory. The lake was visible on the pilot's radar. We commenced the climb, throttling forward over the lake. I looked through a porthole at the two port engines, silenced. The speed read 149 knots. I saw sunlight and earth and water. Each of these long climbs had its reciprocal run as a double-check.

Cairns to Musgrove: 'It's all yours.'

The RAF pilot took over for the 'third segment final stage climb-away'. This one was a ten-minute climb at a lower degree of power. Although the aircraft remained steady, I could somehow sense the strain on it; a ten-minute climb on only two of the four engines.

He read off the time of the climb against the altitude reached: three and a half minutes 9,000 feet; seven and a half minutes 13,800 feet; eight and two-thirds minutes 15,000 feet; ten minutes 16,400 feet. Then the inevitable reciprocal run. Then set for home. I went up front for a fast brakeless landing without reversers. In a few seconds we were down and rolling on and on and on – to a halt.

The afternoon consisted of more tests along the same lines as earlier, with an overall weight of 275,000 pounds. Three-engine take-offs, climbs to clear hills on overshoots and a recorded landing. We were coming down for the final landing of the day – touchdown, and a brake failure. A boom like an anti-aircraft gun across the airfield as a tyre burst . . . We taxied to a stop. They said it was a fairly routine mishap, especially when tests were at 335,000 pounds instead of the normal 235,000 pounds.

I flew home from Madrid in a prototype BAC1-11 which had been undergoing similar 'hot-high' tests while we had been there. I could not help remembering soberly that only eighteen months earlier, on 22 October 1963, Mike Lithgow and Dickie Rymer had taken a BAC1-11 on a test flight from Wisley. During the same stall trials as we had flown on the VC10 from that same airfield, their planes had got into a deep stall, descended at high vertical velocity, and the whole test crew had been killed . . . I felt rather relieved to land on English soil a couple of hours later, even though the airfield was Wisley.

The following year, 1966, the RAF got delivery of its very first VC10. As the design varied from the commercial versions, the aircraft had to undergo the same full programme of tests to prove its own airworthiness. I accompanied the test crew of this first prototype on some of the trials. The two chief RAF officers responsible for this arduous schedule were Squadron Leaders Brian Taylor and Alf Musgrove. We were about to take-off on buffet boundary tests. Buffet as in being knocked about – not as in smoked salmon canapés. This meant subjecting the VC10 to severe gravity strains in turns, dives and climbs to confirm its capacity to withstand them without causing unacceptable wing buffeting – and thus possible operational danger.

Thumbs up from Alf Musgrove. Turning on to Wisley's main runway, we taxied in a semi-circle as the sun streamed through the portholes. The usual take-off angle. Surrey was spread below in the ice-blue winter light. We were in a steep climb as the morning mist draped the Downs. A tiny smoke trail wormed its way westward – a train. All dead smooth as the Isle of Wight lay framed in a single porthole. Visibility was virtually limitless to Poole Harbour and beyond to Portland Bill. We reached 40,000 feet. The buffet tests were about to start, to be conducted through the 'flight envelope' from 40,000 down to 17,000 feet.

'You'll feel just a shade of G', Alf told me in the usual understatement of a test pilot.

Straight and level flight is reckoned as 1G. These tests checked the

VC10 at 1.35G. We were going into our first test. Our speed was Mach .8 or about 470 mph. We went into a tight turn, screwing round hard. Things revolved quite abruptly, but the aircraft continued to purr, as if pleased at its performance. That was at 40,000 feet.

At 36,000 feet: turned tight left, dived, climbed. A switchback sensation again. Climbed, levelled, over the top. Patchwork of fields at forty-five degrees. Then the second test at the same altitude. The speed was Mach .86 or 500 mph. Round, down, up, over, level. Not much buffeting but again the feeling was stomach-turning. I was glad to get on the level after the jet had corkscrewed its way through cubic miles of upper air.

At 30,000 feet, after another tight turn, a shudder rippled through the fuselage. As we swung from left to sharp right, the sunlight through the portholes moved in parallel ovals rapidly to and fro across the empty cabin floor, like marbles rolling with the aircraft. They were back to the port side as the sun returned to starboard. A factory chimney smoked miles below.

At 25,000 feet, more violence. We dived faster, came out of it, levelled, slowed sharply, then went down again with the cabin swaying. We slowed and shuddered over the dark tones of the New Forest. At 17,000 feet, the cabin creaked on the final run. Still all was well. Measurements were taken and the buffet boundary tests were over. Final low-level runs were made westward and eastward with constant power setting.

We took off at 10 a.m. We landed at 12.30. By one o'clock I was drinking lager with the crew in an old country inn not far from Wisley. I had forgotten how refreshing it could taste.

Another sobering postscript to these tests came four or five months later. Anyone who knows about British aircraft will recall that our three great rear-engine airliners of the 1960s and beyond were the BAC-111, the Trident, and the VC10. The BAC-111 suffered that tragic crash during stall trials in 1963. The VC10 managed to go into service without any fatal accident. But on 3 June 1966 a Trident test crew were putting the three-engine jet through its stall trials from Hatfield. Somehow they got into a superstall, the Trident developed a flat spin and it crashed killing everyone on board. So the VC10 was the only one of the three not to experience a fatal crash during stall trials . . .

My rewards for surviving those varied tests were at least a couple of pleasanter flights. The first one was a day return trip of nearly 7,000 miles – from London to Lagos and back. We left Heathrow at 8.13 a.m. on a wet Saturday morning and returned there fifteen hours later. It was still raining. But we had been nearly to the Equator and back in between. The second of these VC10 flights gave me a day in New York, my very first visit to that thrilling city. I shall never forget the intense impact of that day in New York. Nor shall I forget any of those pilots of the Royal Air Force who flew me with such skill and care.

38

THE CONCORDE IS BORN

Concorde combines the art of its aesthetics with the genius of its engineering. It is the world's only supersonic commercial aircraft. It can cruise at more than twice the speed of sound at an altitude of 60,000 feet – eleven miles high. A typical flight from London to New York takes a little less than three and a half hours. Concorde made its fastest flight across the Atlantic on 7 February 1966, when it completed the eastbound direction from New York to London in the astounding time of two hours fifty-two minutes fifty-nine seconds.

Only a decade or so after the end of the Second World War, Britain and France both started work separately on the idea of supersonic airline research. That was in 1956. The best way to convey the Concorde achievement is to record the milestones that flashed by from then on. In 1960, British Overseas Airways Corporation accepted its first Concorde reservation – though the aeroplane still existed only on paper.

Britain and France found that they were working along such similar lines that in 1962 they decided to develop a single supersonic design. The two governments signed an agreement for joint design, development and manufacture – which of course cut the costs dramatically. This partnership between the British Aircraft Corporation (now Airbus UK) and Aérospatiale (now EADS) eventually led to twenty Concordes being built. Each country made one prototype, one pre-production aircraft and eight production.

1967 saw the roll-out of the first prototype at Toulouse. The first flight of Concorde 001 from Toulouse took place on 2 March 1969, while the equivalent maiden flight of the British prototype, Concorde 002, was logged the following month on 9 April 1969. Filton, Bristol, marked the airfield for this and many successive test flights. In fact Concorde was subjected to 5,000 hours of testing by the time it qualified for passenger flight certification. This made it easily the most tested aircraft in aviation history. The key date for its first actual supersonic flight was as early as 1 October 1969.

While the test programme progressed, BOAC became the world's first supersonic airline. Of the sixteen production aircraft, fourteen were made available for sale. BOAC (BA) ordered five Concordes in June–July 1972. Thirty years later, British Airways owned and operated seven Concordes.

The milestones continued to fly past. On 20 September 1973, Concorde 002 landed at Dallas/Forth Worth on its first-ever visit to the USA; on 17 June 1974, the first double Atlantic crossing in one day and in 1975 on 5 December, the UK Civil Aviation Authority awarded the Certificate of Airworthiness to Concorde.

The commercial supersonic travel era was inaugurated simultaneously by Britain and France. British Airways, by flying from London to Bahrain, and Air France, by flying from Paris to Rio de Janeiro. This historic date was 21 January 1976. That same May marked the first transatlantic service to Washington. And eventually agreement was reached for the London to New York service to start on 22 November 1977. Continuing the list of aviation records, the first round-the-world flight by a British Airways Concorde dated from 8 November 1986. The staggering statistics of this sortie read like something out of a latter-day Jules Verne: 28,238 miles covered in twenty-nine hours fifty-nine minutes! The first woman pilot flew Concorde in 1993.

How many flights have British Airways' Concordes operated since entering commercial service? Almost 50,000. And in so doing, they have clocked up more than 140,000 flying hours – 10,000 of them at supersonic speeds. Their total travel distance has been some 14,000,000 miles. More than two and a half million passengers have flown supersonic in BA Concordes since 1976 – the current most frequent passenger being an oil company executive, who makes almost seventy round-trip transatlantic crossings a year. Concorde of course additionally operates a range of charter flights which have taken the aircraft to more than 250 other destinations worldwide.

It was a charter flight on that fateful day, 25 July 2000, when an Air France Concorde crashed outside Paris. On 15 August British Airways withdrew Concorde from service. This followed a special notification from the Air Accident Investigation Branch of the Department of Transport. The AAIB stated that they had received new information which warranted, in its view, a recommendation to the UK Civil Aviation Authority to suspend the airworthiness certificates from Concorde. The CAA accepted this recommendation and it was duly implemented on the next day.

Following this enforced grounding of the Concorde fleet, the manufacturers worked very closely with the regulators and both British Airways and Air France to develop measures to allow the airlines to return Concorde safely back into service. The programme of measures focused mainly on preventing massive fuel leaks like that in the Paris accident – and to eliminate any potential ignition sources.

New fuel tank liners were fitted by EADS (the former Aérospatiale) in Toulouse. These are made of a Kevlar-rubber compound. They have been designed to contain the fuel should the wing skin ever be punctured – an approach already adopted successfully in military helicopters and Formula One racing cars. The aircraft have also been fitted with new Michelin Near Zero Growth tyres, which are much tougher and less likely to explode in the unlikely event of being punctured.

By the year 2002, Concorde had resumed operations between London and New York and also Barbados. The scheduled flights to the latter exotic destination makes the following day trip a reality – breakfast in Britain, a swim in the Caribbean before lunch and back home again in Britain for supper!

Let us end by looking in detail at the performance of Concorde. The aircraft measures 204 feet in length. But this stretches six to ten inches in flight, due to heating of the airframe. The characteristic droop nose is lowered to improve pilots' visibility for take-off and landing. The four Rolls-Royce/SNECMA Olympus 593 engines each produce more than 38,000 lbs of thrust with reheat. This adds fuel to the final stage of the engine to produce the extra power required for take-off and the transition to supersonic flight. They are the most powerful pure jet engines flying commercially. The following are the rest of Concorde's specification:

Capacity: 100 passengers, and 2.5 tonnes of cargo.
Seating: 100 seats, two either side of the aisle, with a 37 inch (98 cm) pitch. The front cabin has forty seats, and the rear cabin

sixty seats, both offering a single-class R, or supersonic, brand of service.

Range: 4,300 miles (6,880 kms).

Take-off speed: 220 knots (250 mph/400 kph).

Cruising speed: 1,350 mph (2,150 kph/Mach 2), at 60,000 feet (18,181 m).

Landing speed: 187 mph (300 kph).

Length: 203 feet 9 inches (62.1 m).

Wingspan: 83 feet 8 inches (25.5 m).

Height: 37 feet 1 inch (11.3 m).

Fuselage width: 9 feet 6 inches (2.9 m).

Fuel capacity: 26,286 Imperial gallons (119,500 litres/95,600 kgs).

Fuel consumption: 5,638 Imperial gallons (25,629 litres/20,500 kgs) per hour.

Maximum take-off weight: 408,000 lbs (185 tonnes).

Landing gear: Eight main wheels (tyre pressure 207 lbs per sq in), two nose wheels (tyre pressure 181 lbs per sq in.

Flight crew: Two pilots, one flight engineer.

Cabin crew: Six.

Concorde is the flagship of the British Airways fleet and a large programme in progress is aimed at ensuring that its interior is as exciting and elegant as the exterior. New seats have a cradle mechanism, footrest and contoured headrest. The design uses new technology and materials that are twenty per cent lighter than previously – leading to large fuel economy through weight-saving. New interiors are lighter and brighter, with improved illumination filters for a fresher look. New washrooms will be more spacious, less cramped. Cuisine and wine lists are also being refreshed and revived. So Concorde represents the ultimate in speed, service and style.

What will the next hundred years yield in aviation history?

39

FLIGHT 93

11 September 2001

The world's worst ever terrorist outrage was perpetrated on 11 September, 2001. This involved four separate but coordinated commercial jetliner hijackings, all flying from airports along the Eastern seaboard of the United States. These four flights have already gone down as the most infamous in civil aviation history – despite Lockerbie and the many other cases of terrorism in the air. The justification for including this tragedy in an account of heroic flights is that it is known beyond question that innocent passengers of these flights displayed dramatic courage in terrifying and ultimately fatal circumstances.

The total of nineteen hijackers operated in bands of four or five on each plane. All belonged to the hated al-Qaida terrorist network. Security experts now say that the terrorists certainly scouted their locations with care and well in advance. They chose the three airports and four flights that would give them the maximum chance of success in an enterprise unbelievably evil.

The American Federal Bureau of Investigation (FBI) now knows from witness accounts of cell phone conversations with passengers on the airliners that the terrorists eluded all security measures at each of the airports before boarding. As well as using cardboard-box cutters and razors to help take control of the four aircraft, they had also managed to smuggle other types of knives through airport security. Tragically these lapses of vigilance by security staff helped to compound the developing disaster.

According to investigation and records of the cell phone calls made by passengers later, the hijackers used all the weapons at their disposal to wound and kill passengers, pilots and other aircrew. Once airborne and in control of each airliner, they are believed to have turned off cockpit transponders to evade detection by air traffic controllers on the ground. With the aircraft commandeered, they were ready to transform all four planes into huge fuel-laden missiles – aimed at destroying their pre-selected targets.

But to go back to the beginning . . . to Boston, Massachusetts, one of the cultural cores of the United States; famed for the Arts, the Boston Symphony Orchestra, Harvard University and so much more. In other words, civilisation.

It was a fairly typical Tuesday at Boston Airport on 11 September, a week after the Labor Day weekend. Five terrorists had pre-booked their seats on American Airlines' early morning Flight 11 westbound across the continent to Los Angeles. As with the three subsequent flights, the terrorists were neither stopped nor searched before they boarded. All was still peaceful, or seemed so.

At 7.45 a.m. Flight 11 took off from Boston according to schedule. None of the passengers or crew yet knew of the five aliens in their midst. The normality was destined, doomed, soon to change. While Flight 11 was gaining speed down the runway, five further terrorists had already got through security to board United Airlines' Flight 175, also bound for Los Angeles.

At 7.58 a.m. Flight 175 took off from Boston roughly to time; just thirteen minutes after the first flight to be hijacked.

World focus would shortly be on these two airliners, but before this two more took off mere minutes later. The next was from Newark Airport, New Jersey, down the east coast near New York – and the fourth from Washington, Dulles International.

United Airlines' Flight 93 departed from Newark at 8.01 a.m. and headed on its course for San Francisco. The Boeing 757 was weighed down with more than enough fuel to carry it across the American continent.

The hijackers had chosen busy metropolitan airports like Newark to avoid undue attention. They picked planes that were all due to make nonstop long-haul flights and furthermore, all were departing early on that Tuesday morning. These factors almost ensured fewer passengers and accordingly less numerical opposition to overcome when airborne.

The terrorists must also have had prearranged help from fellow-conspirators on the ground. Sources said later that the Federal Aviation Administration (FAA) received false bomb threats relating to three or four other planes already in the air that morning. These hoaxes all helped to create distractions that would give the hijacked planes additional time to change course without being noticed instantaneously. And every extra minute would be crucial in carrying through their lethal plans.

8.10 a.m. With Flight 93 barely airborne from Newark, five more terrorists from al-Qaida were seated ready for take-off aboard American Airlines' Flight 77. This plane left Washington, Dulles Airport scheduled to fly westward for Los Angeles; once again, a cross-continental flight with a heavy fuel-load.

Meanwhile, a flight attendant aboard Flight 11 from Boston was making a desperate cell call saying 'several Middle East men' had suddenly brought out knives and wounded some passengers. This initial call shed light on how a few men – in this case, five – armed only with concealed knives or cardboard-box cutters could quickly commandeer and terrify an entire airliner. The terrorists did not hesitate to draw blood.

The precise pattern of these attacks can never be known, which may be just as well. But they were all pre-calculated and all barbarically brutal. The hijackers either killed or wounded the pilots, stabbed passengers and took control of the flight deck.

Reports were almost too painful to hear or read. They confirmed that in several cases the terrorists bound the arms of flight attendants behind them – and then slashed their throats . . . Subsequent ground investigation showed that luggage left behind by one of the killers contained messages that included the following inhuman exhortation: 'Let each find his blade for the prey to be slaughtered'. The rest of the civilized world would ask: 'How is it conceivable for human beings to think and act like this?'

The course of both Flights 11 and 175 have become engrained in the universal collective memory. The time was approaching 8.46 a.m. . . .

8.40 a.m. Two US Air Force jet fighters were scrambled and flew at top speed towards the track of Flight 11 – New York. They could not intercept it in time.

8.44 a.m. Radar logs showed Flight 93 well airborne and heading west.

8.45 a.m. About an hour after take-off from Boston, Flight 11 reached the airspace of New York City. Some workers making their way downtown stood aghast for a moment as the terrorists now piloting the plane steered it deliberately into the North Tower of the World Trade Center. The time: precisely 8.46 a.m. The result: premeditated mass murder on an unprecedented peacetime scale.

At about this fateful time, Flight 93 was apparently still flying fast and without any special incident until it reached the skies over the environs of Cleveland, Ohio. Unseen far below ran the shoreline of Lake Erie.

9.02–9.03 a.m. United Airlines' Flight 175 crashed into the South Tower of the World Trade Center. Unknown to anyone at that instant, both towers had less than an hour-and-a-half survival time left.

Some while after their Boeing 757 had departed from Washington, Dulles, ostensibly en route for Los Angeles, the passengers of Flight 77 suddenly saw and heard hijackers with knives and cardboard-box cutters screaming at them. They were hustled to the rear of the jet, where one passenger was able to call by cell phone to report what was happening.

9.10 a.m. About an hour after take-off, the Boeing had become a massive missile now flying low over afforested terrain and aimed apparently at Washington DC. Fighter pilots were ordered up to take any action necessary against a plane approaching the capital. The terrorist pilot then performed a pivot so tight that observers on the ground watching by chance were reminded of a jet fighter rather than a large airliner – normally much more unwieldy.

9.30 a.m. The plane suddenly cut sharply 270 degrees with the aim of approaching not the White House or other Washington landmark targets, but the Pentagon Building at Arlington, Virginia. It was flying in quite fast from the south-west. But being below radar level, it had vanished from the screens of air traffic control. Aviation experts observing the manoeuvre had to admit that the airliner was being flown with skill. More light on the terrorists' training would be shed later. But if a plane's pilots were killed, forced out of the cockpit, or otherwise incapacitated, it would be relatively simple to steer an airliner into the Pentagon. The next few minutes would confirm this. A government spokesman said later: 'We have to assume that the pilots were no longer a factor; they were either shot or killed somehow.'

9.34 a.m. Back aboard Flight 93, this plane was also presumably intended for an unspecified Washington target. Passengers risked using their cell phones bravely in terrifying circumstances to report

267

that hijackers had suddenly brandished cigarette lighters containing hidden switch-blades. As they tried to take control of the plane, pandemonium flared. Four men wearing red headbands and speaking with foreign accents went wild. They killed one passenger at once as an example, rushed the cockpit, injured both pilots and took over the aircraft.

9.35 a.m. All this was happening now in a mere minute or so. The unfolding horror of the twin towers had already alerted the US Air Force everywhere. Jet fighters took off from Andrews Air Force Base.

9.36 a.m. Flight 93 was in the hands of the hijackers within two minutes. They turned the plane through almost 180 degrees towards the south. It headed back the way it had come, now aiming also in the direction of Washington.

9.37 a.m. After the initial terror of the murdered passenger, those remaining passengers and crew were split into two groups. A few were held in the first-class compartment, but most were herded to the galley in the rear of the plane. The terrorist charged with watching these passengers in the galley had a small red box tied to his waist by a belt. He told them in a frenzied tone that this box contained a bomb – which it presumably did.

9.39 a.m. American Airlines' Flight 77 was pointed directly at the Pentagon Building – heart of the US defence system. The symbolism could hardly have been clearer. The plane made a steep decline and accelerated. It struck in seconds, killing 189 persons including all who were on board the plane. Within seconds it left a great gash in a section of the Pentagon. Chaos ensued. Debris and dust enveloped ground-floor level. The four storeys above lay destroyed and exposed on either side of the impact. Thousands of windows were jaggedly blasted by the eruption. An eerie grey haze hovered around the whole area. The fighters were still over ten minutes' flying time away.

9.40 a.m. So three of the four airliners had now crashed into their appointed targets. There remained only Flight 93 airborne. Cable News Network (CNN) later reported that it had obtained a partial transcript of cockpit chatter and also talked with a source who had listened to the air traffic tape. This source said that a man – clearly a terrorist – announced in broken English:

'This is the captain speaking. Remain in your seat. There is a bomb on board. Stay quiet. We are meeting with their demands. We are returning to the airport.' Presumably this was intended to try to stop passengers from panicking or trying to counter-attack.

Still about this time, at least one US Air Force F.16 was reported to be only 125 miles distant; less than a quarter-hour flying time.

The terrorists aboard Flight 93 could not keep passengers pacified. Already several were somehow using their cell phones. They had learned of the two crashes into the twin towers. The official account reports that they 'formulated a plan to respond to the hijackers'. Soon afterwards, the plane made a number of manoeuvres in midair. These were thought to suggest a struggle to gain control.

9.48 a.m. Two fighters took off to try to intercept Flight 93.

Frantic calls were still being made by passengers. Thomas Burnett had three small daughters and his wife Deena. He got through to Deena. He told her of the situation on board and said that he and some fellow passengers were 'going to do something' because if not the hijackers 'were going to run this plane into the ground'. Others aboard included a typical cross-section of Americans – Todd Beamer, who had two young children at home as well as his pregnant wife; Barbara Olson; Mark Rothenberg; Waleska Martinez; Louis Nacke. Their situation was critical.

9.58 a.m. 'We're being hijacked', a male passenger called to the 911 emergency number. He was locked in the toilet while he dialled the three digits. He added that he had heard some sort of explosion in the cabin and thought they were going down.

That was the last contact with Flight 93. So all that was known for sure was that some passengers said they intended to try to storm the cockpit. No one knows what happened in the next minutes. Or no one has been told fully. The *New York Times* said that the plane's voice recorder registered 'a desperate and wild struggle'.

Official accounts still say that the passengers – alerted to the other three hijacks by their cell phone calls – stormed the cockpit with a terrorist already at the controls. In the ensuing minutes, they forced the plane down to avoid it being crashed on Washington – possibly even the White House. A later transcript claiming to come from the original voice recorder refers to sounds of fighting aboard the plane and prayers uttered in both Christian and Muslim terms. This was based on interpretation of what was going on from the sounds on the recording.

9.59 a.m. Back in New York, the South Tower collapsed completely. Before this, many had already jumped from it to their deaths. Now hundreds more perished.

By this time, too, it was clear that Flight 93 was being aimed back for Washington. The official order was given to bring down the airliner. US Air Force jets were nearly within range to fire missiles. The official account says that fighters did indeed reach the area of Flight 93, but only moments before it crashed. They did not shoot it down.

10.06 a.m. While the presumed life-or-death drama was proceeding in the cockpit and cabin of Flight 93, the plane swiftly lost height. Lee Purbaugh says he saw it strike the ground in fields near Shanksville, rural Pennsylvania, at this very time of 10.06 a.m. An official version records that it slammed, nose-first, into the field at 10.10 a.m., adding 'It is believed that passengers overpowered the terrorists, thus preventing the aircraft from being used as a missile'.

Little was left of the plane or the people. Part of one engine landed over a mile away from the scene of the crash-site; some fuselage, 'the size of a dining-table' also survived, otherwise, nothing else remained visible that was bigger than two or three inches. Debris had been displaced over a wide acreage. Was a bomb set off aboard the plane? Did a missile bring it down at the last minute or two? Did the passengers actually attack the cockpit? The last is still the official version of those last, lost minutes – and is presumably the truth.

Two other strange factors were reported, too. Observers in the area saw a small white jet flying low over the site soon after the crash. And then almost an hour after the actual impact, US mail and other papers from the plane fluttered down to earth eight miles away. As the local coroner Wally Miller said: 'I do not rule anything out.'

So questions still remain – in the air. Yet whatever the whole truth, nothing can detract from the undoubted intention of some heroic passengers of Flight 93 to tackle the terrorists. Surely that is the way to treat this tragedy – not to speculate further on what might or might not have been?

10.29 a.m. As this horror ended, another was still developing in New York. Many hundreds had been trapped and killed following the impact of the original two Boston planes into the twin towers. Forced by the furnace-like flames, some people fell or jumped from windows on high floors of the buildings. The visual images are still shattering on the emotions. One man wearing a light jacket and dark trousers is falling head first past the sheer vertical parallels of the doomed tower.

After the collapse of the South Tower at 09.59 a.m., the intensity of the flames in the North Tower had also weakened its structure that survived the original strike. It, too, collapsed at about 10.30 a.m.

In the tragedy of the twin towers, 343 firefighters, as well as many police, other rescuers, and citizens of seventy-eight countries were killed; people of virtually every religious faith and ethnic group in the world today. Up to 200 actually jumped from the towers. Add all those perishing in the Pentagon and at Shanksville, and the total loss of life has now been put at 3,047.

The terrorists may have been led to believe that, in attacking the World Trade Center, they were attacking 'a symbol of America'. They weren't. Instead, they attacked an institution of international trade, prosperity and economic opportunity. Along with government offices of Thailand, Chile and Côte d'Ivoire, for example, the World Trade Center housed offices of 430 companies from twenty-eight countries. In short, the terrorists attacked not just the United States – they attacked the whole world.

On the very next day, President Bush said: 'Freedom and democracy are under attack'. And leaders from around the world called the events an attack on civilization itself. The British Premier, Tony Blair, was quick to speak in support of Mr Bush, and flew to America to underline Britain's solidarity with the United States.

'The coordinated attack was an act of war against the United States', President Bush said in an address to a joint session of Congress on 20 September. 'Our war on terror begins with al-Qaida but it does not end there. It will not end until every terrorist group of global reach has been found, stopped, and defeated.'

Virtually every nation condemned the attack and joined the US-led coalition to fight terror on several coordinated fronts; diplomatic, economic, intelligence, law enforcement and military. Operation Enduring Freedom, the military component of the coalition, began on 7 October, 2001. The first targets were the al-Qaida training camps and military installations of the Taliban regime in Afghanistan. Islamic extremists from around the world had used Afghanistan as a training ground and base of operations for worldwide terrorism activities. Within months, the Taliban was driven from power, and nearly 1,000 al-Qaida operatives were arrested in over sixty countries. Meanwhile, the world will never forget the people who lost their lives on 11 September, 2001.

This story of heroic flights has lasted for a century since the Wright Brothers first flew. And in many ways, the history of flying and fliers has reflected world history over the same period from the earliest pioneers of all, the military fliers of the First World War, the heroes and heroines of the pioneering '20s and '30s, the famous fliers – and the unsung – of the Second World War, the post-war world of jet propulsion, the expansion of world aviation, supersonic air travel – to terrorism in the air. Throughout all the challenges and changes, there has run the one unbroken thread of human heroism in the air.

INDEX

277

278